1993 Edition

Coping With Unemployment

Brian Jud

Cover by
Concialdi Design

Text layout by
Ellen Gregory

Edited by
Charles Lipka

D0143963

First Edition
Published by Marketing Directions, Inc.

Other books by the author:
Job Search 101
The Career Action Plan
The College Action Plan
The Art of Interviewing (video)

ISBN: 1-880218-03-8
Library of Congress Catalog Card Number: 92-083975

Coping With Unemployment
Brian Jud

Table of Contents

PART THREE: How to Restore and Maintain a Good Attitude

PART FOUR: Financial Planning During Unemployment

Introduction

Millions of people are out of work during the tough times we are experiencing today. But this probably doesn't matter a great deal to you because you're concerned about only one of them: **YOU.** When you are unemployed, your thoughts and actions revolve around one thought: the immediate future that is in store for you and those who count on you. The events of the world and community around you cease to exist as your attention is devoted to finding a job that will enable you to maintain your relationships, pay your bills and restore your self-esteem.

Perhaps the fact that you're not alone, that someone else experienced and coped successfully with the negative job-search feelings, pressure and self-doubt will help you through this tough time. Many other people, including myself, have experienced the sequential job-search feelings of confidence, apprehension, worry, fear and dejection. These are as unavoidable as receiving rejection letters from prospective employers. If you recognize and learn to deal with that fact, you'll get through this situation and become a stronger person as a result. As Robert Schuller said, "Tough times never last, but tough people do."

You may be in a situation where you are about to be unemployed, recently unemployed or in the throes of a prolonged period without a job. In any case, Coping With Unemployment will help you deal with the emotional roller coaster on which you find yourself.

If you are just beginning your job-search journey, Coping With Unemployment will prepare you for the frustration and rejection inherent in your quest for employment. You will also learn how to meet and overcome the obstacles that would otherwise cause a gradual erosion of your self-confidence, regardless of the level at which it is now.

If you have been unemployed for an extended length of time, Coping With Unemployment will help you triumph over the negative emotions and financial pressure intrinsic to your situation. It will help you renew your determination to find a new position and the confidence to make that occur.

During unemployment, your positive attitude is gradually eroded. If certain indicators are not heeded, this deterioration could cause frustration, dejection and even depression. Coping With Unemployment shows you how to recognize these red flags and deal with your failing emotions. It contains hundreds of ideas you can use to reverse this erosion and restore the confidence you had earlier in your search.

I dare to make my dreams come true.

Coping With Unemployment is not "another positive thinking book." Although an optimistic attitude is important to job-search success, it alone will not cause you to succeed. You can only hear the words "stay positive and everything will work out for the best" so many times before they lose their significance and actually become discouraging.

Nor is Coping With Unemployment an instructional book that will show you how to write a resume and cover letter, or how to interview effectively. The focus of Coping With Unemployment is on the management of the changes in attitude and emotion that result from a typical job search. A successful outcome will result only if you take charge of your attitude and implement actions to create your own success.

Coping With Unemployment recognizes that your family and friends are also affected by your unemployed status. Therefore, you'll learn techniques you can use to get through this difficult time period with all your relationships intact. It's not easy, but you can do it. And you'll become a greater, stronger person for it.

When you finally accept a job offer, you'll look back on this time of your life and see how much you've grown. You can't go through this trial without becoming more resilient to the challenges life holds in store for you. Your self-respect and self-image will rise to a level until now you felt was impossible to achieve.

Throughout the next thirty eight chapters you will find examples of techniques that I have used to manage my mental state successfully, while experiencing several lengthy periods of unemployment. I've gone through prolonged job searches with two mortgages and twin sons in college, during the Christmas holidays and with only a year of employment between those searches. I've felt my personality turn inward while the days, weeks and then months passed by without any sustaining positive feedback.

Yes, I know how you feel. But I'm not going to commiserate with you and metaphorically place my arm around your shoulder and tell you that it's not your fault, you should be patient and everything will work out for the best. Everything won't work out for the best until you take control of the situation and work as hard as you can to turn it around. And I'll show you how to do that.

Re-program your mind.

You'll notice that at the bottom of each page is a phrase or sentence. These are self-affirmations that can help you maintain your

---

I am the best "me" I can be and that's all that's necessary for success.

direction and attitudes of control, commitment and confidence. Self-affirmations are meant to help you condition your mind to believe that you can succeed. They state a goal, attitude or event in terms that force you to maintain a positive focus on your immediate purpose. If you don't direct your attention to a positive outcome or action, your thoughts will take on a life of their own. This could cause you to look to the past with regret or anger and to the future with uncertainty or distress. More information on self-affirmations is found in Chapter Thirteen.

You may not choose to share your affirmations with other people and it's not necessary that you do so. But if you share the information in Coping With Unemployment with your spouse or friends, you may find them more empathetic with, and helpful in your search. You don't have to go through this period alone. Use all the resources at your disposal, especially the human ones. With "a little help from your friends," work hard at maintaining a realistic, positive attitude that will enable you to perform all the activities necessary to get yourself back on the job. With all the work you have ahead of you at this point, it will seem like a vacation when you again become re-employed.

Every mountain has a peak.

Your job search can be equated to climbing a mountain. After struggling for a period of time, it may seem as if you're making little or no progress and the top of the mountain is no closer than when you started. And if you slip and fall it's a long way down to the bottom, most likely resulting in serious injury.

Yet there are also positive analogies to climbing the mountain. First of all, it takes planning and teamwork to succeed in your journey. Next, success is achieved by taking one (sometimes laborious) step at a time. And finally, your goal is always there, even though it may not be visible at all times. It could be buried behind some dark clouds, but you know that it is still there, somewhere.

One thing every person does when climbing a mountain is to protect himself from falling by securing a lifeline at regular intervals. That is your task at this point of your search. You must create a lifeline to limit the distance of your fall, to prevent serious or permanent injury and to provide the means to regain your former position. It's not easy, but you can do it.

I am greater than anything that can happen to me.

PART ONE:

The importance of a good attitude

Chapter One

"Ours Is Not To Reason Why..."

"You wake up every morning, and you summon up the energy from somewhere, even when you think you haven't got it, and you get through the day. And you do it day after day."

Does that quotation summarize your thoughts after a prolonged period of unemployment? It was actually said by Terry Anderson (Newsweek, December 16, 1991) upon his release from captivity as a hostage.

There are many similarities between being taken hostage and becoming unemployed. You are placed in a situation against your will, and you worry every day about what will happen to you. You feel alienated from family and friends, and your future is placed on hold. It's difficult to make long-term plans since you don't know what your situation will be even a few weeks hence. The loss of a job is also accompanied by self-doubt and a feeling of loss of control over your life. And perhaps the most devastating element is that there is no definite date upon which you will be "released."

But unlike a hostage, you can take specific actions that will help to free yourself from your bondage. You can use a variety of techniques to develop and maintain a self-confident, energetic state of mind and translate those thoughts into strategic actions directed toward achieving important goals.

Soar or be sore.

Your attitude during a job search can be compared to a balloon with a slow leak. You have to keep replenishing it or it becomes deflated. Your "attitude" can be as big as you want it to be, and you can also shape it. If you fill it with the right stuff it will soar, but you have to control it, or it could get away from you. In any case, you must attend to it to maintain the correct pressure. Too much and it will explode, not enough and you won't get the desired results.

I always look to what is good in my life today.

Understanding your initial reactions.

Once you become unemployed, your attitude can take a variety of directions based upon the circumstances of the separation and the strength of your personality. Most people leave their jobs with feelings of anger, shock, fear or shame. The important point is to recognize and accept your feelings and learn to deal with them. It's not wrong to feel angry with your previous employer, but if you persist in allowing that emotion to remain, you're less likely to get on with your life successfully. Similarly, if you dwell on your fear of an unknown future, it could lead to a more intense feeling of panic. This might in turn immobilize you and prevent you from trying.

After you go through the ordeal of cleaning out your office and leaving it for the last time, there are two things that you must do. The first is to come to grips with yourself about what has happened. Secondly, you have to explain it to your family or significant other. Perhaps three brief case histories of my initial reactions to becoming unemployed will best demonstrate what can happen and how you can deal with it.

For example...

Early in my career I was let go by my employer. I was given a 30-day severance package, which set my deadline for finding another job. At the time, I was married, had six-year-old twin sons and was attending night school to finish my college education.

I was notified of my fate while on a business trip with my supervisor. We had our discussion at an airport, and he flew to his home while I drove back to mine. As I left the airport, I actually felt relief that I had finally been removed from an oppressive job and a supervisor whom I disliked. But while driving home, the reality of my predicament hit me. I had nothing in savings and had only the income from my severance package (equal in amount to my expenses for one month) to live on.

My initial feeling of relief turned to fear as I started thinking about the bills that were due shortly. Once I realized that I could make all my payments for the next month, my anxiety became more general as I contemplated the negative consequences of not finding a job in four weeks. The pressure to find something was great, and I allowed myself two hours (the time it took to drive home after being notified) to feel "down."

I knew I had to begin immediately to find a new job. I sent resumes to all the help-wanted advertisers in the newspapers and regis-

---

I accept the challenge to find another job and I am confident that I will succeed

tered with all the employment agencies in town. But I knew that if I was to find a new job in the time I had allotted I would have to do more than sit home and wait for people to call me. So I went to the library and found a book on job-search techniques which I began to undertake.

Performing what was necessary to find a job kept me busy literally every day. This had two major benefits. First, my efforts resulted in two job offers. Second, and equally important, I was so busy finding a new position that I didn't have time to worry about what would happen if I didn't. Since I was constantly seeking employment, all I could see were the opportunities "out there" and not the pitfalls.

Deja Vu all over again.

During a different separation, I went into shock. I was the leading U.S. sales representative for a company based in England, and had recently consummated an order that increased their gross sales by 25%. The president of the U.S. operation gave me the news that my position was being eliminated and that the Managing Director of the corporation was flying over to explain the circumstances personally. I was astounded by the news, and had no choice but to meet with the Managing Director.

Before he arrived, I created a plan to purchase the distribution rights for their product in the United States. I arranged financing that would make an attractive offer. When the Managing Director met with me and officially told me the news, I countered with my offer. To say the least, he was shocked. Since it was a sincere and well-financed proposal, he had to take it back to his supervisor for evaluation.

The company eventually turned down my proposal, but I had a renewed feeling of control. I was back in the "driver's seat" of my life and this feeling remained with, and motivated me until I finally found a new job.

Just one more time.

On another, more recent occasion, I had been working with a company for eleven months when I left for a two-day business trip. I drove through my territory and arrived at my hotel that evening. Just after 6:00 pm the telephone rang in my hotel room. I answered it to hear that my employment was terminated as of that moment, with no severance pay or benefits. It was a short, terse and final conversation that had a dramatic impact on the rest of my life.

I am a good person and nobody can take that away from me.

First reactions.

Again, the first feeling I had when being told that I was being released was one of relief. I had seen this coming and had been disgruntled with the job and the company's president (my supervisor). For a number of reasons, I initially felt as though a large weight had been lifted from my shoulders. But it wasn't too much longer before I felt a larger weight. In fact, less than an hour had passed when I began to think about all the things that could go wrong.

Although it was not unexpected, it was still difficult to comprehend that I had no income from that moment on. I sat on the bed thinking of a thousand things, thinking of nothing. I just wasn't prepared for the actual event no matter how many times I told myself to begin making plans.

I knew what was ahead of me, since I had been in this position before. I felt some confidence, but then I began thinking that this search was different from earlier ones. I wasn't sure that I could go through it all again.

Shame on me.

My feelings quickly changed to humiliation. I had been on this job for less than a year and before that had been unemployed for five months. I began to wonder what my family was going to think of me. Would they think I was an unworthy provider who could offer them no security? And what about my networking contacts? Now I had to go back to them and again ask for their help in finding another job. What were they going to think of me?

I knew I had to take some immediate positive action in order to begin on the right track. My first decision was to leave immediately and make the four-hour drive home. At least I could get a head start the following morning (Friday) and begin my job-search program in earnest. I packed, checked out of the hotel and began the journey home.

While driving home, it wasn't long before I was overcome by the "Lonely-Driver's Trance." Mesmerized by the regularity of the windshield wipers, I began to lose control of my thoughts, allowing them to wander from fact to fiction. I thought about how little money was left in my checking and savings account, and I couldn't remember whether or not I had used up all the cash-value of my insurance policy during my previous bout with unemployment.

Then my mind drifted to the expense column. I knew my fixed costs were high, with monthly payments for my twin sons' college

---

I control my emotions and thoughts.

tuition, house and car alone at several thousand dollars. It didn't take long for me to understand that the two columns didn't balance, and I would be in financial trouble shortly.

Thankfully, I was able to regain control of my thoughts and redirect them to a more positive track. Although I couldn't think of one thing that was going well for me, I knew I had to try to find something. I took out a piece of paper and wrote one question across the top of it: "What is good in my life now?" Then down the left column I wrote the numbers one through twenty, one number on each line. I was determined to come up with that many items or events that I thought were good. Here is the list I compiled during the drive home:

What is good in my life now?

1. Family support.
2. Experience in getting a job.
3. Self-confidence.
4. The chance to start my own business (something I had always wanted).
5. I had a directory of all the companies in my field of interest that I could use as an immediate prospect list.
6. I had suspected this decision was forthcoming, and I already had several leads in place.
7. I had a good reputation in the business, and I knew I could get good references.
8. Friends whom I knew would offer support .
9. My computer was in good working order since I just had it serviced.
10. The local print shop had existing mechanicals for my personal letterhead, and these could be re-ordered immediately.
11. Knowledge that I could always get "a job," perhaps not one that would pay as well, but one that would support me until I could get something better. (This is not a good approach to a job search, but at the time it offered me consolation.)
12. Enough money available to cover at least one month's expenses.
13. Good health.
14. Faith in my ability and attitude.
15. My brother had offered financial support to help get my twin sons through college if this expected unemployment eventually hit me.
16. Eighteen years of experience in my chosen industry.
17. A car that worked properly and was in no need of immediate major repair work.

I am a good employee, and any company would be lucky to have me.

18. No significant personal expenses (other than college, home and cars) that would come due in the near future.

19. My wife was working, and her insurance covered the entire family.

20. I had a library of self-help books and tapes that I could read and listen to.

The items in the list are not as important as the fact that you begin to immediately control your thinking constructively. Once you begin visualizing all the positive elements of your current situation, your mind dwells on what is good about you now. As you contemplate your strong points you begin to sense a reduction in the pressure you initially felt.

An equally vital consideration is the way you make your list. Writing an objective at the top of the page will keep your mind focused. Write it in the form of a question and keep asking it to yourself over and over again. Each time you do so, you will stimulate new answers.

Similarly, if you begin by writing the numbers one through twenty down the left-hand side of the page, you presuppose that you can think of at least twenty answers. This in itself has a motivating effect.

Once you have gone through the list, take it one step further. Rephrase several of the most important twenty items in the form of a question, and list twenty ways to respond to them. For example, if you wanted to start your own business, write it as a question at the top of another page: "In how many ways could I work for myself?" Write the numbers one through twenty down the left-hand column. Then start listing the ways, such as starting your own company, buying an existing company, purchasing a franchise or any other ideas you have.

How to perform a reality check.

Since your initial thoughts will tend to be negative, you must take immediate steps to reverse that thinking. Here is another technique that can help you perform an objective review of your current circumstances:

Step 1: Define the worst thing that can happen if you don't find a new job soon.

Is it bankruptcy? Divorce? Depression? Write down the worst possible end result you think could happen to you.

Step Two: What is the likelihood of this happening?

On a scale of 1 (least likely) to 10 (most likely), what is the chance of this worst-case scenario actually occurring?

I am a good friend.

Given your current mental state, it is probably 9 or 10. But for now just give yourself a benchmark so you have something to which you can compare your later scores.

Step Three: What can you do to make sure Step One doesn't happen?

Again, given your present state of mind, you may not be able to think of anything you can do that you haven't already tried. This stage in your reality check might be more accurately completed after you have taken other steps to improve your thinking. But carefully think through all the activities you can perform to get back on track and get another job.

In a marketing sense, there are four areas under your direct control. These are the product (which in this case is you), its price, where you want to sell it and the promotion techniques you can use to communicate your skills and achievements.

You have to work at getting control of your job search in these four areas. The best place to start is with your "product," the most important part of which is your attitude.

Then take another look at the geographical area where you can market your skills. In what other ways can you create greater value for your services to justify the price you are asking for them. And how can you more creatively and effectively promote yourself among potential employers? There may be many different possibilities out there since the last time you actively searched for opportunities.

*Step Four: What is the **new** likelihood of the worst-case scenario?*

If you actively pursue all the techniques you have developed in Step Three, what are the revised chances of the situation you described in Step One actually occurring? Most likely, they have dropped down to somewhere in the 5 or 6 range. This is a good sign. Now you have a 50/50 chance of recovery where before you felt you had less than a 10% chance. Once you begin to implement all the actions you described in Step Three, you'll find that you have even a greater chance for success.

I have high energy.

There is a technique you can try that will make Step Three easier. Don't try to master every element of your life at once or the task will become overwhelming. Instead, break your life down into the areas you have control of and those you don't.

Have a mental break-down.

It's unrealistic to set a goal to move yourself immediately from a one (lowest) to a ten (highest) on a general scale of life. Most importantly, if you rate yourself on the way you feel about yourself now, you'll probably grade yourself as being at 1 or 2. But you can try a technique that will help you break down the various segments of your life into more manageable parts and deal with each more effectively. Then if you add up all your individual scores, you'll find that you're better off than you thought.

Separate your life into four (or however many you want) major segments and give each a numerical rating. In this case it would range from 1 to 2.5. You may decide to use five different categories and rate each on a scale of 1 to 2. It matters more that you divide your life into manageable groupings. Just make sure the maximum of all categories together is 10. Those groups you could use are the following:

Person. Think about yourself as a multi-faceted individual, comprised of emotional, physical, spiritual and social aspects. Are you an honest, caring person? Do you take care of your health, eat and sleep properly? Do you try to do the right thing whenever you can, bettering yourself but not at the expense of the feelings of others? Then evaluate your performance in each of these areas and rate yourself on a scale of 1 to 2.5 for this category.

Spouse. Obviously this doesn't apply to everyone, but it might have at some time in your life. If you're not married, think of being a good best friend to someone. Do you try to be a good partner? Do you snap at your mate or do you share feelings constructively? Do you feel that it's "you and me against the world" or have you alienated yourself from your spouse so that you feel that you're alone in your battle against the world? Rate yourself on a scale of 1 to 2.5.

Parent. If this applies, honestly critique your skills as a parent. What have you done that you are proud of and how

---

I am a winner.

do you feel that you might improve? Again, rate yourself on a scale of 1 to 2.5.

Employee. Think about how you performed when you were employed. How would you rate yourself at that time?" Then think to the future. If a company hired you now, what kind of an employee would you be? One more time, rate yourself on a scale of 1 to 2.5.

If these categories don't apply to you, make up your own. Then add up your scores in each. If you feel that you're a good person, you probably gave yourself a "2." Your recent past as a spouse might have been better, so you gave yourself a mark of "1." You've been an above-average parent, so you feel a rating of "2" would be accurate. But try as you will, you can't get yourself to score anything as an employee, given your current circumstances.

Adding your scores, you're up to a rating of "5." This should make you feel better already. And you should realize that even though you've had trouble finding and keeping a job, all is not lost. You're still a good person, spouse/friend and parent and you have accomplishments in each of these areas that nobody can take away from you.

Interrupt your habits and patterns of thinking.

In order for these concepts to be most effective, you have to take steps to stop the negative thinking that may have come to dominate your attitude. Since this happened over a long period of time, you probably created some habits you are totally unaware of.

You may ask yourself, "How could I not be aware of such a negative habit?" The answer is found in the word "accommodation." In order to explain this theory, think of your wrist watch. When you first placed it on your wrist you probably thought it felt odd. Then as time passed you forgot that you had it on and your frequent glances to check the time went unnoticed. You don't even realize you have the watch on until it breaks and you send it out for repair.

Habits evolve through similar stages. For example, one day you may have nothing to do so you sit down in front of your television and watch "whatever is on." As you begin to do this more frequently, you may actually start to look forward to following your favorite characters on the "soaps." Then you enter the "Soap Zone" and begin to get angry if someone or something interferes with your new daily routine. Conse-

---

My actions change my life for the better.

quently, if an event doesn't occur to "snap you out of it," you won't even realize you are wasting time you need to spend on something more important.

That's why you have to interrupt your habitual (negative) response and become aware that your anxiety has distorted what's real. You need to alert yourself to the fact that rejection and lack of response on the part of employers to your overtures have lead you, little-by-little, to depression. It's difficult to change the way you respond, but rewarding, and you can have fun doing it.

The idea is to recognize when your thinking is taking a negative turn and to immediately "shock" your train of thought so it goes in a new direction. Remember that motion begets emotion. You can start to develop a new attitude by taking some action that will force you to gain a different perspective. For example, you could do the following:

- Put a suit on in the morning even though you're not going to the office (this could also help you maintain your self-esteem).
- Don't watch television for an entire day.
- Drive your spouse's, son's or daughter's car for the day.
- Plan a day together with your family or friends.
- Get up early and watch the sun rise.
- Get in the longest line for the toll booth or at the grocery store or bank.

If you've ever seen the movie "All of Me," you have a good visualization of this happening. In the movie, Lily Tomlin's spirit enters Steve Martin's body. He falls asleep during a court proceeding, and she has to scream in order to wake him up. That's just what you have to do to yourself so you can interrupt your negative thinking and start yourself on a new path.

The Six-Step Program.

Once you have a realistic picture of your current position, continue the process with another few steps that will help you organize your thoughts and create a plan of action. If you look at your "Reality Check" as the first step, here are the remaining steps for you to take.

Step Two: Create a plan to apply the tactics you just identified in step three of your "Reality Check." Write them in the order in which you want to perform them and

---

The actions I take lead me to success.

then begin doing so. What else can you do to re-stabilize your position and then move back toward a position of relative security?

Set an objective in each area and write down the actions you can take to restore your feelings of early confidence. Try what worked for you before, but don't ignore what didn't work. Perhaps the conditions have changed and previously unsuccessful tactics are now applicable.

Step Three: Implement your plan. It's important to focus your activity so your efforts are more likely to be successful. Apply your innate innovative skills but control them so you display professional creativity.

Step Four: Evaluate your progress. Ask yourself: "What actions did I take (or not take) that got me to where I am today?" "What actions can I take today that will get me to where I want to be tomorrow?" What have you always thought you should do but didn't? What can you do right now? How can you do better?

Step Five: Based on your evaluation of your progress, you may need to make changes and corrections. Adjust your tactics rather than immediately discarding those that are less effective than others. Find out what works and do more of it. Learn what doesn't work for you and change it.

Step Six: Consult your circle of close friends. Don't feel you have to go through this all alone. Contact your friends and ask them to help you get started. They can offer an objective opinion of your plan and what you should do to get back on track and similar ideas to help you stay moving in that direction.

Use this plan to get yourself started and moving back toward feelings of improved self-esteem. You must learn to feel good about yourself again. A plan such as the one described above can start the ball rolling. You have to get through each day. If you do that with a positive attitude, productively, and methodically, you're much more likely to succeed.

My habits are positive and productive.

Chapter Two

It's As Easy As PIE

Coping successfully with unemployment may be the most difficult challenge you'll face in your life. You have to be a master in written correspondence, diplomacy, personal communications, and fiscal control. At the same time, you must develop and maintain the emotional stamina to endure constant rejection and frustration. This is a difficult period in your life, one that will test your ability and fortitude.

But in the process of taking this test, you'll grow immeasurably. When you find a new job and re-establish your life, you'll look back on this period with a sense of accomplishment and increased self-respect. You'll have the feeling that you have conquered an enormous obstacle and that you can similarly defeat anything that may later be placed in your way.

Getting through this difficult period is not going to be easy. But therein lies the source of the feeling of invincibility you will experience later. You can only find the true extent of your capabilities by applying them against what appears to be an insurmountable challenge.

Coping successfully with unemployment requires constant attention to your attitude. Over time, the regular pummelling it will take from the stream of rejection letters will erode your initial self-confidence. This occurs gradually and can cause emotional damage if not immediately addressed.

How big is your hourglass?

The continuous depletion of your early confidence is analogous to the sand in an hourglass. It's as if you have a limited supply of "attitude" in your body, and as you begin your search most of it is in the upper (positive-attitude) chamber of the hourglass. As time goes on, your self-esteem begins to empty into the lower chamber of negative thoughts and is drained (not irretrievably) at about the same rate your negative thoughts gain strength. Since this trickle of the sand is almost imperceptible, its full impact doesn't become obvious until some damage has already been done.

I take control of my thoughts every morning.

In addition, every person has a different-shaped hourglass (with varying amounts of beginning "attitude") and different rates of movement from one chamber to the other. These depend on many things including your outlook on life (a generally positive or negative world view), your commitment to your objective and the control you meet the setbacks with.

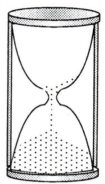

Your task is to stop the drain of your reserve of confidence before you lose all the grains of your "positive attitude." In a sense, you must figuratively turn it back over to restore your original enthusiasm and optimism. To do so, you must exercise confidence and control over your creativity, concentration, commitment, courage and competitive attitude as you use the techniques that will help you reverse the depletion of your positive attitude.

That's the essence of <u>Coping With Unemployment</u>. In it, you'll find ways to recognize the erosion of your self-esteem. And once you perceive that you are sliding away from your feeling of initial confidence into a state of frustration, you must take control and be creative in finding ways to help you turn your hourglass over. This will replenish your original self-esteem, commitment and confidence.

It's time to take control.

Depending on the circumstances surrounding your separation, you could feel a wide variety of emotions. Regardless of your initial reaction, you'll eventually recognize the reality of your circumstance. Depending on the terms of your separation, you have a limited number of days until your funds are depleted, in turn effecting your attitude and consequently your actions. As a result, you have one major objective at this point and that is to gain control of yourself in three major areas:

1) Your **ATTITUDE**

2) Your **EXPENSES**

3) Your **ACTIONS**

If you have been unemployed for a long time, you probably already feel dejection and perhaps even depression. It's time to renew your search. Go back to the basics. Make today the first day of your new search. Plan new actions, reorganize your finances and restore your attitude so you can proceed.

I am totally dedicated to resolving my present situation.

Signpost For Success:

An old proverb says success occurs where opportunity meets preparation. If you work hard to prepare your strategy, you're more likely to create your own opportunities and subsequently become more successful.

Avoid the "Ready. Fire. Aim." attitude.

There are many benefits to planning your journey properly. First, your tactics will be based on an objective foundation, not on a subjective analysis of your financial and emotional situation. By accurately defining your current status, you're more likely to set realistic goals and plan the actions that will get you there. Secondly, your activities will be coordinated and synergistic.

"I only have 'ize' for you."

A complete job search is made up of a series of methodical and sequential steps that must be performed early in your quest. Many times this preparation is abandoned in order to get right to the "meat" of your search, such as sending resumes and interviewing for jobs. But if you skip the planning steps, you may be heading off in the wrong direction without the necessary tools, perhaps damaging your progress.

You can think of this as the **PIE** technique, where you **P**lan, **I**mplement and **E**valuate your search. Then you're likely to succeed more quickly than you otherwise would have. This theory is covered in greater detail in the book <u>Job Search 101</u> but can be summarized in just a few words:

_____

I evaluate and respond to every event in a positive way.

- Crystall*ize*:   Begin with a clear image of what you want to do. This should be based on a thorough under-standing of your strengths, weaknesses and goals.

- Strateg*ize*:   After you thoroughly understand your present situation, create different ways in which you can most successfully market your skills and ben-efits to the highest bidder.

- Organ*ize*:   Once you have all your strategies designed, you should organize them into a written self-market-ing plan that will direct your efforts toward specific objectives.

- Energ*ize*:   Now you may start the implementation of your plan with a 100% commitment to success. You'll find the pursuit of employment is a full time job in itself and requires hard work and long hours to achieve your goals.

- Advert*ise*:   In the shortest amount of time you should tell the greatest number of people about your skills and availability. This requires a combined thrust of both mass and personal communication tools.

- Rev*ise*:   You should experiment with your efforts and evaluate the relative success of each in its ability to achieve your goals. Do more of what works and less of what doesn't.

- Real*ize*:   The realization of your goals will be a combina-tion of many things including detailed prepara-tion, creative implementation and constructive evaluation. This takes hard work and a positive attitude, so if your attitude is negative and self-defeating, your search will be unnecessarily prolonged.

Don't hurry. Be happy.

Take your time to get through the early preparation. Give due consideration to your strengths and weaknesses and plan to use the former and improve upon the latter. Determine the optimum price range in which you can sell your services for your best long-term interests.

I project the positive feelings I have about myself.

Consider the geographical location that provides the best opportunity for your career goals. And plan all the promotional activities that will make the most people aware of the benefits you can bring to them.

Your plan charts your course for success, which presupposes that you have a destination in mind. So begin by establishing a goal that defines the end result you are seeking, and take the time to plan your job-search activities. You'll find that the process of reviewing your skills, setting goals and creating the plans to achieve them has an energizing effect on your attitude and confidence.

It's at this time that the test of your character begins. Human nature dictates that one's attitude deteriorates in the presence of negative feedback without sufficient positive feedback to compensate for it. The combination of these events begins to wear away at your optimism and enthusiasm. It's up to you to reinforce your self-confidence in the face of a deluge of negative input.

You will learn more about yourself after going through a pro-longed job search than you will from almost any other single event in your life. When you become re-employed, you'll look back on this time with a feeling of self-satisfaction that is hard to explain. You will experience a sense of almost invincibility, that you can face whatever life presents you with. You will get the feeling that you've just gone through the initiation of a very exclusive club whose members are limited to those who have met one of life's toughest challenges, and won.

No failure is ever final.

The important thing is to keep moving ahead. Try and learn. Try and learn. Try again and learn more. Keep your mind active and it won't be invaded by negative thoughts of doom and gloom. Be a "keeper:" keep thinking, keep acting, keep believing, keep going. But at some point you start to question, rather than evaluate yourself. You might begin to blame the poor results on yourself for having chosen the wrong career, writing inadequate correspondence or having improper interviewing skills. It is now more important than ever to "reach down" and take control of your attitude. If you don't do something soon you could be headed for more trouble. You must take responsibility for your situation and reverse the deterioration of your self-esteem.

Don't blame yourself or anybody else for your situation. Blame is a very negative concept. It assumes that someone is at fault for the poor results and therefore should be punished for it. On the other hand, taking responsibility acknowledges that a less-than-desirable outcome

---

I am confident in myself and my ability to find a new job.

has occurred and that you must do something to rectify it. There is a big difference between the statements "Something must be done" and "I must do something." The latter states that you will take the proper action rather than wait until someone else does something to rectify your predicament. Once you accept responsibility for your position, you accept that something can be done and that you must take action.

Stage Left.

Many people do not take any positive action and they give up. They stop looking for a job and wait around for something to come to them. Many declare personal bankruptcy (which may not be surrender, but in some cases a logical choice). Others rely on alcohol or drugs as an escape, but the consequences of choosing one of those alternatives can be serious. In addition to the immediate mental and physical repercussions of substance abuse is their habit-forming nature. Keep your wits about you and you'll be in a better position to deal with what's real.

I monitor my attitude to keep it positive and confident.

Chapter Three

The Anatomy of an Attitude

What is your definition of the word "attitude?" What is a good attitude and what is a bad attitude? If you aren't sure what the answers are, how can you deal with them? You probably haven't thought much before about what makes up your attitude, and now the idea of doing so may be overwhelming to you. But if you break the concept down into manageable parts, you'll find it easier to monitor and maintain a successful job-search attitude. Although there are volumes written on the subject of attitude in general, we'll dissect this concept in terms of what is important to helping you deal with it during your present situation.

Everybody has an attitude. For some it's positive and for others it's negative, but for most it's somewhere in between the two extremes. Most people feel that if they have self-esteem, then their attitude is generally positive and vice versa. But too much emphasis has been placed on self-confidence as the one quality necessary for success in one's quest for employment. Self-esteem is more than self-confidence and as important as self-confidence is, it's not the only emotion that you must support.

Forward ho.

You can view this as you would the spokes of a wheel on an old Conestoga Wagon. All the spokes must be in place for the wheel to work. If one or more of them are broken, the wheel is crushed under the weight of the wagon. Similarly, you have seven "spokes" to maintain for an effective job-search attitude. Each of these must be monitored and strengthened if they appear to weaken. They enable you to remain competent, professional, enthusiastic and successful throughout your journey to employment.

These traits are as follows:

Control	Courage
Commitment	Competition
Confidence	Concentration
Creativity	

I break my search down into manageable segments.

From another perspective, you could look at each of these as an ingredient in a recipe that makes up your attitude. The way that you mix these in your own mind is what makes you unique. If you have one hundred percent confidence and none of the other characteristics, you won't be nearly as successful as someone with a more balanced combination. Your job is to isolate these and concentrate on improving each one.

Divide and conquer.

By breaking your job-search attitude down into these elements you will not become overwhelmed or intimidated by attempting to conquer something you can't see or perhaps even comprehend. But if you understand the characteristics that make up your job-search attitude and strive to strengthen each, you'll be more successful in dealing with their erosion.

For example, you can improve your self-confidence by starting out with minor successes and building on those. Practice with a video camera and go on informational interviews before contacting your most important prospects. Commitment in many cases is thrust upon you by a deadline that is only months away. Courage is demonstrated every time you pick up the telephone and call a person to ask for an interview if you are reluctant to do so. You can develop your creativity every time you look at a bumper sticker or tee-shirt and get an idea for a new job opportunity. You exhibit control by instilling self-discipline to organize your efforts and keep them aimed at your goals. Your competitive attitude shows with every thank-you note and follow-up letter that you send. And you exhibit your concentration by steadfastly focusing your attention on your job search.

You can look at these aspects of yourself without feeling overwhelmed if you address them one by one. Your job search is a way of proving to yourself that you have the power to control your thoughts and consequently your actions. When it's over, you'll have a much greater understanding of your capabilities, and you'll look back on all your efforts with pride and gratitude for an opportunity to find out what you really can do. It's a good feeling when you get there, and well worth the journey.

Being unemployed can take a tremendous toll on your attitude. One of your most difficult yet important tasks is to monitor and correct a deterioration in your attitude. There are "red flags" that surface during a prolonged job search that indicate this "attitude disintegration" is begin-

---

My thoughts remain on what I can do today to be successful tomorrow.

ning. Once these are identified, you can respond positively and redirect your thoughts and actions to more results-oriented activities.

Why a good attitude is important to you.

What you concentrate on grows.

According to Viktor Frankl in his book <u>Man's Search For Meaning</u>, if you focus on a negative possibility, "you could actually enhance the likelihood that it will occur." He calls this "anticipatory anxiety." If you dwell on the bad things that you are experiencing in your life now, you actually stand a good chance of prolonging them or making them worse.

"It is a characteristic of fear that it produces precisely that of which the patient is afraid," adds Frankl. If you are afraid, support yourself in your fear by reminding yourself that you are an empowered adult capable of taking care of yourself. If you must worry, do so about the positive aspects of your situation and <u>they</u> may become your self-fulfilling prophecy. That is why you must reverse any frustrated thinking and restore or create an attitude of positive expectancy. Concentrate on what is good <u>now</u>, or what <u>could be good</u> if you worked to make it so.

It's your response-ability that determines your success.

The response you make to a situation can be an action or it could be inaction. If you decide to do nothing to rectify your situation, some result will still occur. But in that case you relinquish control over the result. Instead, focus on the positive outcome that you want to achieve and the actions you can take to make it happen.

Event ———> Thought ———> Response ———> Result

Whenever an event occurs to you, you immediately begin to think about it. The strength of your self-esteem will dictate the response you make and subsequently the results that occur. For example, if you perform particularly poorly on an interview (Event) you'll mull this over in your mind as you leave the office (Thought). Based on your feelings at the time, there are a variety of different responses you could make with equally different results:

I accept responsibility for my circumstances.

Current Emotional State	Response/Result
Self-confidence:	Objectively evaluate your performance (Response) to see what you did correctly, and plan the techniques you need to practice in order to perform better on the next interview (Result).
Frustration:	Become angry (in your mind) with the interviewer for asking you the wrong questions (Response) and consequently fail to improve your interviewing skills (Result)
Dejection:	Berate yourself for having poor interviewing skills (Response) and further diminish your attitude (Result)
Surrender:	Do nothing at all (Response) because there's no way you are going to get a job anyway (Result).

If you take action based on feelings of high expectation, you're more likely to create a positive result. Conversely, if you take a negative action, or no action, you are far less likely to achieve a positive result. Attitude management requires that you take control of your thoughts, redirect them toward a positive result and thereby create the actions that will lead you there.

Actions speak louder than words.

It's a misnomer that an attitude is intangible, that it can't be seen and described by others. Quite the contrary, your attitude is visible, and changes in it are immediately evident. Attitude management thus has the practical result of others seeing you differently.

If you're not part of the solution, you're part of the problem.

Employers want to hire people who can make a positive contribution to their organization. They want people who will create solutions to their problems and not become part of the problems themselves. If you can demonstrate in your interview that you are a confident "idea" person, you're more likely to make a favorable impression than if you appear uncertain or negative.

I am successful because I persist.

Since your outward conduct reflects your inner feelings, you should work hard to project a positive attitude. This is true, especially when you feel frustrated or dejected. Your lack of eye communication, stooped posture and uncertain verbal communication skills will announce your poor attitude. The interviewer won't know if this is the "real you" or just a reflection of your temporary situation. Since he doesn't want to make a mistake in hiring someone, his doubt will probably take you out of contention for the position.

These initial impressions are vitally important to your job search. They are rarely based on what you say, but on your overall appearance. And the way you look is most often a reflection of how you feel. Your low self-esteem will most likely be reflected in your posture, eye communication, hand shake and general bearing.

Just for a moment, sit up the way you would if you knew you were unable to be defeated. Straighten your back, raise your eyes and confidently hold your arms and hands. Then stand against a wall with your heels, buttocks and shoulder blades touching the wall. Now take a few steps away and feel this new position. How does this make you feel? If it's different from the way you normally feel, you may be inadvertently projecting the image of a defeated person.

Your health is affected by your attitude.

Sustaining a good attitude is important for your own mental and physical health. As you begin to worry increasingly about what "might" happen to you if you don't get a job, you'll laugh less often and make more negative comments (about yourself and others) than you have at any other time in your life. Stress and tension will begin to take their toll unless you have a positive outlet for this aggravation.

While you are in the throes of a job search, you are guaranteed to gain weight. In fact, I know exactly how much weight you will put on and where it will be placed. The amount is 6600 million million million tons (this is the estimated weight of the world) and it goes squarely onto your shoulders. And unless you have a program in place to lose this weight, you are headed for trouble.

Take the pressure off yourself.

Inevitably in the job search, most people will ignore or reject your candidacy for employment. Your attitude will begin to get worse over time. Unfortunately, everybody begins with a different "amount" of

---

I always look to what is good in my life today.

self-esteem, so the effects of extended unemployment affect people differently.

It's not necessary to be 100% positive all the time. An attempt to reach this state of Nirvana will only place unnecessary pressure upon you. Find your natural level of comfort and work on maintaining it. If you're naturally not a confident person, recognize that. Under these conditions, an attempt on your part to achieve total self-confidence will only be self-defeating.

The job search is an emotional roller coaster. Seek only to minimize the ups and downs so you can deal with adversity rationally, objectively and emotionally. Don't try to be somebody you're not.

Try to get the proper amount of sleep every night.

You may find yourself spending eight hours in bed every night, but the chances of sleeping that entire time are not good. As you dwell on the negative consequences of what "might" happen to you, you'll find that it's more difficult to get a good night's sleep. This is a major contributing factor to irritability and fatigue. Addressing your loss of confidence will let you sleep better and improve your attitude and performance during the day.

Your entire family gets laid off with you.

Unfortunately, your aggravation and stress don't only impact you. Marital and family relations can become strained as taut nerves cause friction that would otherwise not have been. You'll find yourself yelling unnecessarily at your spouse and children for minor mishaps that might have previously gone unnoticed. Your subsequent feelings of guilt will increase your anxiety and decrease your self-esteem. Instead, communicate your feelings to your family members. Sometimes just verbalizing them can have a cathartic effect on you.

Deal with the job-search "givens."

There are several basic axioms associated with a prolonged job search, and all of them have a negative affect on your attitude. If you can recognize that these are going to occur, the impact on your attitude may be reduced.

1) Rejection is a way of life.

The largest amount of your correspondence to prospective employers will be ignored. Obviously, this will wear away at your

---

I am aware of the job-search pitfalls and I have a plan in place to deal with them.

attitude. It's imperative to find some way to deal emotionally with the lack of response to your correspondence as well as the rejection. You may find yourself reaching the point where you welcome rejection letters, since then at least you'll know that your correspondence is getting through.

Just be forewarned that you will be rejected far more times than you will be accepted. Don't take it personally. After all, they haven't even met you yet. Accept it as a challenge to improve your correspondence and thereby increase the likelihood that you will be accepted for an interview.

2) Job offers can be rescinded.

There are a variety of reasons for which a job offer may be rescinded. But regardless of the reason why it occurs, the fact remains that it can have a devastating affect on your attitude. This is compounded by the fact that when you accepted the offer originally, you felt the "weight of the world" lifted from your shoulders. Now that it has been "dumped" back upon you, it seems heavier than ever.

3) People make decisions too slowly.

You'll rarely meet an employer who is in as much of a hurry as you are to reach a decision. Vacations, travel schedules, other business and unavoidable emergencies will interfere with the decision process. In the meantime, you have to smile, tell them you understand and continue to bear the pressure of waiting for an answer.

Every time an interview is rescheduled or telephone call delayed, you'll feel a little of the "air" go out of you. Oddly, this loss of air doesn't relieve the pressure on you; in fact it increases the pressure. Your challenge is to deal with it in a positive way and channel it into an energizing force that will sustain your self-esteem.

4) The salary is rarely as much as you had hoped.

A poor economy and an increase in the competition for most jobs will create a "buyer's market," which forces the wage rates down. You may have to call upon your courage and confidence to turn down an offer that is not economically responsible for you to accept. Accepting such an offer may meet your short-term needs, but your long term financial condition may take a beating.

I know that job-search rejection is not directed at me personally.

A positive feeling of self-esteem should not be misconstrued with ego. If you let egoism tell you that an offer is "beneath" you when it is in fact a rational offer, you could be deluded into an extended search. Review your financial situation and objectively determine the absolute minimum offer you can accept. This doesn't mean you have to accept it, but at least you'll know the level below which you cannot go.

If you have the personal resources to make up the difference between the offer and your obligations, the situation may be different. But just make sure you analyze all the ramifications of the offer. When you accept it, know in your heart that it's the best one for you and your family over the long term.

A poor self-image can also cost you money. If you don't feel good about yourself, it's less likely that you will negotiate for a better compensation package. When the question comes around to, "How much money do you need?," your reduced self-esteem could cause you to ask for less than you are capable of earning. As Abe Lincoln said, "People are worth pretty much what they think they're worth." If you have a good feeling about yourself, and you think you are worth a lot, you'll most likely end up with a higher offer than you otherwise would have received.

If you want to pursue it, then you must do it.

A good attitude is made up of many parts, each requiring some degree of attention. Over the next seven chapters you'll see what they are, why they're important to your search and how to strengthen and maintain each segment. Once you have a "grip" on the fundamentals of your attitude, you'll be in a better position to set realistic and attainable goals for yourself as well as the strategic plan to make them come to pass.

No one else can do this for you. Your goals must motivate you to take action, even when you have been without employment for an extended period. Hope and cope, but don't mope. Don't feel sorry for yourself. Feel sorry for the people who have to compete with you for the career opportunity that you choose to obtain. The only thing that can stop you from reaching it is you.

I address my daily challenges with energy and optimism.

PART TWO:
The seven critical attributes

Chapter Four

You're the Captain of Your Ship

The ability to remain in control may well be your most important asset while unemployed. You can think of controlling your life as you would your car. You turn it on, put it in gear, direct it toward your destination, determine the speed with which you move ahead, make corrections in your course, schedule it for regular maintenance and add fuel periodically. You must do the same thing to yourself.

Some people view control as a restraining act, the need to hold or curb something. But control is really a *dynamic* process. It requires adjustments to compensate for predictable and unforeseen circumstances as you move toward your objective. For example, you need to control the use of your time to utilize your twenty four hours per day most productively. You don't spend your time. You invest it in activities that will yield a high rate of return.

With control, you can apply your creativity professionally. It directs your commitment so you can pursue your goals. It helps you use your confidence for productive means. A controlled grip on your anxiety will give you the courage to continue with your efforts even after you have been rejected 99% of the time. And it ensures that you maintain your competitive edge without giving in to tensions that might otherwise cause you to panic.

Control is self-discipline. It helps you create patterns and successful habits that lead you further towards your goal, even though you're worried about what lies ahead of you. During times of reduced self-esteem, you need the discipline to continue working on your job-search program. Perhaps it's because of these feelings that you must continue. You must persist in your actions with a realistically positive attitude during emotion-draining periods. When you accomplish this feat, your self-respect increases as does your feeling of invincibility.

Self-discipline is also the ability to recognize an opportunity that comes to you on the "spur of the moment," evaluate and pursue it even though it wasn't part of your original plan. For instance, my idea to attend a trade show (as discussed in Chapter Twenty Nine) was not in my

---

I am in control of my finances.

original plan, but it did represent a chance previously unknown to me to meet 500 decision makers in my target market. So I did it.

Why control is important in your job search.

There are three major areas where you must exercise control during your job search. These are your attitude, your finances and your actions. It's difficult to separate these three areas because they are all intertwined and effect each other. For example, negative financial performance could adversely affect your attitude. As the domino effect takes place, you could find yourself doing less and less to act on finding a job. On the other hand, an improved attitude will motivate you to take actions that will help your financial situation.

Controlling your attitude can make you more optimistic and confident. Such control recognizes that everything will not go smoothly during your search but that you will be able to deal with whatever does come up. Furthermore, controlling your finances can help you cut back on expenses so you can extend your deadline for as long as possible.

Controlling your actions gives you a sense of mastery. It places you in charge, able to make the correct decisions for your long-term best interests. It's invigorating to know where you want to go, how you are going to get there and then follow through. If you don't seize control of your destiny in all three of these areas, your job search will lead you in a variety of different directions at the same time, adding to the frustration normally associated with an extended period of unemployment.

The keystone state.

Control of your thoughts may well be the keystone to your emotional state. If left uncontrolled, they will take their own course which is (given your current circumstances) usually a negative one. Think about how you think. Learn to listen to yourself. Discipline yourself to recognize the "red flags" that your thoughts provide and immediately take action to re-direct them toward the attainment of your goals. It takes commitment and courage to do this, but it's a critical function to perform. Take charge of your thoughts, and you will control your life.

Put yourself on automatic pilot.

In many airplanes, the pilot has an option to place his controls on "automatic," which means the plane in effect flies itself. Of course the

---

I believe in myself.

proper program has already been installed so the plane's computer can read any changes that show the plane going off course and automatically make the necessary corrections. You can do the same yourself. Program into your mind the parameters that determine success and then go to work acting on what you have planned. Program yourself "automatically" to determine if you're going off course and then make the necessary changes.

Since control begins by establishing parameters, let's see how you can create your own indicators of a successful "flight." For example:

- You could set an objective to make ten telephone calls to prospective employers every day. You could easily make ten calls and never speak to one potential decision maker. Instead, set your objective to call people until you arrange one interview. This could take one call or it could take one hundred. But your actions are more likely to *accomplish* something rather than just keep you busy.

- If you detect someone in your circle of friends commiserating with you by telling you how bad things are in the job market, you may need to avoid that person at least until you achieve your goals. Negative input will build upon itself until it has defeated your resolve to succeed. Associate with only positive people, those who will support and assist you in your search.

- If your intuition tells you that something is wrong with an offer, think twice before accepting it. Listen to your "gut feeling" and do what it tells you to do or not to do. Rely on your intuition to steer you in the right direction.

Learn to recognize when you are giving yourself negative signals. If you hear yourself using the words "always" or "never," they are most likely associated with a negative statement. These are "trigger words" which can warn you that you are thinking negatively. Then you take charge by directing your thoughts more positively.

These words don't have to be related to your search in order to trigger your attention. When you ask yourself "Why do I always get in the slowest checkout line?" or "Why do these things always happen to me?" tell yourself that these events are not "always" the case, though they may be happening this one time. Weren't you ever the first person

I find time to relax every day.

in line or in the fastest-moving line? Didn't something good "ever" happen to you? Of course it did. Think back to those times now that you have alerted yourself to the direction your thoughts have taken.

Become underwhelmed by your situation.

Don't become so overwhelmed by everything in your search that you decide to give up. Success in your search is simply to find names of people to contact and then send them letters. Follow up until you hear from them. Once they respond to your letter favorably, they'll ask you to come in for an interview. If you perform well during the interview, you'll get the job. That's all there is to it. The time-consuming factor is making so many contacts that you find the one job that is out there waiting for you. It takes time, but it's there, and it's up to you to find it.

It's important not to over-manage your efforts. You must give different activities a chance to work. Think of this process as you would think of driving on a slippery road on a rainy day. You can't change the driving conditions, but you can adjust your actions to compensate for the negative external conditions. Don't make major adjustments and don't hit the brakes too hard. Just drive more carefully, "feel" the road and respond as warranted by the feedback you receive from constant attention to your actions.

For instance, you might find that you are not generating as many interviews as you would like from your direct-mail cold-calling efforts. If you test different letters, give them a few weeks to demonstrate their relative success before abandoning them for other approaches.

Your job search is totally under your control. The quality and quantity of effort you apply determines the length of time your quest will last. Discipline yourself to do what you need to do, and take time to rest later, after you are back to work. Never give up and never let up.

But don't overwhelm yourself by trying to control every element of your life all at the same time. Take one step at a time, and **just for today**...

- ...take one action that will lead you back into control of your life.

- ...don't worry about what might occur. The worst has already happened and you lived through it. Today, think one thought about what you could do to make it better.

- ...read something that requires effort, thought and concentration. Use the material to spur ideas about something you could do to improve your situation.

I make the difference in my life.

- ...look and feel the best that you can under the circumstances. Get up earlier than usual, shower and dress up in one of your business outfits. Then go to a telephone and make one networking call. As long as you're up, why not try revising your resume?
- ...plan one more action you could take tomorrow than you did today.
- ...exercise your body by taking a walk, and your character by doing one thing you know is right but that you don't want to do.
- ...smile one more time than you did yesterday.

How to avoid surrendering control.

Think of your mind as a bank filled with a reserve of self-esteem. Deposit into and withdraw from it only positive "currency." Maintain a positive balance by depositing more reinforcing information than you extract. And be aware that others can deposit into and withdraw from your account. So you have to be on the lookout constantly for people and events that are attempting to steal self-esteem from you. Review your "balance" each evening by <u>objectively</u> evaluating the transactions that occurred that day.

Review your day to see what happened that caused you to feel badly about yourself and take steps to diminish the negative effect on your attitude. For example, if you didn't receive any rejection notices, perhaps you should follow up on some of the letters you sent previously. Or if you stayed in bed later than you normally do, set your alarm clock for an earlier time tomorrow. Regularly evaluate your progress and plan ways to improve your performance and attitude.

Divided we stand. United we fall.

You have to separate the events that you can control from those which you cannot. Don't dwell on troubles like the increasing rate of unemployment or the lack of response to your letters. These are out of your control, and worrying about them will only cause you undue frustration. On the other hand, you can control your response to these events, just as you can influence your attitude toward them. Determine what is under your control, and work hard to exercise your powers in those areas.

I seek the advice of interested people.

It always comes back to this point. You have to first take action on your own behalf if you are to correct and redirect your thinking. Pressure is generated internally by dwelling on the uncontrollables or the negative "what ifs" in your life. Similarly, relief is generated internally by controlling your response to the words and events that bombard you every day. Make a decision to exercise authority over your thoughts (and therefore your response), rather than surrendering control to forces beyond your influence.

How to take control.

The feeling that you are losing control of your job search may be caused by a variety of factors. The source of each may be internal or external, but the effect could be the same if you don't exert and maintain your self-discipline. During your job search, be careful that you **DON'T SURRENDER CONTROL TO...**

1) **...negative statistics.** The media are full of stories and negative facts related to the current job market. The headlines will proclaim the number of large companies that are laying people off, the continuing rise of the unemployment rate, the monthly decrease in the number of help-wanted ads appearing in the paper and many other articles proclaiming doom and gloom in your city and the country as a whole.

Maintain control by evaluating statistics.

There's an old proverb that states: "Don't believe anything that you hear and only half of what you see." While this is an extreme view, it does address the point that you should not accept as gospel everything that you read or hear. Evaluate any information to determine its validity and importance to you.

For example, you may read that unemployment has reached 8% and that this is the highest percentage since World War Two. But if you evaluate this in another way, it states that 92% of all the people in the work force are still employed. While this may offer little solace if you're one of the 8%, it should establish or reinforce your confidence that the future holds greater opportunity than if a significantly larger percentage of people were unemployed.

Similarly, if you have an average of one *second* interview for every ten *first-interviews* you attend, you could view that as a failure rate of 90%. On the other hand, had you evaluated your performance on each one and tried different tactics, you might interpret the results as having been given nine opportunities to see what didn't work. And if your one

---

I maintain control by taking positive action.

second interview occurred on the tenth try, it should indicate that your constant evaluation and practice were successful.

Learn to separate fact from "hype." Newspaper headlines are written specifically to get the attention of many people as quickly as possible. Therefore, they are written in a provocative manner so you will stop what you are doing and read the copy. For example, the headlines may proclaim that a large local employer is eliminating 3000 jobs. People might understandably assume this to mean they are laying off 3000 people, and that could reinforce their negative concept about the future of the economy.

But further perusal may demonstrate that the reduction will occur over three or more years and be accomplished primarily through normal attrition and voluntary departures. Therefore, read the entire article and evaluate its contents. Headlines are written to attract attention, not necessarily to impart all the facts. Don't assume anything, but interpret the information according to its relevancy to your particular situation.

In the job search, it doesn't matter who is right but what is right. Make a habit of evaluating your activities and the feedback you receive. Interpret everything according to your own situation. Don't accept negative input without questioning it, and rely on deduction as well as intuition to determine what the statistics mean to you. Then respond accordingly.

2) ...**predictions.** Opinions and forecasts of any kind should be submitted to the same scrutiny and evaluation you apply to statistics. If a noted expert in a field predicts that the unemployment "picture" will only get worse before it gets better, recognize the fact that it is only his opinion. There is no way to validate its accuracy no matter how educated his judgement may be.

Maintain control by setting goals.

If you listen to the forecasts of continued unemployment, you could become less sure of attaining your job-search goal. These predictions refer to possibilities and generalities. They do not refer to your specific situation because the person who has proffered his opinion is not aware of your skills or your determination and commitment to succeed. You are a uniquely qualified individual who can succeed where others didn't. You are an individual who is out-performing your competitors in a world of negative soothsayers who are not aware of your tenacity and self-discipline when confronted with adversity. Follow the path you have set to reach your goals, and don't be side-swiped by professors of negative thoughts.

_____

I interpret events with a positive and open frame of mind.

Develop yourself into the person you want to be. The job search is
analogous to the way a professional photographer seeks the one photo he
will use. He may take one hundred or more different shots of the same
thing, each time changing the aperture setting and shutter speed. But he
always maintains his focus on the target. Similarly, you can (and should)
evaluate your relative results and change your tactics accordingly, but
you should always do so with constant attention to your goal.

3) ...increased anxiety. The pressures of an extended job search will
create many anxious moments. As your deadline approaches and no job
offer is in sight, you could lose sleep and become more apprehensive.
You may also react with more irritation to the innocent queries of friends
and relatives.

You'll wait by the telephone, hoping that today will be the day
you hear from prospective employers. When they don't call, or call with
information that the decision will be delayed, your level of anxiety will
increase a notch.

Maintain control by relaxing.

Tension is an every-day event during your search. The important
point is that you must manage your tension and use it for productive
purposes. Denis Waitley asks the question "Is tension good or bad?" His
answer is "yes." Tension is either good or bad depending on whether you
control it or it controls you. Tension you control keeps you performing at
your top level. It helps you make that extra effort that allows you to
accomplish more. It helps you listen and generally perform better on an
interview because you have that sharper "edge" about you. On the other
hand, tension that controls you can lead to serious emotional and physical problems if you allow it to continue unchecked.

Conventional wisdom tell us to stop and count to ten before
responding to an event or the words of other people. This has never been
more true than it is in a job search. If you react too quickly it could cause
you to over-correct the issue. By accurately assessing the positive and
negative aspects of different events, you can control your response and
its effects.

There is a difference between a reaction and a response. The
former is an immediate action taken without sufficient forethought about
the impact or damage it could have upon the recipient (who could be
you). The latter is a reply which has been given adequate consideration.

For example, you can respond to your tension in at least two
ways: A) adopt an exercise routine that will help you release tension and

---

I budget my money and my time.

pressure in a positive way; B) maintain a sense of humor. Don't make fun of yourself, but find humor where you can and thereby release tension and enjoy yourself for the moment:

A) Get up and do something. It matters less what type of physical conditioning program you choose (walking, tennis, gardening, bicycling, etc) than it does that you do it on a routine basis. Regular exercise will relax and invigorate you in addition to providing many other benefits.

Related to this subject is your intake of alcohol. Don't have a drink because it "helps you to relax." You may find that as you do this more frequently, the "cocktail hour" begins starting earlier than usual. There is no moral message intended here, just the fact that alcohol is a depressant, affects your health and can be addictive. It won't make you feel better, only worse. It will sap the energy from you and reduce the productive hours of your day by the number of hours it affects you.

B) Don't knock your humor senseless. The ability to have fun will be a valuable asset during these times. Having fun doesn't mean making self-deprecating comments that make people laugh at your expense. Nor does it mean that you should start telling jokes or making puns at every opportunity. It does mean that you should develop the capacity to see the lighter side of things.

Having a sense of humor can't come from the conscious decision that "from now on I'll have a sense of humor." It is the result of self-confidence and the realization that there can be a humorous way to make your point. For example, during one interview with two interviewers, I mentioned that I had just completed an extensive sales-training course. One interviewer said that I must therefore be a good listener. I responded by saying "What?" Both interviewers chuckled. That one response proved my listening skills more than if I had told them what a good listener I was.

A healthy sense of humor will also help you when you inadvertently do something "stupid." Instead of berating yourself, you can enjoy the humor of it. It's also more likely that you'll be able to relieve the embarrassment of the moment by responding with humor.

One of these events occurred to me when ordering food at a speaker in the drive-through lane of a fast-food restaurant. I placed my order and added that I wanted it "to go." The attendant asked "What?" and I repeated that I wanted to take the order with me. It wasn't until I began making my way to the window that I realized it had been unnecessary to state that I wanted my food "to go" when going through the drive-

---

I feel good about myself.

through lane. I made some comment about this fact to the attendant collecting the money, and we both got a chuckle out of it.

4) **...fate.** Don't give in to a feeling of inevitability. If you begin to think that it doesn't matter what you do because "What will be will be," you will cease taking action on your own behalf.

Work hard at whatever it is that you must do, and then deal with each obstacle as it presents itself. If it's "to be," it's up to you to make it happen. Don't surrender control to your astrological sign or any idea of predestination which causes you to cease working on your own behalf.

Maintain control by breaking the fickle finger of fate.

Other than the loss of a loved one, there are few events in life that will cause as much mental anguish as a prolonged period of unemployment. In both cases, you have to "reach down" for that inner strength to get you through. You must take control of your thoughts and actions and build upon what you have left without dwelling on what you have lost.

In another example from his book Man's Search for Meaning, Viktor Frankl said, "We must never forget that we may also find meaning in life even when confronted with a hopeless situation.... For what then matters is to bear witness to the uniquely human potential at its best, which is to transform personal tragedy into a triumph, to turn one's predicament into a human achievement."

You can make a difference in your life. It's easy to feel that "my situation is hopeless because it's different from everyone else's. I can't apply the techniques others have used since they won't work for me." But this is not at all true. Granted, there may well be unique aspects of your situation, but there are principles of achievement everyone can apply.

One of these is that you can make a difference in your life and that no one else can do it for you. Certainly other people can help, but it's like quitting smoking. Everyone is cheering for you to make it, but only you will experience withdrawal and reach down inside for the strength to withstand the desire for another cigarette.

Today is the tomorrow you thought about yesterday. Don't surrender your self-discipline to thoughts of inevitability. You can't change past events, and the future is of course uncertain. But controlling what you are able is the action you can take right now. This will in turn create your future, and when tomorrow comes you can deal with it. Immerse yourself in what you can do today to solve your problems.

I am proud of myself because ...

Look to the credo found in Chapter Thirteen and evaluate each segment of it, particularly the words:

"When tomorrow comes, this day will be gone forever, leaving in its place whatever I have traded for it. I pledge to myself that it shall be for good, gain and success."

This means that whatever you have tomorrow is a direct result of what you do today. If you prospect today, you'll have opportunities tomorrow. If you reduce expenses today, you'll have more to spend tomorrow. If you network today, you'll have leads tomorrow. Take action. Don't leave anything up to fate. Don't "have a good day" but "make it a good day."

Look to the good in other people and yourself. Further analysis of the credo brings us to these words:

"I am tolerant of other people, their shortcomings and their mistakes, and I view their actions with the most favorable understanding possible."

With these thoughts, you can view a prospective employer's lack of response in a different way. It's no longer "your fault" that the responses are not forthcoming. It's just that the recipient didn't have time to respond because of all the other things that were on his mind. This will encourage you to create new ways to get his attention as you follow up on your initial correspondence. Now you are back in control.

When you're feeling down, change bats. The great New York Yankee baseball player Yogi Berra has had many interesting quotations attributed to him. One of them is particularly helpful in explaining not only how to keep from blaming others, but how to keep from blaming yourself as well:

"I never blame myself when I'm not hitting. I just blame the bat and if it keeps up, I change bats. After all, if I know it isn't my fault that I'm not hitting, how can I get mad at myself?"

Don't get mad, get even. Don't get angry with people when they don't respond to you, and don't get angry with yourself either. Pick up a different bat. Keep writing and calling until you embarrass them into responding to you. At least you will have the feeling that you took control of an event and didn't allow it to take its own course.

Keep your senses about you. As the credo concludes, it reminds you to *respond* instead of *react* to a situation. Even if you can't control the event itself, you can always control your response to it:

I control my response to external events.

"I will respond in a calm and intelligent manner, without alarm, no matter what the situation. If I cannot control the situation, I will respond in a positive manner, even to negative facts."

When bombarded with thoughts of inevitability, reach down for the fortitude to counter with a positive, offensive attack. This knowledge furthers the essential understanding that you are in control of your destiny and you have not surrendered to the idea that your future is in the hands of fate.

5) **...other people.** The underlying principle of success in your quest for employment is that you are totally responsible for its success. You should seek assistance from other people and rely on them for emotional support, but you are the one who must go on the interview and, eyeball to eyeball, convince the prospective employer that you are the best person for this job.

Even your best-intentioned friends could at some point play Devil's Advocate with you. They will point out all the reasons in the world why your new idea won't work. If this continues to occur, you will begin to doubt your abilities.

Similarly, your family members may, with increasing frequency, ask you what is going to happen if you don't get a job. As you search for an adequate answer, you will begin asking yourself this same question. The more you do that, the less likely you will be to come up with a reassuring answer.

Maintain control by listening to an Angel's Advocate.

If you play golf, you may have asked your fellow players what club you should use in a particular situation. With the intention of helping, they will tell you what club they would use. This may or may not have any bearing on the proper club for you to use under the same conditions.

It is good to seek the advice and opinions of interested people, but just recognize that it is their opinion only. It is founded on how they see a situation. They are describing what they would do if they were in your situation based on their knowledge of their limitations and abilities. So, seek their advice but evaluate it in light of your strengths and weaknesses before accepting or rejecting it.

I am in control of my plan and my thoughts.

There are many human resources at your disposal, and all you have to do is ask for their assistance. These include members of the clergy, family, friends and professionals. Many times you'll find that people feel flattered when asked for their opinion and they truly want to help you. When you seek advice from someone, you'll often find you've gained a valuable ally.

There are numerous ways to seek new input. For example, you can circulate in new groups. Accept invitations to parties and events at which you know there will be many strangers. Go to PTA meetings, industry-association conferences, even a different gym to meet new people. Attend meetings of different unemployment-support groups. Network with unemployed people who have more recent information about the status of the job search in your area.

6) **...intimidation.** Some people view themselves as inferior to others simply because they are unemployed. They feel they are not a productive member of society, therefore, they are not quite as good as those who are. And if they also believe that they are responsible for their unemployed status, their feelings of inferiority are reinforced.

If this is true in your case, your self-esteem can be undermined even further in the interviewing process. You'll then give the interviewer psychological power over you by virtue of the fact that he "controls" your destiny by deciding whether or not you will be given the job offer.

Many interviewees allow this feeling to frighten them and consequently cause them to perform less adequately during the interview. Much of the self-inflicted intimidation that occurs in your job search can be caused by fear of rejection, criticism or failure that results from the feeling that you have lost control over your future.

Maintain control by taking positive action.

The sense of intimidation can be intensified in many ways. For instance, it could be an interviewer in his large office who appears less-than-friendly upon your arrival. Or it could be the initial impact of the enormity of your task when you realize that you may have to make five hundred or more contacts to receive a job offer.

Regardless of the threat, it will damage your self-esteem unless you move to diminish it. "Easier said than done," you say? Perhaps not. Try these techniques for remaining in control of yourself even when you feel intimidated in the face of "looming danger:"

I only think about good, gain and success.

1) <u>Renew your efforts to locate and approach prospects</u>. If you always have another potential opportunity on hand, you can be more confident while on an interview. There will be less pressure that "you have to get this job, or else." As long as you continue to contact and create new prospects you always have a sense of choice. If you keep this feeling of opportunity alive inside you, you will be less intimidated by the interviewer and more likely to make the interview a mutually informative discussion instead of a one-sided interrogation.

2) <u>Take action to stay in control</u>. Isaac Newton found that "for every action there is an equal and opposite reaction." For every action you take in your job search, it may seem as if this "equal and opposite reaction" is the word "No." Instead, think that for every action you take, there is a change of status. The degree and direction of that change depends on the effort you put into making it happen.

For example, when you send a prospective employer a letter announcing your candidacy for employment, several reactions could be forthcoming. The first may be rejection and notification. Another might be rejection without notification. Or you could receive a positive response.

In the first case, you simply send a thank-you note to the person for notifying you of his decision. In the second case (which is by far the most likely to occur), your unsolicited correspondence will receive no response. You don't know if the reason is that the recipient was disinterested or wanted to keep your information for some possible future use. Your continuous follow-up will coax them into making a decision. You'll be surprised how many prospective employers are simply waiting for the "right time" to make their move to ask you in for an interview.

3) <u>Begin chemo-therapy</u>. Most hiring decisions are not made logically but are made on the basis of emotion. Creating the proper "chemistry" between you and the interviewer is vital to success in your job search. If you're intimidated or hold otherwise self-limiting concepts, you're less likely to perform in a way that will lead to this intangible bond between you and the interviewer.

If you have ever tried to impress someone, you probably found out that it rarely works. The best way to impress someone is not to try to impress him. The interview is not a one-sided discussion. It is a mutual transfer of information that will help both parties learn more about each other so that an intelligent and long-lasting decision can be made (by both of you).

I can change anything I want to change to anything I want it to be.

Make sure that rapport is established. You have to help him sell himself on you. As you respond to the interviewer's questions with confidence and build rapport, he will gradually develop a positive impression of you. Abide by the simple rules of common sense and courtesy. If nothing else, say "please" and "thank you" frequently and you'll be amazed at how favorably people respond to you.

If you feel competent, you can respond to an event in a confident manner. The interviewer will sense if you treat yourself with respect, and respond similarly. Through your words, gestures and deeds, you signal how you want people to treat you. Believe in yourself, treat yourself with respect and you will not be intimidated by them.

7) **...excuses.** As you experience job-search rejection, you may begin to create excuses for your lack of success. These may begin to surface as one of the Terrible Toos (too old, young, etc). Or it could be evident in the way you think you are being treated by others. If you think that you cannot get a job because you are female, black, a single parent, handicapped or for any other reason, you are relinquishing control of your future. This is not to say discrimination does not occur, but you have to succeed in spite of it. The discriminator is the one who suffers in the long run and it is incumbent upon you to rise above the prejudice of others.

Maintain control with the knowledge that "it's up to you to make it through."

You must accept personal responsibility for your success (or lack thereof) in your job search. No one else can interview for you. No one else can make the telephone calls or send out the letters that you must send to be successful. You must take the bull by the horns and take charge of your quest for employment.

A variety of negative circumstances could provide you with an excuse to relinquish control over and responsibility for your success. These include procrastination, feelings of futility, perfectionism and blame. However, you must be able to overcome these obstacles and become accountable for the actions you take and the results you achieve.

If you snooze, you lose.

If you delay performing the tasks necessary for reaching your goals, you will only extend the time you will be unemployed. Plan your daily activities; then make every telephone call and do everything you planned. Don't put off anything but procrastination, and develop the habit of doing things now.

I am good at creating rapport.

<u>Frustrate your feelings of futility</u>. When you accept responsibility for your results, you're less likely to experience feelings of futility. In fact, you'll become invigorated with a renewed sense of being your own master. You'll write more letters and "dare" people to respond negatively because you have a plan in place to deal with them positively.

As you evaluate your results and make the necessary changes in your actions you'll begin to anticipate future success. You'll anxiously anticipate the response to each wave of letters you send with your new attention-getting opening paragraph. And your revised cold-calling script will knock 'em dead. Each trip to the library will uncover many more leads for you to follow.

Just keep at it and you won't have time to experience futility. When well-meaning people ask you how you are maintaining your positive attitude, you'll tell them that you don't have time to feel depressed. You have so many things going for you that one of them is sure to work out. And this will indeed be the case if you never give up and keep working at finding that elusive opportunity that is waiting out there somewhere for you. All you have to do is find it.

<u>Don't expect perfection but strive for it</u>. You may hesitate to take action because you don't want to do something imperfectly. Expecting perfection will create anguish and lead you to inactivity. It's more important to your success that you take some action and correct your mistakes as you proceed.

If you understand that nobody ever was, is or will be perfect, it may take some of the pressure off you. But you shouldn't go to the opposite extreme and allow yourself to produce poor work. You should do your best given all the resources at your disposal and then make changes that will lead to improved performance in your next attempt.

Every cover letter doesn't have to sound as if it was written by a professional writer, but it should be better that the last one and not as good as the next. This same principle applies to your interviews, resumes and any other activity you undertake. It's better to do something imperfectly (and then correct your mistakes) than do nothing perfectly.

<u>Don't fix the blame, fix the problem</u>. Early in your search, define what you can and cannot control. You can control your weight, wardrobe, attitude, actions and finances. You cannot control your race, sex, height, physical handicap or other factors that are not yours to change.

People tend to make excuses for poor results in areas in which they can control and to blame their lack of success on what they can't control. Don't get caught in this negative quagmire of blaming. Instead,

---

I overcome obstacles that hinder my progress.

strategically manipulate the elements that you can regulate in your life and take responsibility for the results of your action. Also, plan to deal accordingly with elements that are out of your control. If you can separate and deal with these circumstances, you'll be able to take charge and choose the course of action that is best for you.

8) **...frustration.** It is inevitable that you will become frustrated in your search for a job. You know that you are uniquely qualified for a job and that you would make an excellent employee. Why can't these people recognize that fact? Why don't they at least have the courtesy to acknowledge that you sent them a letter?

If you allow these and other legitimate questions to get you down, your frustration will only increase. There are no logical or suitable answers to them. You have to make up your mind to continue in your quest regardless of all the negative feedback that will occur.

Maintain control by dealing with frustration.

An inevitable consequence of your job search is that you will be rejected 99% of the time. This rejection rate is realistic though disheartening. And being aware of the odds when you begin your journey doesn't prevent frustration from setting in after you start it. However, not dealing with frustration could strike a fatal blow to your attitude.

Learn to deal with change. You have probably developed routines and habits during your years of employment. Now that unemployment has been thrust upon you, you may not cope well with the loss of routine. You no longer have the structure that previously arranged your life for you. You now determine what new patterns will replace the old, including when you get up and what you will do all day. Vacations must be placed on hold as do spontaneous dinners out with your spouse or friends. And you have to be more frugal than you otherwise might be.

One of the hardest changes you'll have to adjust to is that you are now in control of your time and actions. No one else will tell you what time to get up and when to write your letters and resume. You don't have to be anywhere at any particular time and there is nobody to notice if you leave early.

Try to get out of bed at the same time you did before becoming unemployed, and continue the routines you had as much as you can. If you normally got up early to jog or walk, persist in doing that. Some people even continue to wear a business suit even though they never leave their homes. There's no problem with doing that at all. You're the one who now makes the rules.

I always do my best.

If you usually do your creative work in the morning and repetitive work in the afternoon, plan your days the same way now. Don't change your routines dramatically, but watch because they may begin to change little by little. Like the sand leaving the upper chamber of your hourglass, bad habits are formed one small, unnoticeable step at a time. They don't become obvious until some damage has already been done.

Good habits are hard to come by but easy to live with, and bad habits are easy to come by but hard to live with. Stick with the good ones you have and replace the bad ones with something more constructive.

Time: use it or lose it. It's important to have a monthly, weekly and daily plan. At the beginning of each month, set aside certain days for prospecting, networking or reviewing out-of-town newspapers. Then as you begin to plan your week, be more specific about the hours per day you will spend doing those same events. Block out an hour each day for exercise, perhaps two hours for cold calling and networking, another half-day at the library to locate prospects and research potential employers.

And as you prepare your daily plan, actually write out the names of the people you will contact and their addresses and telephone numbers. Prioritize all your actions in A, B or C categories depending on their likelihood of being productive and successful. Cross off each as you complete it and transfer those remaining unfinished at the end of the day to tomorrow's plan. Organize your time carefully and you'll be efficient and effective.

Budget your money as well as your time. Limit your spending to items that are absolutely necessary for you to exist comfortably, although the definition of the word "comfortable" should be more austere at this point. Work out a budget that will accommodate you and your family, but allow you to extend your deadline.

No one likes to have an external event or person dictate to him what he has to do. But in this case you have no choice. Your life has been changed dramatically, and you must respond accordingly. If you manage the impact of the belt-tightening, this period will be less difficult than it otherwise might. Welcome this change in lifestyle as the transition price that you must pay to move on to bigger and better things.

There are no guarantees. The fact that there is no definite time when you will find a job can lead to frustration and anxiety. Even if you work every available minute of the day to find a new position, there is no way to tell exactly when it will surface. Even a prisoner knows when his

---

I create my own routines.

sentence will be up, but your situation is more analogous to that of a hostage. You just don't know when you will be released, but you continue believing that the day will arrive.

Don't let the little things get to you. You have too many important things to deal with to let minor ones get in your way. Yet in your frustrated state of mind, small irritations you would have previously ignored now seem to loom as apocalyptic. Don't allow minor events to grate on you. If it's your turn to make the bed or mow the lawn, do it. If someone cuts you off while driving, don't allow it to affect your attitude for the rest of the day.

Concentrate on resolving the major challenges that face you and leave the insignificant ones for later, if necessary. Someone once said, "Worrying must help. Nothing I ever worried about happened." Work instead of worrying. Keep yourself busy and you won't have the time or the inclination to become frustrated.

9) **...fears.** Frustration leads to worry, which leads to fear, which leads to immobility. All these negative emotions are usually based upon your (subjective) concept of what might happen in the future. As the negative "or elses" begin to enter your mind, you may become paralyzed with fear that your deadline will arrive and you will still be without a job.

Fear causes you to evaluate a neutral event negatively. For example, you don't know when your time as a job-search "hostage" will be over. This is a statement of fact. You could assume that because you don't know how long you will remain unemployed, finding the right job will take a long time. On the other hand, you don't know how long your unemployment will last, and it may end tomorrow. There is no proof or evidence that either event will occur. But if the more negative variation is the one you believe, then it will be the one guiding your thoughts and actions.

Maintain control through belief in yourself.

If you do what you fear, you can overcome it. If you are reluctant to call prospective employers on the telephone because you fear rejection, begin by calling some of your friends and talking to them first. Or, write an outline for a script and practice it. Then as you call people, you will feel more comfortable knowing that you are prepared.

If you are afraid to interview, you should practice interviewing. Prepare a list of questions which you think an interviewer could ask you. Prepare a response to each and have someone ask you the questions. Make a list of the questions you could ask an interviewer and practice

---

I invest my time productively.

asking them. Anticipate the objections an interviewer could have about you as a candidate and develop ways to combat each. Have someone video-tape you during a practice session and then evaluate your performance. The more you do whatever it is that you are afraid of, the more quickly you will overcome it.

10) **...fatigue.** Acquiring a job is a full-time job in itself. You have to work long hours every day without any compensation or positive feedback in order to find a new position. Even if you decide to work on your job search only from Monday through Friday, you'll think about your concerns for the remainder of your waking hours. This will obviously take its toll on you.

Maintain control by stretching your perspectives.

You need to condition your mind and your body for success in your search. Set aside quiet time to relax and do whatever it is that you do to unwind. Read a book, work on your hobby, read to your children or talk to a friend about something other than your quest for employment. Get your mind off your job-search efforts for a little time each day.

Use this time to stretch your perspectives. Read books to learn about topics you are not familiar with. Go to an art show or a football game if you have never been to one. In addition to broadening your horizons, these atypical events may offer a different idea for your search. A book of poetry might provide you with a new way to express yourself in your cover letter. An art gallery could help you generate new ways to design the layout of your resume.

Knute Rockne got the idea for a shifting backfield from watching a ballet, and the idea for velcro came to a person as he tried to remove a common bur that was stuck to his clothes. The more you look in unfamiliar areas, the more likely you will be to find a new approach to your search that will help to move it ahead more quickly or to overcome some obstacle that is impeding your progress.

You can also use your downtime to continue your education. It's been said that the half-life of knowledge in the computer industry is three years. So after three years, 50% of the previous knowledge is obsolete. What is the half-life of knowledge in your field? What can you do to remain current? Find magazines in your specialty and read them thoroughly. Join associations that are related to your industry and get involved with them. These are both also good sources of prospects for potential employers.

I work instead of worry.

Go back and finish college or high school, whichever is the case. Enter graduate school if that is your need or desire. Do what is necessary to improve your formal and informal education.

Maximize your windshield time. A way to continue your education (as you improve your attitude) without a great deal of effort is by listening to motivational and educational tapes in your car as you drive. If you don't have a tape-deck built into your car, bring a portable one with you. If you drive 20,000 miles per year at an average speed of 40 MPH you'll spend 500 hours behind the wheel annually. How much better could you be if you spent another twelve work-weeks every year improving yourself?

One of the best investments you can make is to purchase a hand-held dictating machine. As you drive, record your ideas and use the time to dictate letters or take notes. You'll find yourself arriving at your destination with pages of notes, ideas, plans and goals. You'll also arrive with a feeling of productivity and accomplishment rather than just a blank mind.

Listening to educational and motivational tapes while driving will also keep you from listening to the radio. Although there are news programs, few radio stations are informative on a regular basis. In fact, some can have a negative effect on you if particularly antagonizing music causes you to get keyed up or annoyed. On the other hand, "elevator music" may make you feel depressed. Control what goes into your mind and you will control what comes out of it.

11) ...**fantasy.** If kept under control, your imagination can be a tremendous source of ideas during your search. It can stimulate your creativity and lead you to think of new careers to pursue. But left unchecked, it can lead you to live in a Walter Middy-like world. If you dream without taking action to make your dreams come true, then you are less likely to realize them.

Maintain control by learning from yesterday, acting today and enjoying tomorrow.

Fantasy and dreaming are good for your creativity. They can help you set goals that will guide you to become what you truly want to be. But don't waste your time thinking about what you could have been. Dream about what you can be and fantasize about doing what you truly want to do. Then do it.

If you always wanted to design a boat and sail around the world, do it. If you want to get your license to fly and become a commercial

---

I look in unfamiliar areas for new ideas.

pilot, do it. If, for example, either of these dreams is yours, go to a nearby marina or airport and take pictures of the plane or boat that you eventually want. Keep these photos with you and study them regularly until you can visualize yourself in them.

Whatever it is that you want to do, visualize yourself accomplishing it. If you want to start your own business showing others how to sail and fly, then see yourself doing it. In your dreams you can become whatever it is that you want to be. Listen to yourself and follow your instincts.

Focus your attention on what you can do today that will bring you closer to success in the future. You should have long-term goals as well as intermediate and short-term goals. Every action you take should reach today's goals and help you achieve your ultimate objective.

Control of your attitude and actions is so important because it forces you to perform activities today that will move you closer to a new job tomorrow. It focuses your attention on what you can control in the present, which keeps you from agonizing over what "might" happen in the future. Constant purposeful activity will keep your mind active and attentive to your current work.

Be aware of the conditions that can cause you to lose control of your attitude and consequently reduce your ability to perform the tasks that you must in order to succeed in your quest. Strengthen your defenses and reach down for the toughness that will get you through this difficult time. You are the final authority in your life. Only you can take and remain in control of your attitude, finances and actions.

I make my dreams come true.

Chapter Five

Batteries Not Included

Commitment is second only to control as the most important characteristic necessary for success in a job search. If you keep working at your search even though you don't have the self-confidence to do so, that's commitment. Conversely, if you are self-confident but aren't committed to your goals, you're less likely to achieve them. And continuing to call people to get a job even though you feel afraid of doing so, that's commitment.

Commitment is the power behind the control you exert in your search. Just as the batteries are rarely included in the products you purchase in the stores, you have to seek to create your internal power if you don't already have a sufficient supply.

Commitment is the ability to entrust yourself with your future. It's the knowledge that if something is to be accomplished, then you have either to do it or see to it that it's done. You must believe in yourself and your ability to reach the goals you have set for yourself.

Commitment is the ability to devote your entire focus on the attainment of your objective. It is the discipline to continue trying in the face of adversity. It's the desire to succeed even when it seems that failure is certain. Commitment is a pledge that you make to yourself to succeed in spite of seemingly insurmountable odds.

Commitment is the knowledge that you're not perfect, and therefore you must continue evaluating your results and trying different tactics, using trial-and-error and learning from your mistakes. Your commitment to the attainment of your goals will sustain you through temporary setbacks and keep you moving forward to success. Remember, the way you think when you lose determines how long it will be until you win.

If you put all your effort into trying to get a job working for one particular company and don't receive an offer, it should bother you. If it didn't, it would indicate that you weren't sufficiently committed to win. Commitment to the attainment of your goal will keep you working toward it because you know it is the only way you'll eventually succeed. You must be committed emotionally to your chosen course of action.

I have a firm will to achieve success.

A boxer will give 100% of his available energy during every round. He may take many hits and even get knocked down. Then the bell rings and he takes time to consult with his advisors, evaluate his performance and readjust his strategy. Then he goes back into the ring to give this new approach 100% of his remaining available energy. Approach your job search with this same commitment. Give it your full attention.

Why commitment is important in a job search.

Those who fail in their job search do so because they don't have the commitment to succeed. In order to be successful in a job search, you have to have a burning desire to reach your objective. The fuel for this fire is the commitment to keep taking the action necessary to find another position in the face of continuous rejection.

If you are committed to achieving your goal, you will continue contacting people after being rejected or ignored by the first five hundred people you contact. You'll keep calling on people even after you've had a job offer rescinded. You'll answer every telephone call with the positive anticipation that this is the one you've been waiting for. And when it's not, you'll answer the phone the same way next time.

Don't give it a piece of your mind.

During a recent trip to a shopping center, I saw a window display with odd-looking mannequins in it. They were odd because on each one half of it's head was missing. I chuckled to myself that these were probably unsuccessful at their work because they only had "half a mind" to become full-fledged mannequins.

Have you ever had "half a mind" to do something? What happened? You probably thought about what you could do and then went on doing what you were doing already. Commit to doing what you know you must do to become successful and you will be. Have a full mind to get what you want.

What you can do and what you actually do are often two different things. You must strive to do more to attain your goals. Force yourself to make the first few telephone calls and you'll find that most people respond sympathetically or are flattered that you would call them for advice or for employment.

I always do what I am capable of doing.

Commitment creates action which in turn may bring accomplishment. The fact that you are busy doesn't mean you are getting something productive done. Plan, manage and make the greatest use of your time, and you will find employment more quickly. Always implement purposeful activity that brings you closer to finding a fulfilling career position for yourself.

If at first you don't succeed, change the rules.

100% commitment doesn't refer to adhering blindly to one course of action until you create final success or failure. It requires that you plan your actions realistically, implement them with confidence and evaluate your relative success objectively. If the results are not what you want, try something else. Evaluate the new results, then continue this new approach or change it as necessary.

Don't just aim for success. Pull the trigger.

A sharpshooter may or may not improve his score by adding a telescope to his rifle. The fact that he now has a better picture of the target doesn't guarantee that he's going to hit it. He has to adjust the scope by aiming, firing, evaluating, re-adjusting, aiming and firing again. But nothing happens unless he pulls the trigger. This ignites the gunpowder to force the bullet toward the target. Become committed to hitting the bulls-eye of your target through this same sequence and you'll become re-employed sooner than you thought.

As Yogi Berra said, "It ain't over 'til it's over."

How many times have you heard that? It's as true in your job search as it is in any other competitive event. You may be given and actually accept a job offer and later find that it's been rescinded. One time I arrived at a company on the first day of a new job only to find that the person who hired me was no longer with the company. Another time I was hired pending the results of a background search. I expected this to be positive, and it was. But at the time I worried that through some "glitch" there might be an erroneous entry into my records that would eliminate me from the position.

The simple fact is that there are many events that can occur after you are given an offer that could dismiss you as a candidate. You have to remain committed to your quest until you have actually started on your new job.

I demand the best from myself every day.

Inactivity and negative thinking sap energy.

If you are thoroughly committed to success, you're more likely to "keep at it" during an extended period of frustration. As the rejection letters continue pouring in, as the bills keep mounting up and as your self-confidence dwindles you have to redouble your efforts to succeed.

Sustained and regular activity is invigorating. If you remain active in your pursuit you won't have time to worry about the negative consequences, and you'll also be getting closer to your objective. When you become inactive, your thoughts lean toward the negative.

I recall one trip to Las Vegas, about a four-hour flight from my origination point. I had prepared to be productive during the flight by bringing with me enough reading material and other work to keep me busy even if the plane was delayed for an hour or two. I read positive-thinking books and wrote letters and memos and made the use of my time as productive as possible. As we were on our final approach, I overheard the passenger sitting in front of me say to his friend, "Flying really takes a lot out of you, doesn't it." Of course, the friend agreed and they both sank a little lower into their seats.

From my perspective the flight didn't take a lot out of me, it got a lot out of me. I was productive, stimulated and had improved the level of my thinking and activity. Here were two people (me and the passenger in front of me) that spent the identical amount of time on the identical flight who had totally different reactions to and results from their experience. This impressed upon me the importance of being committed to becoming better at what I do and using every available moment to do so.

How to develop commitment.

Coping With Unemployment describes techniques that you can use to develop the commitment to complete your job search successfully. You can do this by setting challenging yet realistic goals that are important to you (Chapter Eleven). Then you create innovative plans to achieve them (Chapter Fourteen) and begin enforcing your tactics. As you evaluate some actions as being more effective than others, you perform more of the former and revise the latter.

You can develop job-search commitment by visualizing a future that is rewarding and under your control (Chapter Twelve). Your affirmations (Chapter Thirteen) and supportive self-talk (Chapter Seventeen) reaffirm your desire to succeed.

I act and feel successful every day.

Try reverse-networking.

The cheering you receive from your friends and members of your Brain Trust (Chapter Twenty One) is extremely valuable. Friends would call me during periods of unemployment just to say "How goes it? Is there anything I can do to help?" This show of concern meant a great deal to me and helped sustain me through some low periods. I was also invigorated with a renewed spirit not to let them (or myself) down.

But what if your friends don't call you? Attend unemployment support groups or call someone else who is unemployed. Trade success stories and leads. Offer advice about techniques you have tried that worked for you and mention others that didn't. Perhaps your friend will make suggestions, too. Soon he'll be calling you.

Manage your time.

You can't develop commitment by setting a deadline and then just sending your resume to companies advertising in the help-wanted ads. You can generate commitment by planning and managing your time one day at a time (Chapter Twenty Eight). This means that you set aside a few hours every day to search for new prospects and write letters to (or call) them. Plan time to do everything you need to do to reach your goals.

Commit yourself to becoming committed.

You can become more committed to your search by managing your tension and re-directing it by taking positive action (Chapter Twenty). Work to build your confidence (Chapter Six), courage (Chapter Seven), creativity (Chapter Eight) and competitive attitude (Chapter Nine). Draw on the support of family members (Chapter Twenty Seven), members of your reference groups (Chapter Twenty Six) and read motivational books and listen to the tapes (Chapter Thirty One). Utilize the techniques described in these and other chapters to generate the internal commitment to succeed in the attainment of your goals.

"... and then some."

If you want to be successful in a competitive job search, you have to work harder than the next person. You have to give more to your quest than you have to any other challenge in your life. If you practice three words, you will be more successful: "And then some." Whatever actions you take, give it all you can "and then some." Go the extra mile. Go over your resume one more time to make it a little better. Proofread your cover letter one more time to check for errors. Prepare and practice

---

I know that success requires persistence.

for your interview once again. Do all you can to be successful, <u>and then some.</u> Total commitment to your success will enable you to do this.

You have to develop a strong belief that you can and you **will** succeed. It's not just positive thinking. It's a conviction in your own mind that you can be greater than anything that can happen to you. You can do better and you deserve to. You will succeed if you're committed to becoming the best you can be.

I do all that I can to succeed, and then some.

Chapter Six

Believe and Achieve

The dictionary definition of confidence is "trust in a person or thing." You can make this more specific to your job-search by stating that if you trust in yourself and your close allies, you'll eventually find a new position that will meet your long-term requirements for career success.

A general feeling of confidence in yourself and in your future will help carry you through these tough times. Unfortunately, this is the very attribute that takes the greatest abuse from all the rejection and lack of response with which you must deal. All things considered, you'll be more successful, more quickly, if you approach your search with a confident, optimistic attitude.

Why self-confidence is important to your job search.

There are two vital points to keep in mind about confidence (or lack thereof). The first is that many interviewers equate confidence with competence. These are not synonymous terms but given the choice between two otherwise equally-capable candidates, an employer is more likely to choose the one who comes across as being more confident. He assumes that this will translate into greater competence on the job.

The second point is that your opinion of yourself shows. That's why it's so critical to _feel_ confident during an interview. If you feel down on yourself, others will be able to sense it and that will negatively affect your image as a competent, enthusiastic professional. There are visible signals people use to detect what they define as the lack of confidence in others. These include such things as the inability to maintain eye contact, poor posture, a weak hand shake or the inability to smile.

Interviewers view these signals as symptoms of the inability to communicate with others in the work place or of becoming a potential "bad apple" employee. Your job is to examine and restore your inner self-confidence and the results will show themselves externally. You can begin this journey to recovery by thinking about all the benefits you will receive as a result of restoring your self-esteem.

I am the confident person I aspire to be.

What confidence will do for you.

There are many advantages to maintaining a self-confident attitude during your job search, not the least of which is that you'll feel better about yourself and your future. You'll also experience these benefits:

1) Confidence will keep you motivated to perform the actions that you must for job-search success. For example, you may find it difficult to contact your creditors to tell them you're having trouble making your payments after a long history of prompt payment. But if you have the viewpoint (bolstered by self-confidence) that yours is a temporary situation, you'll find it easier to make those necessary calls.

2) An enhanced feeling of self-confidence will bolster your courage to perform all the tasks you are reluctant to do. It will enable you to cold-call on people in person or by using the telephone. And it will allow you to be more open and inquisitive during interviews, making each one a mutually-beneficial exchange of information.

3) Belief in yourself could improve your financial situation. When I was on the interviewing side of the desk I found that people with an apparent (by my definition) lack of confidence seemed to ask for less money when I asked them what their salary requirements were. On the other hand, people who I felt had greater self-esteem tended to ask for a higher level of income.

4) Confidence helps you perform better during interviews. Did you ever go on an interview for a position that you didn't want? Most likely you performed better because the "pressure" was off you. When you have a sufficient level of confidence, you'll perform well even when you are interviewing for a position you do want. Self-confidence acts as a release that enables you to build up <u>steam</u> instead of pressure.

5) Your fundamental belief in yourself will help you deal better with rejection and frustration. I've said it before and I'll say it again, you'll be rejected far more times than you will be accepted during your search. You can't let this get to you. Accept and believe the fact that the company is not

---

My confidence does not waver in the face of adversity

rejecting you personally but only the fit between your qualifications and the specific needs they have for an open position at this time.

Confidence will help you strengthen your "risk" muscle.

A successful quest for employment is made up of a series of decisions and choices that you have to make. Each time you choose one alternative, you are choosing not to take another alternative and its possible benefits. Don't second-guess yourself. Once you make a choice, stick with it for as long as is reasonably possible. Then as you continue to evaluate the results of your decisions, make minor changes to keep yourself moving toward your ultimate objective.

For instance, you may decide to include only Fortune 500 firms in your search. This obviously narrows down the number of opportunities for which you might apply. Given your career aspirations, this may or may not be a bad decision but once you make it, stick with it until you have exhausted all the opportunities among those companies. Then you could expand your list to include companies in the Fortune 1000 and so forth.

Don't try to eliminate risk in your job-search decisions. Instead, carefully evaluate all possible alternatives. Then make a choice based on calculated risks which may or may not be the "safest" choice but the one that is best for your present and future situation.

When you make a sensible gamble and it doesn't work out as well as you had planned, don't berate yourself. In retrospect, the decision may have been wrong. But don't allow that to affect your next decision. Go back to the steps you took to make the original decision. Most likely you'll see that it was the correct decision to make, given the facts and information you had at the time.

Perform an autopsy on your decision *process* and see if there is an error there. The system you use is more important than the actual information because the latter will change in almost every case. Don't inter the system (or yourself) for making what was at the time your best choice.

There is an old proverb about getting ahead that could help you: "Behold the turtle. It only makes progress when its neck is out." I'll amend that to include the caveat that "It only makes progress when its neck is out *and its eyes are open.*" Confidence will help you keep your neck out and enable you to realistically evaluate what you see.

I choose to succeed.

Choose to succeed.

A fear that many people have about making decisions is that by doing so it removes any excuse for failure. By making a choice to pursue one alternative, you can't later say "I didn't really want that job anyway." Instead, tell the world "I chose this alternative and if it doesn't work it's my fault." Taking total responsibility for their own success or failure is difficult for some people. Is it difficult for you? Is that what is in the way of your decision to begin a new career or start your own business?

In most cases you really know what it is you want. Your "gut feeling" will tell you if you made the correct decision just by making any decision. To illustrate this, there's a story about the time a friend walked into my office in a quandary about a decision he had to make between two alternatives. I pulled out a coin and said "If it's heads, choose alternative A. If it's tails, choose alternative B." As I flipped the coin I said, "Call it." He called 'heads' because he really wanted to choose alternative A anyway but didn't realize it until that split second. This is not the most sophisticated decision-making process, but it worked.

There are many factors that determine your system for making choices. Self-confidence will help you make those decisions that are best for your long-term career. Unfortunately, people make choices based on their beliefs about themselves at a time when their self- esteem is low. Consequently, their decisions may not be the best ones for their ultimate happiness and success.

Instead, try this methodical decision-making process. Write each major choice at the top of a piece of paper. Before you go to the next step ask yourself one question: "If I take this alternative, will it lead me closer to my ultimate objective?" If the answer is "no," go to another alternative. If the answer is "yes" or "maybe," go to the next step.

Divide the page into two separate columns. At the head of the left-hand column write the words "Positive Benefits" and at the top of the right-hand column write the words "Negative Consequences." Then list possible entries under each. For example, a page could look like this:

I am taking control of my life today.

Possible choice: Lower my salary request.

Positive Benefits	Negative Consequences
Perhaps become re-employed more quickly.	Have more difficulty meeting my current financial obligations
	My future earnings will be reduced since raises are made as a percentage increase of salary
	There is no guarantee that I'll be employed faster
	My savings will be depleted at a faster rate to help make ends meet

Although this example makes the ultimate decision fairly obvious, not all your choices will be as clear. Show your chart to people in your Brain Trust. They can help you evaluate your results and assist in listing other alternatives that you may have overlooked.

Make the right choice for the right reasons.

If you enter into this decision-making process with a low level of self-esteem, you might find yourself settling for a position or salary that will solve your short-term problems but that is not good for your long-term career. Don't limit your future based on your feelings about yourself at this difficult time in your life. As confidently as possible, make decisions that are best for you and your immediate family. And don't make these mistakes in the process:

1) Choice by consensus. People who are not sure of themselves tend to seek others' support for their decisions. It's good to seek advice during the information-gathering stage but the decision itself should be yours.

In many cases you've already made the decision. If so, you'll phrase the question in such a way that the respondent will reaffirm it. So listen to the way that you phrase your question, and you may find that you've already answered it. If you have confidence in yourself, you won't seek reassurance after you have made the choice. Instead you'll seek informed advice before you make your decision.

I act in a calm and intelligent manner no matter what the situation.

For example, if you seek help in deciding which job offer to accept, you could consult a member of your Brain Trust. Don't pose the question as a "set-up" by saying something similar to "Should I take Job A with all these challenges and benefits or Job B with all these risks?" This is obviously an overstatement but it illustrates the point. When you seek advice, present the facts in an objective way. And also be willing to objectively consider the answer.

Assess the available information and choose a course of action based on what you really want. Then you're more likely to succeed. Otherwise you won't be able to generate sufficient commitment or enthusiasm to sustain the level of activity necessary for successful performance.

2) Choice by default. Indecision caused by lack of confidence may prohibit you from making any choice. If you know there are actions you must take but choose not to perform them, you have in fact made a choice to prolong your search or perhaps even to fail. For example, you could choose to stay in bed later in the morning, refuse to engage in physical exercise, refrain from making the necessary telephone calls or personal contacts and neglect the preparation that's necessary before you implement your job search. If you do this, you're deciding to extend your search.

3) Conditional choices. If you don't have the confidence to pursue one path to its completion, you may decide to pursue several different paths and take the one that becomes successful first. By dividing your energy, time and financial resources you may not be able to achieve either one.

During one search I spent several thousand dollars and many hours of time pursuing my dream of starting my own business. Since I wasn't totally confident that this business would work, I concurrently spent a significant amount of time seeking employment through the traditional means. I eventually found employment with another company and abandoned my plans for starting my business.

I am responsible for my actions and therefore my success.

You can more effectively utilize your resources by deciding what you want and then going after it. Then apply all your effort to making that choice succeed. If you get to a point where it makes no sense to continue in that direction, then you must make another choice and seek a different opportunity.

4) Choice by reaction. Confidence will give you the desire and ability to objectively weigh alternatives, make choices and create plans for their attainment. Once your plan is in place, you'll be able to purposefully respond to opportunities rather than react to imagined consequences.

For example, if you don't perform an analysis of your finances, you won't know how much time you have left before your financial resources are depleted. As a result, early in your search you may choose to accept a job offer that you know is not really the best one for you. But "it's a job." Confidence, combined with appropriate planning, will enable you to respond to the same situation with a more calculated decision.

Almost by definition, a confident attitude will cause you to focus on what you want. A negative attitude will force you to think about what you don't want. The difference is more than just semantics. Maxwell Maltz said that "you always find what you think about most." What do you think about most:

> The benefits of success or the consequences of failure?

> The income you're worth or the amount you need to get by?

> A challenging career position or a "job" to provide some income?

If your lack of confidence causes you to make choices based on a negative interpretation of your goal, that's what you'll get. This increases the chances that you'll be unhappily employed, and perhaps unemployed again in a few years.

I look people in the eye when they look at me.

Confidence helps you decide what you want, to focus not on the problem but on the solution, and to choose what's best for your long-term success and happiness. Decide today to restore and maintain your confidence, regardless of the internal doubt or external forces that conspire to reduce your feelings of self-esteem and self-worth.

Sail on an even keel.

When you do this, you'll be better able to deal with the expected (and unexpected) ups and downs of a typical job search. For instance, picture a sailboat rolling on the waves during a storm. It will toss and turn but will always return to an upright position if it has adequate ballast and a sufficiently-deep keel. A deep-seated foundation of well-armored confidence in yourself will enable you to similarly maintain your balance during these tumultuous times.

How to maintain job-search confidence.

There are two ways to describe the challenge of maintaining a successful level of self-confidence. The first is from the perspective of an historically self-confident person who goes into his search with a stable level of self-esteem. The second is from the viewpoint of a person who has historically held a lower level of self-confidence, who enters his search with greater apprehension. Of course, there are all degrees of confidence in between but these represent the two extremes.

Regardless of which group you feel best represents your level of confidence, the terms of your separation will have great bearing on how long it takes you to re-establish yourself. Even an extremely confident person can be emotionally devastated at the unexpected loss of a job.

In any case, your goal should be to establish and maintain a "working" feeling of self-confidence. This is defined as a level sufficient to sustain an optimistic feeling about yourself without trying to be 100% confident at all times. The latter position is a worthy long-term goal but is unnecessary for your purposes now. What you need is emotional stability, an inner knowledge that if you work hard at finding a new position you will find it.

If you have generally been a confident person with an optimistic view of yourself and your future, you are in a better starting position than those at the other end of the continuum. Once you have organized your financial program and your actions, you can spend more time implementing your plan.

I do everything in an excellent way.

Confidence is an attribute that every person has but in different degrees and in different areas of life. You may be very confident in the way you drive a car but not in the way you play golf. You may be a confident parent but not sure of yourself when asked to speak before the members of the PTA.

As you can see, you have confidence in what you feel you are good at and lack confidence in what you haven't tried before. Since you may never before have experienced unemployment, you probably lack confidence in this area. Your goals should be to transfer confidence from your familiar area of life to your job search. The good news is that once you have stretched yourself to a new level of ability, you'll permanently raise your overall level of confidence a notch or two. This is one of the major benefits you'll experience from your job search.

Look at the job search as analogous to something with which you are familiar and you'll be able to approach it more methodically and confidently. It's not necessary to develop a feeling that you are totally confident and competent in your search. You only need enough "spunk" to get through this struggle.

Prepare your job-search recipe.

For example, if your (off-the-job) strength is in shopping and cooking for your family, you can equate your search to that area of expertise. You begin by visualizing the end result, i.e., the completed meal. Then you look in the recipe book to make sure you have all the ingredients. If you don't have everything it takes to complete the desired result, you go out and get it.

When you go shopping, you make a list of items to buy. This ensures that you get everything you need, without wasting time. As you buy each item you cross it off your list, and if you can't find it in one store you go to another. You may go to a supermarket or to a specialty store to locate a particular item.

The analogies to your job search are obvious. In it, you begin with a vision of the end result. If you don't have the wherewithal to achieve it, you go out and acquire it. If you need assistance preparing your search, you can consult a job-search book, one that provides step-by-step directions for pursuing your desired result.

Before you go out shopping for a job, you create a list of everything you should do and cross each off as you perform it. As you seek your new job, you go to the supermarket (i.e., the newspaper) or to specialty shops (industry directories, trade shows, etc.).

I have the habit of winning.

If you have a background in sales, look at your job search as reaching your annual quota. You know what the end result must be and the amount of time allotted to achieving it. Break it down into a series of monthly goals and plan your time so that you can develop prospects and turn them into satisfied customers. You do a lot of work but you don't get your commission check until the sale is made.

If you're a pilot, make an analogy to your pre-flight checklist. If your expertise is in building, create your job-search blueprint. You may have been confident as a student in college. Here you had to plan the courses you'd take over the four-year period, and then you had to work hard to achieve the grades necessary for success. Or, if you are more familiar with driving, think of your job-search plan as the map leading you to your destination most directly. If you're an athlete, prepare your game plan and utilize the talents of your teammates. Whatever it is that you are used to doing well, make an analogy of it to your search. Plan, practice and implement your activities just as you would in your familiar area of confidence.

Find out what skills you are lacking and go out and acquire them. If you're not confident of your eye communication, practice it. Begin looking at yourself in the mirror every day. Then practice with your spouse, children and friends. Practice with the clerks at supermarkets and banks, and then with complete strangers. Build your confidence little by little and by the time you go on an interview, successful eye communication will be second nature to you.

If you're not confident on the telephone, call a friend and talk to him or her. Then call strangers who will be glad to hear from you, such as sales clerks. You don't have to buy something each time but inquire into the availability or price of different items. Then talk into a tape recorder, pretending you're on the telephone. Talk as if you're explaining to someone why you would be a good employee. Practice answering some "hypothetical" questions. Once you feel comfortable doing this, make an outline of your conversation and use this as a script when you begin calling people.

Confidence is something you already have. Develop it one step at a time, building on your inherent strengths. Transfer the knowledge and enthusiasm you have in your particular area of competence to your job search. Perform all the techniques suggested throughout Coping With Unemployment and you'll have sufficient confidence to get through all this. You'll also increase your fundamental self-confidence in a way that will remain with you even after your quest for employment is completed.

Every day I grow wiser, more self-confident and emotionally stronger.

Chapter Seven

"A coward dies a thousand deaths..."

Courage is the spirit that faces adversity. It suggests a reserve of inner strength you can draw on when your world seems as if it is falling apart. This is not to suggest that you can eliminate fear, but you must face it and control it. You have to make the apprehension you feel about your future work for you.

If you worry about every negative consequence of unemployment, you'll torture yourself daily. I remember at one point thinking about where I could find shelter on cold nights and how I would go about getting food if I lost my house and had to live on the streets. I caught myself and turned my thinking around. It doesn't take courage to give up. It takes courage to keep fighting even when in the back of your mind you're thinking about losing everything you've worked for. It takes courage to reach down inside and make a commitment to yourself that you won't ever let anyone take away what you have.

Why courage is important to your job search.

At times it may seem easier to quit. But quitting is never the easy way out because it creates additional, more serious problems. The difficult decision is to keep doing what you need to do in order to succeed in your search. There are many adversities that present themselves in diverse ways. In a job search it takes courage to...

- **...get back up every time life strikes another blow.** At times you'll get the feeling that "somebody is trying to kick you while you're down." You must realize that a continuous search for employment will never leave you the same way it found you. Some day you'll look back on all this and realize how much you've matured and grown because of the struggle. Your job search doesn't do something <u>to</u> you; it does something <u>for</u> you.

I have the courage to look to the future and pursue a goal I can only imagine now.

- **...seek assistance in your quest.** You don't have to go through all this alone, and you shouldn't. Call a member of your Brain Trust when you're having a bad day and need someone to talk with. You'll find that saying something out loud makes it seem less devastating than you originally thought. Your sounding board may not even have to say a word, but just listen. If you need professional help, seek it too.

- **...accept responsibility for your situation.** Blaming previous or prospective employers for your predicament will not solve your situation. Only when you accept that your future is entirely in your hands will you be free to take positive action.

- **...go on the offense.** At times you may feel as if you've lost control of your search and that the potential employers "hold all the cards." If you relinquish control of your actions, you will end up responding only to the help-wanted ads rather than soliciting your own opportunities.

  One way to go on the offensive is to be assertive during an interview. An interview is analogous to a sporting event, i.e., you can only score when you have possession of the ball. Consider the concept of the "ball" as the topic of conversation. If the interviewer controls the ball for the entire game, you may not get answers to all your questions. If you simply "attend" an interview without actively participating, you won't score many points.

- **...try different approaches.** During an extended search, you may begin to feel comfortable with various tactics. You'll get some solace out of knowing that these activities provide a constant in your life. But it takes guts to try something untried, and this is exactly what you have to do to shake up your thinking and be creative in the action you take.

  People are creatures of habit. Once they find something that works they continue in that rut. If you find yourself responding only to the help-wanted ads, ignoring all the other means of prospecting, you're dramatically limiting your opportunities. Push yourself to try new and different tactics and you'll be more successful in less time.

I keep doing what I must even when I don't like doing it.

- **...be flexible.** You will be confronted with a variety of challenging circumstances during your quest for employment. These may show themselves in the form of different types of interviews, such as interviews over a meal or with multiple interviewers. When these occur, your steadfast courage will enable you to be flexible enough to succeed in these circumstances.

  Events will always occur for which you have not planned. For example, the day after being laid off, the transmission of my car went bad, and I had to pay almost $1000 to have it repaired. That shortened my available job-search time. Later in that same search I was told that I had to repay all my unemployment benefits because I was self-employed while searching for another job.

  These events could have been demoralizing had I not developed the flexibility to bounce back and regain my composure. I found a temporary position (as explained in Chapter Thirty Four) which allowed me to cover the unexpected expenses as I continued my search for full-time employment.

- **...act in spite of overwhelming odds.** You may think you're too old, young, experienced, inexperienced or anything else. But you can't let such biased self-evaluation get in your way. You have to eliminate anything (through all legal and moral means) that gets in your way of finding a new position.

  The odds may be in the form of a recessionary economy. The newspapers abound with stories of ever-increasing numbers of layoffs and business closings. By objectively evaluating what you read and surrounding yourself with positive people, you can prevent negative feedback from eroding your attitude.

  Or the odds may appear in the form of a shy personality. If this is the case, you have to recognize that fact and work within the boundaries you feel comfortable. You may have to force yourself to do more prospecting through the mail rather than in person, attend job fairs or work through employment agencies. These are just a few of the ways you can still apply yourself if you are shy. It's difficult, but you can't give up.

I always take positive action even in spite of overwhelming odds.

Don't try to conquer self-consciousness; develop it. Become more aware of your limitations and create ways to deal with them. Always be aware of your strengths and weaknesses and utilize the former while improving the latter.

Similarly, don't mistake excitement for fear. If you truly want a particular job, the situation will make you feel more apprehensive. Recognize that what you feel is anxiety and that can actually work in your favor to make you sharper. Excitement can be motivating, while fear can be debilitating. Sometimes the only difference between the two is your reaction to it and the way you handle it. Practice and prepare before you go on an important interview and you're more likely to relax.

- **...to ask for the order.** When your interview is about to conclude, you should ask the interviewer to agree to take some positive next step. When the time comes to negotiate for a higher salary, you should stand your ground for as long as is reasonably prudent. And if you want the job, you have to ask for it.

- **...smile, even when it "hurts."** This may be one of the most difficult yet rewarding parts of your search. You've finally "made it" if you can take your lumps, get back into the game and still smile. There is something invigorating about surviving a difficult event and handling it well that will sustain you through other tough times. Minor problems no longer seem as bad and major problems no longer seem insurmountable. You feel as if you can handle anything that happens to you all because you had the courage to face the challenges of your search, succeed and smile as you did so.

How to develop job-search courage.

Fear tends to feed upon itself and grow more ominous as a result. If you constantly worry about something, the fear of that event grows. Therefore, an excellent way to eliminate fear is to face the event you are afraid of. This takes courage. For example, if you dislike contacting people on the telephone, you must start calling people to realize that it's not as bad as you thought it would be. In most cases, people are polite and nice to you because they sympathize with your position.

Also, if you spend the bulk of your time involved in activities that will enhance your search, you won't have time to worry. You will

---

I have the flexibility to deal with any job-search challenge.

have the satisfaction of doing everything you can to further your quest. It takes courage to do what's necessary for success, especially if you have not had experience with something.

If you can generate the courage early in your search to meet certain events head on, you won't allow fear to build up. Below are ideas that you can use to help you begin to take control of your search. Once you take charge of what you do, you'll find that you will fear it less.

1) Keep your mind from dwelling on negative possibilities by preparing a list of twenty things that are good in your life right now.

2) Determine how long you have to find a new position by performing an analysis of your finances.

3) With your family members, discuss finances, expense reduction, the time you have to find a new position, your plans for finding it and the list of things that are going well in your life right now.

4) Send letters to your creditors alerting them to your situation.

5) Create weekly and daily plans to organize your time.

6) Spend time in the library reviewing directories and making copies of pages with names of potential employers. Then send letters to them.

7) Register with an employment agency.

8) Call your friends to let them know about your situation and ask them to let you know if they hear of any opportunities.

9) Practice talking into a cassette recorder and create a telemarketing script to use when contacting prospective employers by telephone. Anticipate possible objections and list your responses. Begin calling the people you previously contacted and follow up on the letters you sent to them.

If you make a habit of performing these activities on a regular basis, you'll overcome your general fear as well as your specific fear (for example of contacting unknown people by telephone and in person). You create courage by taking action on what you fear and continuing to do so until you no longer are afraid of it.

––––––––––––

I am successful in my job search because I believe in myself and my goals.

The character-building key to success in the job search is to keep working even when you're concerned about what's going to happen to you in the future. It's the ability to keep moving ahead when you don't know what's in your path. Try to isolate the function which you are afraid to perform and then take action to overcome that fear.

I always take the initiative to meet new people.

Chapter Eight

Make a Mole Hill out of a Mountain.

The dictionary defines creativity as this: "to cause to exist; bring into being; originate." If you are to be successful in your search, you must cause opportunities to happen, bring offers into being and originate professional ways to gain the prospective employer's attention.

Creativity is essential to success in a job search. Yet this attribute is an early casualty to the constant barrage of negative feedback. Creativity suffers when you lose the confidence to seek new ideas, the courage to implement them and the commitment to make them work. But without innovation in your job search, you are just another applicant.

You can apply innovation in your search during any stage. Early in your quest you can develop new sources of income or additional ways to cut expenses without significantly diminishing your life style. Creativity is particularly helpful later when you need to search for employment in the hidden areas your competitors are ignoring. Creativity can also help you develop actions to reverse your slide into frustration and restore an enthusiastic demeanor.

If you think you've depleted all the avenues you could possibly think of to find employment, you must seek other paths creatively. One of my favorite quotations is an anonymous one that has helped me stimulate my thinking. Perhaps it will do the same for you. It says: "Do not follow where the path may lead. Go instead where there is no path and leave a trail."

When your paths are obstacle-ridden or you feel that you've reached a dead end, embark in uncharted territory and leave a path for others to follow. A hard person to beat is one who combines and supports creativity with confidence, commitment and courage.

I creatively seek new opportunities to differentiate myself from competitors.

How to develop job-search creativity.

Don't ask "What's the Problem?" Ask "What's the solution?"

Don't waste time thinking about what will go wrong if you don't reach your goals. Instead, spend your time developing new ways to achieve them by changing the way you phrase the questions you ask yourself. "How can I keep from going bankrupt?" will lead you to different solutions from the question "How can I increase my income?" Also, a question phrased to stimulate multiple responses will enable you later to go back and choose the one that is best for your situation. Ask yourself, "In how many ways can I ...," and you'll find yourself generating more options.

Look at the present with a long-term perspective.

A critical part of managing your mental state is to evaluate your efforts constantly and continue using those methods that work for you while eliminating those that do not. This could be called the new KISS principle, which is an acronym for Keep Implementing Successful Strategies. Try something and learn from it. Then try something different and learn from that. If you keep gaining more knowledge from your mistakes and trying new approaches, you will succeed. This technique forces you to reflect on the past, using it to direct your actions today to provide satisfaction in achieving your goals in the future.

Look at your current status as part of the "Big Picture" of your life. Your predicament at this moment is a mere "glitch" in the long-term scheme of things. You have a past that brought you to this point and a future that, once you overcome this short-term misfortune, will be both long and profitable.

Analyze your past, but don't dwell on it. Use the information you glean from prior mistakes only to help you avoid them in the future. As Ben Franklin said: "Learn from a lesson only that which is meant to be learned. A cat, once burned, will never jump up on a hot stove again. Neither will it jump up on a cold one."

Think of your view of the past as you would a glance at the rear-view mirror in your car. If you stare at the mirror, you'll have an excellent view of where you have been. But you are very likely to crash into something ahead of you. On the other hand, if you direct your attention to where you are going, but periodically glance into the mirror to assess your progress, you are more likely to proceed without a mishap. Remember:

My resume and cover letter are creative, professional and persuasive.

Hindsight without foresight is not good.
Foresight without hindsight is not good.
Some hindsight with more foresight is good.

Poverty is in the eyes of the beholder.

Creativity can help you have fun in your current circumstances. By using or cultivating your sense of humor, you can release some pressure and at the same time generate new ideas to solve your problems. For example you can dwell on the fact that you have "money problems." If you think of it in a different way, you don't have money problems, you have "lack of money problems." You can take this one step further and imagine that what you really have is "lack of <u>idea</u> problems."

Now you have something you can work with. Create a logical syllogism and <u>prove</u> to yourself that ideas will help you become more successful and subsequently make more money:

Major Premise: Ideas create opportunities.

Minor Premise: I can create an idea.

Conclusion: When I create new ideas, I develop more opportunities.

Have some fun by approaching your job search creatively. You'll give yourself new direction, positive feedback and even more reasons to smile. Try these techniques for stimulating your idea-generating abilities:

- Always have an objective in mind. Don't say to yourself, "Think of an idea to help my situation." Instead say, "In how many ways can I locate new job opportunities? In how many ways can I improve my resume and cover letter? In how many ways can I improve my listening skills?"

- Once you have this objective in mind, write it at the top of a piece of paper and list the numbers one through twenty down the left-hand column. Then begin filling in the blanks.

- Purchase Roger von Oech's <u>Creative Whack Pack</u>. This is a deck of cards, each serving as a creative stimulant. As you're walking or riding your stationary bicycle, review these cards and generate new ideas to solve your specific challenge.

I am good at coming up with creative solutions.

- Purchase a cassette recorder to record your thoughts while driving in your car. The monotony of a long trip behind the wheel can be broken with creative idea-generating.
- Always look for new ideas. If you live in a small town where the library is not as complete as you would like, take a day and drive to a library at a nearby college or in a larger city. Call Nightingale-Conant for a list of their cassette tapes. Subscribe to out-of-town newspapers. Purchase directories of companies in your field of interest (also available in libraries) or contact similar associations and get their mailing lists.

Don't untie what you can cut.

According to history, King Gordius of Phrygia created an intricate knot without any visible ends. His Gordian Knot presented a challenge and an opportunity to the people of ancient Asia. As an oracle proclaimed, the person who could untie this enigmatic ball of rope would be ruler of Asia. Apparently nobody could untie the Knot until a person, later known as Alexander The Great, came along and cut it with his sword. He went on to fulfill the oracle's prophecy.

Similarly, you may feel that your life is entwined in a seemingly endless loop of anxiety and frustration. You now have an opportunity to resolve your situation by taking innovative and bold measures. You can become the ruler of your world by creatively restoring control of your commitment and confidence. Create new ways to solve your problems and then dare to implement them.

I am relaxed, confident and creative.

Chapter Nine

You're Guaranteed to Win

Competition is the spirit of vying for a prize. But competition doesn't have to be against others in order for you to win. You can compete with yourself so that every day you get better at doing whatever it is you need to do to get a job.

Why a competitive spirit is necessary in a job search.

In his book <u>The Inner Game of Tennis,</u> W. Timothy Gallwey says that you can be sure to win every time you play if you never compete with anyone nearly as good as you are. This applies to your job search in the sense that you can always get a job if you lower your standards enough. You'll compete against people who are not nearly as qualified as you, and you'll eventually be hired. But I think you'll agree, doing so would not create long-term success.

In your journey to employment you obviously compete with others for a job. But success in your endeavor will be more readily assured if you direct your competition toward yourself instead of them. This means that you should always try to be the best "You" that you can be. Always try to improve on your actions and skills, and you're more likely to become successful more quickly.

Compete with yourself to contact one more person per day this week than you did last week. Look for ways to make your cover letter and resume better than they were yesterday but not as good as they will be tomorrow. Seek one more idea to solve a problem. Find new ways to inspire the "... and then some" spirit. Always attempt to improve yourself in some way, every day.

If you stretch yourself to perform at the highest level you are capable of, you'll make mistakes along the way. But you'll also improve and eventually succeed. A high-jumper doesn't know how high he can really go until he misses. Only by failing on that last try can he find out how high he can truly jump.

I always evaluate my performance and make necessary changes.

Strive for goals that are important to you.

If you set goals that are important to you, you're more likely to succeed. If you try to reach goals set for you by someone else, you cease to compete with yourself but with the image someone else has of you. It's very difficult to win under these circumstances.

Decide what you want for yourself and go for it. If you've always wanted to start your own business, do it. If you're an accountant who wants to try your hand at selling, do it. If you're a housewife who wants to get back in to the business world, do it. Compete with yourself and you will grow and succeed. If you try to compete for what others think you should be, you won't have the commitment to succeed.

One essential result of a competitive attitude is that you'll be doing something. As we've seen before, action tends to beget action. With action comes either success or failure. If you fail, you learn from it and take other action. If you succeed, you continue doing more of that same action. It all starts with taking that first step and your competitive nature will enable that to occur. It's better to do something imperfectly than to do nothing perfectly. As Robert Schuller says, "I'd rather try something great and fail than to do nothing and succeed."

You also compete with others for limited opportunities.

Competition shouldn't mean there has to be a winner and a loser. In a competitive environment there can be several winners. In the Olympic games there are gold, silver and bronze medals for every event. The gold-medal winner may be .005 seconds faster or jump 1/2" higher than the silver-medal winner, but I don't consider the latter as being unsuccessful.

In the job search, you must deal with two concepts that are difficult to comprehend. The first is that in most cases you'll never know who your competition is. You won't know what special skills and experience they bring to the bargaining table. Consequently, you may never find out the real reason why you weren't hired and the other person was.

The second fact is that you'll never know how close you came to actually getting the offer (if you were turned down). For your own mental well-being you have to believe that you were one of the finalists in the decision-making process.

You can still be a winner in this situation by evaluating the skills and attitude with which you went into the latest round of interviews. In

---

I learn from my mistakes so they don't happen again.

how many ways can you improve to make sure you get the gold next time. Call the interviewer and ask for his opinion about how you could improve. Place yourself in front of a video camera and practice your questioning techniques. Remember that the job doesn't always go to the best candidate, it goes to the one who can sell himself the best.

How to develop a competitive attitude in your job search.

The great thing about competing against yourself in your job search is that you can't lose. If you constantly evaluate your performance and improve on your weaknesses, you have to increase your competence. This should subsequently improve confidence in yourself, too.

Listed below are two checklists you can use to evaluate your relative progress in your search regularly. These are partially reprinted from the book Job Search 101 and you can use them to review your performance objectively. They will help you focus on what is going right in your search as well as on what techniques need improvement.

The first is the Job-Search Progress Checklist. You can use this throughout your quest for employment to help you evaluate your forward motion and make corrections as you proceed. You may find that you set many self-improvement goals. Then you probably started off in one direction and may have forgotten to work on all the areas in which you first intended. This checklist will force you to evaluate your progress regularly in all the areas that are important to you, which should, in turn, keep you focused on improving yourself in each.

JOB-SEARCH PROGRESS CHECKLIST

- ❑ How can I better present the skills that I possess and the benefits of these skills to the interviewer?
- ❑ Have I made all the changes to my "product" that I had planned?
- ❑ Is my attitude sufficiently positive and enthusiastic?
- ❑ Have I priced myself properly?
- ❑ How else can I better utilize the members of my "Brain Trust?"
- ❑ How can I more properly balance my mass- and personal-communication techniques?

I evaluate everything I see and hear to determine its truth and relevancy to me.

❑ Have I listed all my tactics and generated at least twenty ways to accomplish each? What else could I do?

❑ Are all my communications creative, credible, complete, current, convincing, concise and clear?

❑ Does my resume adequately portray my accomplishments?

❑ How could I re-write my cover letter to address the issues that regularly surface in interviews?

❑ Have I recorded all the contacts I have made and followed up with each?

❑ What else can I do to control my voice during an interview?

❑ Where else can I look for names of prospective employers?

❑ What else can I do?

❑ Do I regularly review my Career Journal (Chapter Fifteen) to re-evaluate all the aspects of my job search?

❑ What other occupations might I consider?

❑ What other role models can I contact for information about how they succeeded?

❑ What other techniques could I use to practice my interviewing skills?

❑ Is there a support group nearby that I could join for more objective information and assistance?

❑ What else can I do in order to be more successful?

You may find yourself coming out of an interview saying to yourself how "stupid" you were to answer a particular question so foolishly. Surely, they'll never call you back now. This self-diminishing feedback can force you to concentrate on the negative aspect of your performance while ignoring all the things you did well.

You can use the Post-Interview Checklist to critique your performance on the interview. This will force you to evaluate the positive elements as well as the areas in which you may need more work. As long as you keep the proper perspective and change only that which needs changing, you will find yourself improving after every performance you make.

I have the need to succeed.

POST-INTERVIEW CHECKLIST

❑ Did I properly prepare for this interview, including a review of the company's literature? Did I spend enough time practicing?

❑ What was my objective for this interview? Did I achieve it?

❑ Did I call to confirm the interview beforehand, and did I arrive on time?

❑ Did I scan the office to find something with which to open the interview personally?

❑ How could I have more effectively opened the interview?

❑ Did I use the interviewer's name frequently enough? Did I pronounce it right? Did I get a business card to get the proper spelling for my thank-you note?

❑ How can I ask better questions?

❑ Did I discuss the benefits of my skills and my accomplishments?

❑ Did I use reference letters and testimonials effectively?

❑ Did I adequately handle the objections? Which ones have come up often enough that I should anticipate more effective ways to handle them?

❑ How can I improve my skills in asking questions that will commit them to hiring me?

❑ Did I actively participate in the interview? How can I do better next time?

❑ How should I follow up on this interview? When? To whom should I send a thank you note?

❑ What is the commitment for the next step?

❑ How did I look? Was my suit clean and pressed? What about my shirt/blouse? Were my shoes shined?

❑ Did I adequately listen to the interviewer, or did I find my mind wandering to what I was going to say next?

❑ Did I anticipate the questions sufficiently? Which ones gave me trouble answering? How can I do better next time?

❑ Did I ask the right questions and obtain all the information I wanted?

❑ What else can I do to improve my performance on my next interview?

❑ Would I accept this position if offered to me?

Use the items shown in each of these checklists as a starting point. Add and delete questions that will force you to probe into and evaluate the areas in which you need more development. Then as you

---

I focus on my strengths, accomplishments and goals.

review each, make specific plans on how you can improve what you need the most help on.

The result is that you will be constantly <u>evolving</u> during your journey towards employment. You will change for the better every time you evaluate and improve your performance in your search in general or in the specific areas that need more development. When you carry this technique with you into your next job, you'll create the habit of improving your performance every day in some way. How can you lose?

I am constantly evolving as a person.

Chapter Ten

Success: Made From 100% Concentrate

When you concentrate your thoughts on your goals, you direct your attention to the actions that will achieve them. This presupposes that you have set a goal and that you have planned the strategies and tactics that will lead you to it.

Progress during your period of unemployment has less to do with speed than it does with direction. Concentration serves as the compass that keeps you headed toward your end result, with the arrow pointed directly at your goal.

It's been proven that the most points scored in a football game are made in the final two minutes of each half. The players are concentrating on getting the points on the board before the time runs out. They are not thinking about what happens if they lose, but on scoring the points necessary to win. You have to play the job-search game as if you are always in the last two minutes of the second half. Concentrate on the rewards of success, not the consequences of failure.

Why concentration is important to your job search.

Once you have determined what you want to do with your future, you are more likely to achieve your goal if you concentrate all your thoughts and efforts on pursuing it. Place your full attention on performing as much purposeful activity as you can today, and you will reap the rewards in the future. By so doing, you'll keep your mind focused on what you need to do today to become employed tomorrow.

Lack of concentration can cause a well-intentioned plan to fail. For example, years ago I tried to start a business. Since I was unsure of how well this would turn out, I also took a position as a full-time college teacher (which only demanded about twenty hours a week of my time). But this did two things. It eliminated twenty hours of prime time that I could have otherwise applied to my business. Second, it gave me an avenue for retreat if my first choice didn't work out. Consequently, I

My concentration keeps me in control of my life.

didn't concentrate exclusively on my goal, and when my plans didn't go as well as expected, I chose the path of least resistance and went back to work for another company.

You always find what you concentrate on.

I was once asked if I thought there was a job "out there" for everyone who was unemployed. My answer was that there is a job available or that can be created for every unemployed person who is willing to command of himself the self-discipline and concentration to seek it. You have to work hard enough to find a new job. Concentrating will help ensure that your efforts are most effective and efficient in finding it.

For example, the month of April, 1974 was my first period of unemployment as a married adult. There were only 30 days in that month, 22 of which were work days. I broke my available time down like this:

$$720 \text{ hours} = 30 \text{ days}$$
$$- 240 \text{ hours} = \text{time for sleep}$$
$$- \underline{176 \text{ hours}} = 22 \text{ work days @ 8 hours}$$
$$304 \text{ hours} = \text{evenings and weekends}$$

I concentrated my time during business hours from Monday through Friday calling people in their offices, contacting employment agencies and doing whatever else I could to maximize my time with potential employers. I spent evenings and weekends at the library reviewing directories and at home looking through newspapers and typing letters. These were the days before word processors and I had to type every letter individually.

My severance package and savings all were depleted on the last day of the month (which was a Friday). The day before that occurred, I received a call from a company I had contacted the previous week, and we arranged an interview for the following day. The interview went well, and they asked if my wife and I could have dinner with the president of the company and his wife on Saturday night, which we accepted. That went well, and my supervisor-to-be called me on Sunday to offer me a job, starting the next day. I accepted the offer.

This is an example of the results that can be achieved if you believe that you will succeed and then work as hard as you can to make it happen. If you concentrate your efforts on finding new ways to locate

---

I always achieve what I concentrate on.

potential employers and then contact them, you will become re-employed. Concentration on your efforts also has these benefits:

• *Concentration puts you back in control of your life.*

One element of unemployment is that your focus is directed on present-day events and you lose the ability to plan for the long term. But if you set long-term goals and seek to reach them, you can take back control of your future by immersing yourself in the present. Then you are less likely to think about the unchangeable "catastrophes" of the past and the uncertainties of the future. Concentrate on what you can control today, and you'll be in charge of yourself and your future.

Job-search success begins with setting goals and steadfastly adhering to what will make them occur. It's important to set goals early in your period of unemployment so you establish your direction and motivation right from the beginning. Take control of your journey as soon as you can and you will take less time to arrive at your destination.

• *Concentration helps prevent you from becoming overwhelmed.*

If you think too far ahead, you can lose control and become demoralized by your inability to deal with everything all at one time. Think only about your current efforts and results and you can more readily deal with the reality of your situation. Concentrate your efforts on achieving one small step at a time and you're less likely to feel overwhelmed. Don't think about the entire challenge facing you. Break your activities down into small steps, and think about what you can do to implement each.

For example, if you know you have four months to get a job, that you will average one offer for every five hundred contacts and that the interview process takes about two months, your plan is simplified. You now know that you must begin interviewing within two months and therefore must contact five hundred people during the next sixty days. This is less than ten new contacts every day and certainly you can do that. The more contacts you make exceeding the ten every day, the more quickly you will find employment. That fact alone should offer some solace.

• *Concentration assures you won't divide your actions between two goals.*

You'll save money, time and energy by focusing all your actions on one objective. If you decide to work for someone else, apply yourself totally to doing so. If you choose to work for yourself, devote 100% of

---

I concentrate on my goals.

your concentration to succeeding in that task. Don't allow multiple goals to distract you from achieving the one goal that is best for your long-term personal needs.

- *Concentration on positive actions will prevent your mind from wandering.*

Have you ever driven over a long stretch of road without thinking about what you were doing? If you could retrace your thoughts, they probably wandered from topic to topic without direction. The next time you begin a long drive, take along a cassette recorder and direct your thoughts to what you can do next on your job hunt. Depending on what mental state you find yourself in, you should concentrate on ways to improve your lot.

Instead of thinking "Why me?" Answer these questions:

> *What do I want to do with my life? What else could I do to improve my financial situation? In how many ways can I improve my attitude? What else can I do to communicate my skills and achievements persuasively?*

Instead of "I've run out of newspapers to look for help-wanted ads in, now what am I going to do," concentrate on these thoughts:

> *Where else can I look for a job? How can I get more done in the same amount of time? What directories are available to provide additional names for prospecting?*

Instead of dwelling on the negative, for example, "This search is taking much longer than I thought it would," think about ways to reverse the turn of your emotions:

> *What action can I take to get more potential employers to respond to me? In how many other ways can I productively follow up on my contacts? In what other ways can I deal with the rejection that I know is part of my job search?*

Instead of "If I don't find something soon, I'll lose everything," dwell on ways to reverse your spiraling attitude:

> *What other positive books can I read and tapes could I listen to? What can I say to myself to improve my self-talk? What physical exercise can I do to relieve the stress I'm feeling?*

Instead of "What's the use? I'll never get a job. Nobody wants to hire an old guy like me," think about what you can do just for today.

I succeed in activities that combine attention to detail with creativity.

What one action can I take today to feel better, network and smile more? What are the positive aspects of my age?

How to develop job-search concentration.

In most quests for employment, concentration will be thrust upon you by virtue of the limited amount of time you have to find a new job. Given a large severance package and equally stable financial position, you may have a year or more to find employment. But most of us are not in that condition and must locate a job in a relatively short period of time. Therefore, we become focused on our efforts almost immediately.

The first action you can take to instill greater concentration in your search is to set goals. You should determine how much time you have to find a job by performing a cash-flow analysis of your situation. This will set one goal, i.e., your deadline.

But it does not set your career goal. Early in your quest you should try to determine what it is that you intend to do for the remainder of your working life. If it's to pursue exactly the same type of position you had before, then do it. If you have always wanted to try something else, now you have the opportunity to do so.

Try something and make changes as you proceed.

Following my lay-off on November 9, 1990 I decided what I didn't want to do. That was to go back to work for somebody else. I didn't know what I wanted to do, but I did have over twenty years of marketing experience, so I started a consulting business. As time went on, the economy took a downward turn and several banks in New England became insolvent and folded, causing the remaining banks to be more conservative in their loans. Consequently, I was refused financing by every bank I applied to.

Since I needed funds, I began a resume-writing service. And during this entire time I was writing a book for my twin sons who were about to graduate from college. It was a book about how to find a job, based on my own experience in the job market. Since the other business was slow in starting, I devoted more and more time to writing the book which I eventually self-published with the title <u>Job Search 101</u> in July of 1991. It wasn't until that time that I found my career focus and have subsequently committed myself to marketing that book and writing <u>Coping With Unemployment</u>.

I approach my search with perspiration and inspiration.

So, if you aren't sure what it is that you want to do, try <u>something</u>. In my case I concentrated on proceeding toward my goal of self-employment, although I wasn't sure at first how that would occur. As I continued with my end result in mind, I responded to opportunities as they arose and changed my strategy (but not my ultimate objective). Remain in an action mode and new alternatives will present themselves to you.

If you're one of the lucky ones who knows exactly what it is that you want to do, then do it. Concentrate your full attention, efforts and resources on reaching your goal. It's exhilarating, finally, to do what you love and look forward to each working day. You'll look back on the day you were given your notice and say to yourself that it was a blessing.

Once your goals are in place and you are moving toward them, there are several questions you can ask yourself to help you maintain your focus on your goals. When you are undecided about which choice to take regarding alternative uses of your time, ask yourself:

*"If I choose this alternative, will it take me
closer to my goal or further from it?"*

If your answer is "Closer," then do it. If your answer is "Further," then look for something different to do and ask yourself that question again. In any case, you have to be ready to deal with your answer. If you knowingly choose a course of action that will be *fun* vs. *right*, it will cause a feeling of guilt. For example, if you have a choice between taking the weekend off or remaining home to go through the newspapers, you could ask yourself the question above. And if you do, be prepared to deal with your response.

Another good question is:

"What's the best use of my time right now?"

Your answer will keep you busy for hours. Then when you again find yourself without anything to do, ask that question of yourself. Make sure you define the word "best" as an activity that will lead you closer to your objective, not the one that will relieve your tension most readily.

Pursuing goals is not necessarily a tension-relieving activity. You will find less enjoyment in looking through a directory at the library than if you joined your friends on a picnic. But your long-term satisfaction will be met by reviewing the names of people to contact and then doing so. And you'll enjoy your picnic more at a later date when you know you have a job to go to the next day.

My habits improve the quality of my life.

Don't let it happen, make it happen.

Throughout your entire job search you must take action to establish your control, commitment, confidence, courage, creativity, competitive attitude and concentration and defend them from deterioration. You may find yourself paying more attention to one at the expense of the others. But success in your search means you must develop the entire mix with an awareness that changes in them can occur individually and collectively.

There are two major points you should remember from the information in the past seven chapters. The first is that by breaking your attitude down into manageable sections, you can more easily take control without being overwhelmed. The second is that protecting your attitude is an ongoing and monumental task. You must regularly monitor and correct any deterioration of any segment before it affects the whole.

If maintained, your job-search attitude will sustain you through your present dilemma, and it will have an enormously beneficial after-effect. Once you become re-employed, you will rarely be bothered by minor events again. What were once heretofore "calamities" in your life will now be reduced to relatively minor incidents because they don't compare with what you have just endured. And as you learned and tried new techniques, you improved your skills in many ways. You'll end up being more organized, economical and efficient in most aspects of your life. And you'll have a stronger attitude about yourself and your ability to manage whatever it is the future has in store for you.

Your strategies won't work unless you do.

Whatever positive attitudes, actions or images you create won't help you if you don't put them to work. You must commit yourself to doing all you can every day to pursue employment. Just as you have to put a car into drive to get it to move forward, you have to put yourself in gear. You have to start the car. You have to set the direction and you have to drive it. Take charge of your present and you can control your future. Work diligently, commit irrevocably, think creatively, act decisively, dare boldly, hope eternally and believe completely. You will succeed.

I earn my success through commitment, courage and hard work.

PART THREE:

How to restore and maintain a good attitude.

———————

Chapter Eleven

Reach for the Stars

Goals are very important to achieving success in a job search. They stimulate internal commitment, control and confidence. They direct your actions so that everything you do works toward achieving your objective. And they also keep your mind focused on how you will evolve and when it will happen, helping you become more creative as you define new ways to accomplish your goals.

Why goals are important to your job search.

Undoubtedly you've heard the concept that goals should be specific, measurable, time-oriented, reasonable and written. These are all true, especially during a job search when they serve as a source of both solace _and_ motivation. But there is much more to the importance of setting goals at this time in your life:

1) Goals set your direction and control the actions you take. There is an adage that says a journey of one thousand miles begins with just one step. But what if that step starts you off in the wrong direction? You could spend the remainder of your trip walking away from your objective. If you know where you are going, you're more likely to get there.

As indicated earlier, goal-setting is like using a compass. Your goals create your magnetic north, and you must keep checking to make sure you're still heading in the right direction. If you find yourself heading the wrong way, you should make the corrections necessary to get yourself back on course.

2) Goals make the task of prospecting for potential employers much easier. If you know what you want to do for your career, you can focus your prospecting activities on that industry, allowing yourself to utilize your time and concentrate your limited resources more efficiently.

I have created goals in every area of my life.

3) <u>A solid understanding of what you want in your career will enable you to ask incisive questions during an interview</u>. The interview should be a mutual exchange of information during which each party evaluates the other's ability to meet his needs. If you know what your needs are, you can ask specific questions that will help you determine if this particular company is "right" for you.

4) <u>Goals help you to focus your efforts where they will do the most good</u>. By carefully analyzing the opportunities that are available in other geographical areas, you can enormously improve your chances of finding employment in a shorter period of time.

5) <u>Your actions are more likely to lead you to employment successfully and in less time</u>. As you focus on a goal, you're mind tends to think of ways to accomplish it. Consequently, your objectives will motivate and dictate your actions.

6) <u>Long-term goals help you determine short-term landmarks to keep your search on track</u>. By working backward from a specific long-term goal, you can establish interim goals, the attainment of which provides much-needed positive reinforcement. These interim goals also allow you to evaluate the relative success of your tactics and change them accordingly.

7) <u>Attention to specific goals will enhance your creativity</u>. As you dwell on ways to achieve your objective, your mind will be stimulated to think of new techniques to try. These will in turn lead you to other ideas.

Your goals should be firm but flexible.

When you set a date upon which you will have a job, you create additional pressure for yourself. As your date approaches and you have no opportunities in sight, you may begin to "panic." When this happens you could benefit from altering the deadline, if possible. But if you have a specific date on which you will run out of money, it's difficult to change the deadline. If you have time, alter your deadline to accommodate a change in tactics. Or you could find other ways to extend your financial deadline by taking a part-time or temporary position.

I write my goals down along with written plans on how to achieve them.

Don't let existing resources set your goals.

At this point in your search, you're self-esteem may not be as high as it otherwise might be. Be aware of this and don't automatically lower your goals in order to find something more quickly. Doing so could lead to long-term problems. Of course, what you do depends on the financial resources at your disposal and the level of confidence you have in yourself to find a new position.

You have to let go of limiting thoughts that hold you back from achieving success. Think of yourself as a trapeze artist in the circus. You have to let go of the first trapeze if you are going to reach for the other. Don't be afraid of letting go of an outdated belief as long you have another in sight.

Seek opportunities that that you wouldn't have thought of at first. Set goals that cause you to stretch, emotionally and professionally, to achieve. You may experience greater resistance by doing so, but the opportunities associated with a greater challenge will make it worth your while. One person described this situation by saying that the greater the goal she set, the larger the difficulties that seemed to get in her way. But she turned this into a self-motivational statement by telling herself, when confronted with an enormous obstacle, "I know I'm really on to something big."

Your attitudes are influenced by events that occur to you over a period of time. However, they are not shaped by the events themselves but by your interpretation of them and what they mean to you. In order to change your attitude about your situation, it's important to see how it was developed in the first place, as illustrated in this diagram:

Goal —> Action —> Results (Good   Bad) —> Change in
$$\vdash\!\!-\!\!-\!\!-\!\!-\!\!-\!\!-\!\!-\!\!\dashv \quad \text{Attitude } (\underline{\pm})$$

As this demonstrates, you begin the process by setting a goal, i.e., stating your target date, title and the salary you expect to achieve. Then you take action with some expectation of what the results will be. As actual results are experienced, you subjectively compare the actual to the expected results. If they exceed your expectations your positive attitude is reinforced. If they are less than your expectations your attitude is diminished. It's important that you try to be as objective as possible as you compare the actual results of your actions with the results that you expected.

I read my goal statement every day.

Set your goals at the attainable limits of your ability.

The "Goal —> Action —> Results" series of events causes either an upward or downward spiral of your attitude, depending on your evaluation. Low self-esteem will cause you to assess your performance negatively and consequently lower your goals even further. And if you still cannot find a job (poor results), your attitude is further eroded, which leads you again to lower your standards.

You could reply by saying that if you set low standards for performance, you're more likely to exceed them, and therefore your attitude will always be good. By reducing your salary expectations, you will compete against people who are not nearly as qualified as you for a position, so you are more likely to get it. But this is incorrect thinking because if you set your objectives below your abilities, you'll never experience the exhilaration of competitive victory. You may also suffer in the long run due to being underemployed and underpaid.

Similarly, if you set your performance standards excessively high, you're setting yourself up for regular defeat and your attitude will plummet. Later in their job search, people become deflated when they feel they must lower their salary expectations. But this presupposes they were set correctly in the first place, which may not have been the case. Lowering salary requirements for some people may merely be a function of bringing them back to reality.

Take a strategic setback.

You must seriously evaluate any job offer, but this is even more important when you are in a vulnerable mental state. It may indeed be a wise decision to take a lower-paying or less-challenging job in order to position yourself strategically for greater future success. But this decision should be the result of conscious forethought, not a conclusion reached through desperation and a desire to reduce the tension you currently feel.

That's why it's so important to set your goals at the right level of expectation and objectively evaluate your relative success. Once you establish appropriate standards for success in your life, you can evaluate the results of your actions more accurately. If you later find it necessary to reduce your standards for employment, at least your decision will be based on a more logical review of your performance.

Always keep one point in mind: your goals should be your goals. You won't be sufficiently motivated to reach a goal that someone else set for you. If your parents want you to be a doctor or nurse but you want to become an electrical engineer, that's what you should become. Do what

Every day I take at least one different action to reach my goals.

makes you happy and you'll succeed in it. Do what makes other people happy and that's what you'll succeed in, i.e., making them happy.

Create goals in other areas of your life that are important to you. These should include both your professional and personal aspirations. For example, you may want to set goals in these areas:

Professional Aspirations	Personal Aspirations
Begin a new career	Feel better about myself
Upgrade my present skills	Improve my financial position
Continue my education	Improve relationship with
Improve my time management	my spouse/friends
Practice communication skills	Increase my self-esteem
Improve my listening skills	Take more time to be with
	my children
	Begin a physical conditioning
	program

Prioritize these according to their importance to you and then convert each into a specific statement that establishes a measurable time frame for its attainment. Then create your action plan that outlines the steps you must take to realize your objective.

Your mind is a goal mine.

Setting goals is nothing more than converting your thoughts into words. Ask yourself questions to stimulate these thoughts and then write down what comes to mind. Don't try to think about everything all at one time. Instead, take each of the above statements and interrogate yourself.

For example, if you want to begin a new career, what would you do? You could begin by listing the tasks you like to perform:

Solving Problems	Meeting
Training	Planning
Supervising	Creating
Travelling	Selling
Counseling	Analyzing
Writing	Communicating

Then write down what you like about each. What kind of problems do you like solving? Where do you like to travel? What do you like to write about? One of the most stimulating questions I've found to ask myself is, what I would do if I won $10,000,000 in a lottery? This eventually led me to a career change at the age of 42. Instead of seeking another position after becoming unemployed, I started my own business.

I take time every day to review my goals.

At the time I didn't know what I would do. So I looked back upon what I liked to do in my career and knew that I always enjoyed marketing products. This led me to think that 1) I could market someone else's products or 2) market my own.

Since I had no products of my own, I initially looked into marketing someone else's products and was left with two choices:

A) I could work full time for a company, or

B) I could work as a consultant.

Eliminating the first alternative was not difficult so I chose the latter, i.e., helping companies market their products as a consultant. However, I quickly found that working on this basis was not much different than working <u>for</u> them. They always held power over my income and could sever the relationship at any time.

If you look over this sequence, I had the goal in mind to be an independent businessman. I wasn't sure about the specific position, so I set a goal to try something. As a result of evaluating my progress and results, I made changes in my direction and continuously fine-tuned the actions I took.

Setting goals is worthless.

Goal-setting by itself will not make you more successful in your job search. Goals only become effective when they motivate you to take action on their behalf. Creating a specific goal that is important to you is like pushing the ignition button on a space-shuttle launch. It sets in motion all the power and guidance systems that are waiting to be utilized. Until ignition occurs, you (like the shuttle) are just an expensive piece of equipment waiting for something to start it.

Goal-setting is only the first step in the process. If you don't follow through with all the action steps to keep you moving, the goals themselves won't take you there. Think of goals as verbs, not nouns. Words such as "work, commit, endure" denote actions you can take to reach your goals. Focus on the goal-directed activities and you'll move closer to your objective.

I always create clear mental pictures of my goals.

Chapter Twelve

What You See Is What You Get

Coping with unemployment is like assembling the pieces of a jig-saw puzzle. You begin by focusing on what the final outcome will be, i.e., the picture on the outside of the box. Then you organize the individual pieces into groups that seem to go together and try to make them fit. And if you keep at it long enough, you have a finished puzzle that you can be proud of.

This same concept will help you in your search. Once you set your goals, you should begin by creating a detailed mental image of them. Then you create the pieces and assemble them until you achieve the picture you have in your mind. These pieces are the things you will do to reach your goal, which include your resume, cover letter, interviewing skills and prospecting activities.

Visualization is a technique you can use to form an image in your mind of the goal you want to attain. It's not a new theory; you use it every day of your life. Unfortunately, in your present situation you probably use it to create negative images. For example, if you picture in your mind what will happen to you if you don't find another job, you are using visualization.

The concept of visualizing performance is not new particularly to those of you who participate in sports. For example, when bowling you have to keep your mind focused on the pins and not on the gutter. The golfer visualizes the perfect swing that will send the ball to the pin, not in the traps. Visualizing perfect performance in any sport helps you focus on your objective, not on failure. All you need to do is use the same concept to create positive images of your search so you are drawn to them rather than toward the negative images.

In the job-search sense, the term "visualization" is something of a misnomer because you should utilize all your senses to describe your objective, including touch, sight, smell, sound and taste. Have you ever heard someone say "I want that so bad I can taste it?" You should feel the same thing about resolving your predicament. Use the principles of **sensory projection** to describe your goals in terms of the feelings you

---

I use all my senses when focusing on my objective.

have, the sounds you hear, the images you see, the items you touch, the aromas you smell and the flavors you taste.

The more senses you can involve in your image, the stronger it will be for you. A thorough image of your goal has a motivating effect on your attitude and helps stimulate you to create more "pieces" to your puzzle. And it reminds you of the positive benefits you will receive when you finally become re-employed. This will keep your mind and actions focused on achieving the end result you desire.

Since you are already using visualization, it won't be difficult to re-focus your images in a more positive direction. There are several steps you can take to make this occur:

Step 1.

Begin the visualization process by imagining something you are familiar with. It could be the perfect swing of a tennis racquet, but it doesn't have to be an athletic event. For example, what do you think about when someone says "Think of a dog?" How does that image change when you are asked to think of a "snarling, junk-yard watchdog?" Conjure up in your mind a detailed image of what it would look like. Then try doing the same thing with another familiar object.

Continue practicing this technique by mentally describing what it is that you want from your work. Is it the prestige of a large office, the camaraderie of working with your friends, the boat you want to purchase, the sense of challenge and accomplishment, a feeling of self-worth or the fact that it provides you with a way to meet your financial obligations? Use all your senses in creating this image of what you will have when you become re-employed.

This technique can also help you determine what you truly want to do in your career. When you picture the perfect job, it doesn't have to be one you've had in the past. You can use your imagination to create your ideal position. It could be an image of yourself working behind the counter in your own store. If so, what does the counter look and feel like? What does the bell over the front door signalling the entry of another customer sound like?

Step 2.

Once you have this image firmly in mind, write down a description of your thoughts. Concentrate on what you sense in your mind. As a starting point, think about your "perfect" work area. What does it look

---

My detailed vision of my goal draws me closer to it.

like? What does it feel like? What do you talk about with your co-workers? When you go to the cafeteria for lunch, what do you smell and what does your lunch taste like?

Be as specific as you can when writing your descriptions. You can make it as long as you want because it's not necessary to read it every day. You can accomplish that through the use of affirmations which will be discussed in the next chapter.

Step 3.

Create a "feeling" that brings to life all the sensory perceptions that you wrote about. Be as detailed and complete as you can. If you're artistically inclined, draw a picture of your goal. If not, find a picture or take a photograph of something that closely matches your objective and keep it with you. Use it as a reminder of what you want, and a motivator to keep you working towards it.

This technique worked for my son. Before he started high school he had a goal of working for American Airlines. He wrote them to tell them his goal. He ordered their quarterly and annual reports and read every article he could find on the airlines in general and American Airlines in particular. He pasted pictures of American Airlines planes on his bedroom walls. And he had coffee mugs, bumper stickers and other memorabilia from American that kept him focused on his objective. We even gave him American Airlines stock as a Christmas present one year.

Upon graduating from college and after eight years of visualizing his objective, American Airlines flew him to their Dallas headquarters for an interview. It won't take you that long to attain your goal if you use this technique.

Sensory projection will serve as a motivational device by reminding you about the benefits of success. Since you described what is important to you, your visualization will be more effective in urging you to keep working harder at your search. It serves as the proverbial carrot out in front of you that keeps you moving toward it. But most importantly, it provides hope by focusing your attention on something that is important to you. And describing your goal in such detail makes you feel as if you've attained it before you actually do. This feeling will provide solace and encouragement to you even if you have reached the latter stages of frustration and dejection.

I have a clear vision of my ultimate objective.

Chapter Thirteen

Have you hugged yourself today?

Once you have your sensory image firmly implanted in your mind, you should create a way to remind yourself of it regularly, one that will keep you working to reach your goal. Using positive affirmations will make this possible. These are self-motivating statements that instill in your mind a sense of renewed commitment to your future. By phrasing them so they describe your vision as if it has already occurred, they force you to concentrate on positive, constructive thoughts and lead you to the results you seek.

An affirmation is a statement of a future event in the present tense. You create these by writing a sentence describing each feeling, image, sound, sight, and taste of your sensory projection, as if you are currently experiencing it. Make a list of these sentences and repeat them every day until they become ingrained in your mind.

Why affirmations will help you.

There are several benefits in doing this. First, you'll remind yourself about what you want to become and at the same time help you create new ways to get there. They will also keep you focused on your goal and keep your mind from wandering to negative thoughts. In addition , affirmations keep your mind alert, ready to recognize the opportunities that abound about you. For example, have you ever driven over a long stretch of highway without noticing the billboards? Then when you're running low on gas you seek the information shown on the roadside advertisements to advise you of the location of service stations ahead of you.

Affirmations work the same way. They serve as announcements reminding you of the actions you must take and the emotions you must feel in order to remain on course. For instance, if you regularly repeat to yourself, "I have an exercise program in place that helps me reduce my stress," you are more likely to begin and maintain a physical conditioning program.

Another benefit is that repetition builds belief. If you hear positive statements about yourself often enough, you're likely to believe

---

I seize opportunities by preparing my mind to recognize them.

them. Therefore repeating the words "I am the confident person I aspire to be" eventually leads you to believe that you have the belief in yourself that is necessary to find a new job.

Go ahead and give it a try.

In your present state of mind you may doubt the ability of affirmations to lead you to your objective. In order for these statements to have maximum effect, you must defer judgement about whether they will work or not . Don't try to think about *how* it will happen, think about *what* will happen. You'll feel better, look better and project the positive feelings that will persuade an interviewer to hire you.

When you use them, positive affirmations will motivate you. Imagine how good you could feel about yourself if you constantly reinforced your positive attributes. You'll feel much better about yourself if you repeat these words out loud every day:

I am full of enthusiasm and vitality.

I am a good person and nobody can take that away from me.

I am proud of myself because ...

I am happy, healthy and calm.

I have high energy.

I am a winner.

I feel good about myself.

I believe in myself.

Affirmations also help you concentrate on ways to reach your goals. As long as you focus on your objective and the ways in which you can reach it, you'll get there more quickly. Affirmations such as these can remind you to concentrate on what you want, not on what you don't want:

I know that I will become what I think about the most. Therefore, I only think about good, gain and success.

I set goals in every area of my life.

I write my goals down along with detailed plans on how to achieve them.

I always create mental pictures of my goals.

Every day I take at least one different action to reach my goals.

My expectations are positive and realistic.

I take time every day to review my goals.

I can change anything I want to change to anything I want it to be.

What I will have tomorrow is a direct result of what I do today.

I focus on my strengths, accomplishments and goals.

Your mind thinks at a rate of over six hundred words per minute. But what do you think about? Your thoughts represent one of the few functions of your search over which you exercise total control. Since you direct your thoughts and your thoughts determine your actions, affirmations will give you a sense of mastery. Positive statements such as these will make you believe that you really can control your life:

I succeed by making the most of my time.

I spend my time in productive activity.

I break down projects into smaller, more manageable tasks.

I use my time for good, gain and success.

My thoughts and my self-talk are confident and optimistic.

I am taking control of my life today.

I am responsible for my actions and subsequently my success.

I plan every day with a list of things to do and people to call.

I choose the way I respond to outside events.

I act in a calm and intelligent manner no matter what the situation.

I have a daily plan so that I spend my time wisely.

My priorities are set and I am sticking to them.

I master my emotions as I feed and direct them.

If you don't like calling people on the telephone or knocking on their doors, affirmations can help you develop the courage to do so. They remind you of your ability to do what is necessary to get a job, and they also give you the fortitude to do so. The next time you feel uneasy about calling a prospective employer, repeat these affirmations out loud:

I do what I am capable of doing.

I don't take my eyes off my goal.

––––––––––––

I am grateful for the wealth I have in my life.

I demand the best of myself every day.

I act and feel successful every day.

I feel comfortable looking people in the eye when they look at me.

I have the courage to look to the future and pursue a goal that I can only imagine now.

I know that adversity reveals my true nature and I like what I see.

I know that success requires persistence.

You could approach this as a competitive event. Remember that in the job-search sense, competition is with <u>yourself</u>. You improve your ability by challenging yourself to do better and then evaluating your results. Grow and stretch to be greater than you are now by repeating words like these every day (remember to make up your own affirmations to suit your individual circumstances):

I succeed because I perform to the best of my ability.

I succeed because I pursue goals that are important to me.

I have the ability to recognize and use my abilities.

I do everything in an excellent way.

I have a firm will to achieve success and it can not be broken.

I trust my intuition and act accordingly.

I have a feeling of personal satisfaction today.

Every day I grow wiser, more self-confident and emotionally stronger.

I like myself because ....

I give the best of me in everything.

I have a habit of winning in life.

I regularly read self-motivational books.

I take action that will improve my self-image.

I have a clear mental image of my ideal self.

I objectively evaluate my actions and make appropriate changes.

I approach my search with inspiration.

I use affirmations to invest in myself and my future.

This last affirmation should remind you to include creativity in your search and combine it with the commitment to succeed. With these two thoughts in mind, repeat affirmations that stimulate your creativity and reinforce your resolve to succeed. These may help you do that:

I feel good about myself.

I am good at coming up with creative solutions.

I know that I project on the outside the way I feel on the inside.

I am relaxed, confident and creative.

My habits improve the quality of my life.

I associate with people who are positive, successful and optimistic.

I am a good person (spouse, parent, employee).

I speak with confidence.

My search is easier and faster because of my adequate preparation.

I succeed in activities that combine attention to detail with creativity.

I am successful in my job search because I believe in myself and my goals.

I create my own luck and circumstances through hard work and persistence.

I succeed because my goals are too big to miss.

What I will to be, will be.

Doris Day's song "Que Sera, Sera" contains the words "What will be, will be." While this attitude may be consoling, it's not motivating. You need to control your actions with confident, results-oriented thoughts of commitment, courage, creativity, concentration and competition. Sentences stated as affirmations enable you to do this.

Helpful affirmations are printed at the bottom of each page of this book. Stimulate your confidence and energy by repeating them (or your variation of them) enthusiastically.

There are several techniques for using affirmations. Some people suggest repeating them many times per day. Others take one affirmation and dwell on it for a day. Or you can arrange them in groups and repeat all the positive statements in one group each day. The best technique is

---

I repeat affirmations to remind me of the actions I must take to succeed.

the one that is best for you. If you try someone else's, it may not encourage you to repeat affirmations daily. Use the affirmations stated here to help you write your own. Or create any combination of them that works for you.

In the book <u>Live and Be Free Thru PSYCH-CYBERNETICS</u> (Maxwell Maltz, M.D., F.I.C.S., and Charles Schreiber, F.A.R.A.), there is a credo made up of affirmations that you should repeat out loud every morning while getting your day started. It will have a motivating effect on you as well as allowing you to reach down and begin your day on a positive note:

> *This is the beginning of a new day. I have been given this day to use as I will. What I do today is important because I am exchanging a new day of my life for it. When tomorrow comes, this day will be gone forever, leaving in its place whatever I have traded for it. I pledge to myself that it shall be for good, gain and success.*

> *My thinking and my attitudes are calm and cheerful. I act and feel friendly toward other people. I am tolerant of other people, their shortcomings and their mistakes, and I view their actions with the most favorable understanding possible.*

> *I act as though attainment of my goals is sure to happen. I am the kind of confident individual I aspire to be, and everything I do and the way I feel expresses this individuality, self-confidence and enthusiasm.*

> *I will not allow my thinking or my attitudes to be affected by negativism or pessimism. I will try to smile as often as possible, at least several times a day.*

> *I will respond in a calm and intelligent manner, without alarm, no matter what the situation. If I cannot control the situation, I will respond in a positive manner, even to negative facts.*

Say it out loud.

One of the symptoms of reduced self-confidence is to speak more softly. Therefore, a remedy is to practice speaking with greater volume. Your affirmations provide an excellent opportunity for doing this. Don't just say them; say them <u>out loud</u>, with enthusiasm. Don't *think* them or *whisper* them, but say them as if you're talking to someone sitting in the back seat of your car as you face ahead, and you have the

---

I use affirmations to keep me motivated.

sun roof open creating a lot of extraneous noise. You have to yell in order for that person to hear you, so do it. At the same time you'll have a little fun, and you'll be surprised at how much better you'll feel after repeating them.

Don't be an "if" person; be a "when" person.

Use affirmations, words and thoughts that optimize, maximize and capitalize on your achievements. Never minimize your assets. Think in terms of positive actualities rather than negative possibilities. Write and say your affirmations with enthusiasm to ingrain the feelings, sights, smells, sounds and tastes you described when you initially wrote about your sensory projection.

Don't expect too much.

There are few ailments that modern medical technology can cure immediately. The same is true with affirmations. Don't expect immediate results and then cease to use them when your expectations are not met. Changing your attitudes and beliefs will take time. Affirmations are only one weapon in your arsenal.

For example, I was once participating in a racquetball match (three games of fifteen points each). I won the first but found myself losing the second game to a score of twelve to two. I began repeating to myself: "I am winning this game." I lost the game by a score of fifteen to thirteen. But the affirmations helped me perform better and I eventually won the match. Use affirmations to improve your performance, not as a cure-all for a negative attitude.

Organize them into a system that suits your needs and say them out loud every day to instill a sense of positive inevitability in your manner of thinking. This will snowball and draw you closer and closer to your goal until you eventually reach it.

I have feelings of love, joy, power and confidence.

Chapter Fourteen

Creating Your Personal Marketing Plan

You may be working very hard to find another job but not experiencing success. This in itself will fuel the fires of doom and gloom in your mind. But if you are pursuing tasks that generate results, you are more likely to be motivated to continue doing them. A well-prepared job-search plan helps you do this. It ensures that you are working on tasks that are more likely to achieve the success you desire.

Why planning is important.

Your plan will organize the steps you should take to reach your objective, and at the same time provide the means for evaluating your progress. Then you can start your journey in the right direction and make necessary corrections as you move forward. Your plan doesn't have to be a formal, multi-page marketing program, but it should be a working document that will keep you on course.

Creating your plan is vital to continuing the improvement in your attitude. With renewed vigor, you can accumulate all the pieces of your job-search puzzle and organize them into a plan that will make the actions you take more effective. It will direct them toward the attainment of your goals, which is likely to shorten your period of unemployment. In addition, planning your work has these advantages:

1) Planning insures that your activities lead to accomplishment.

You may find yourself very busy performing all the activities pertaining to finding a new job, yet not getting any closer to landing it. An analogy can be made to sitting in your car in traffic. Your engine is running and you're depleting your energy, but you are not moving.

However, if your actions stem from a carefully planned sequence of steps, they are more likely to yield results quickly. For example, when prospecting for potential employers you could send letters to the people

---

My actions are goal-directed and support the plan I have in place.

listed in directories. Then when you call to follow up on your letter you could find that the person you wrote to left the company six months ago. Had you called first, you could have saved yourself two weeks of time since you must now re-submit your letter to the correct person.

2)Planning maintains your concentration on one goal.

One way to dilute the effectiveness of your actions is to address two dissimilar goals at the same time. For instance, you might decide to start your own business and search for another job at the same time. Or you may decide to look for employment in one career while seeking training in another. Your plan may be to address each with equal vigor and then choose the first opportunity that looks good.

This dual-objective strategy will do nothing but drain your attitude, energy and finances at a faster rate than would otherwise be the case. Instead, decide exactly what it is that you want and devote your complete attention, energy and available funds to its attainment. Only when you do this will your actions accomplish the end result that you truly desire.

3) Making a plan helps you deal with the "uncontrollables."

There are many events that you cannot control in your job search. You'll send out hundreds of responses to ads that seem to be written just for you. Unfortunately, you can't control how the companies respond to your letters. But <u>you can control your response</u> to that situation by following up on every lead until you are sure that it will not yield an opportunity.

<u>You control</u> the way you respond to unemployment and therefore the actions you take to re-gain satisfactory employment in the shortest possible amount of time. Regardless of the detail and accuracy of your current plan, there will always be unexpected events placing obstacles in your path. Therefore, you should have a Plan "B" and a Plan "C" ready as back-up strategies. They will allow you to regroup when something catches you unaware.

4) Planning enables you to turn your stumbling blocks into stepping stones.

Planning enables you to break down your larger tasks into smaller ones, making two things possible. First of all, it makes heretofore insurmountable problems seem more manageable. If you're aware that you may receive one job offer for every five hundred contacts with

---

I always control my response to uncontrollable events.

prospective employers, you can plan to make twenty contacts every day for twenty five days. After that, it takes about two months for the interview process to unfold, so you should have a job in three months.

Secondly, you'll get immediate feedback. If you send out five hundred letters in one week, you're less likely to follow up properly on each. But if you send out fewer letters at a time, you can contact each recipient and find out immediately where you stand with that person. And this approach will give you the opportunity to improve your tactics as you proceed.

As you get this feedback, you'll find that you will be motivated by it. People will make suggestions to you, and you can incorporate some of them into your future correspondence. Then as you send out the next wave of letters or make the next round of telephone calls, you should find that your success rate will go up slightly. If you continue to fine-tune your efforts, you will eventually find another position.

5) Preparation helps you avoid the "Soap Zone."

If you don't plan your time and take positive action to seek employment, you may find yourself falling into the "Soap Zone." This occurs when you spend your time watching "soap operas" during the day instead of pursuing your goals. Once bad habits are formed, it becomes difficult to get back on the right track. The remedy is not to let them form in the first place, but if they exist, do something positive to correct them.

As you "plan your work and work your plan," you will find that it has a cathartic effect on your attitude. You'll wake up each morning more invigorated with the knowledge that today you have specific actions planned that will help you achieve your goal. With a complete day of productive events planned, you won't have time to take part in unproductive activities.

On your mark. Go. Get set.

Too many people fulfill their job search by writing a cover letter and resume and sending them to the companies advertising in the help-wanted ads. Although this is a source of job opportunities, it is not the greatest source. Relying solely on it with hastily-prepared correspondence will only extend your search and increase the frustration and dejection.

Instead, take the time to organize your thoughts and plan your objectives. Then write out a few simple statements that list the activities you should perform in order to succeed. If you are already involved in an

---

My plan keeps my mind focused on my one major objective.

extended period of unemployment, you can create a plan that will restore your confidence and lead you back into the job market. Planning has an invigorating effect that will further your cause.

Creating your plan of attack.

A job-search plan is not something you write and then put away for later review. It's a dynamic document that should stimulate your creative powers to think of new ways to accomplish your objective when existing methods are taking longer than expected. Here is an outline you can use to create your plan:

Step One: Set your goals.

You have already completed this step. If you haven't written your goal down, do so now. This statement serves as the starting point for the remainder of your plan. As an example, your job-search goal could read something like this:

By X/1/9X I will be happily employed in a Big 6 account-ing firm as a (job title) with an annual income of $X0,000.

Step Two: Describe your overall strategies.

In one sentence, define the general direction you will take in each of four primary areas. These convey the overall strategies that will direct your thinking and action.

Self-Analysis: Evaluate the aspects of my personality that affect my ability to become employed and improve those that require strengthening.

Geography: Investigate the geographical locations that would offer me a greater opportunity.

Salary: Establish a reasonable salary range for my ser-vices, including a list of the non-salary items that impact my take-home pay.

Promotion: Put into action a cohesive promotion program utilizing all forms of mass and personal communication

Step Three: What can hinder your efforts?

Anticipate the obstacles that might hinder you in carrying out your plan of action. These could relate to your experi-ence, education, attitude, the lack of emotional support from your family, the local economy, your finances or any other aspect of your life that you feel could create a hurdle for you.

_____

I break down major tasks into manageable steps.

Step Four: What additional information do you need?

Given these potential impediments, how can you better prepare yourself to succeed? Perhaps additional training or education is necessary. Or you might need family, emotional or financial counseling. Also list the places where you might find necessary information, such as your public library.

Step Five: Whose help do you need?

If you feel that your creative skills are lacking, contact a friend or relative who could help you think of ideas. Or you might read a book on creativity. If you feel you need more information on financial planning, who can provide it? Who can assist you in restoring your bruised confidence? Who can help you start a physical conditioning program or provide assistance writing your resume and cover letter? Find the answers and plan to contact each person.

Step Six: List the specific steps you will take.

Using each strategy from Step Two as a major topic, list the things you will do daily to achieve each. Be as specific and detailed as you can.

Step Seven: What's in it for you?

If you follow through with your plans using the resources at your disposal to overcome the obstacles you anticipate, how will you benefit? Write a description of how you will feel when the worry, self-doubt and financial pressure are finally relieved. What will it be like going to work every day, doing what you like to do and feeling productive again? How will you feel about yourself for successfully planning, carrying out and evaluating your job search? How will your relationships with people (including your creditors) improve? Write down in great detail the answers to each of these questions and any others that seem relevant.

Step eight: Reinforce your vision by creating and repeating your positive affirmations.

You can use those found at the bottom of each page or those in Chapter Thirteen as examples to help you create your own affirmations.

I have good habits and I work to strengthen them every day.

Your plan should be a working document.

Your plan will never be finished since you will be constantly updating and adding to it. Review it every day and decide what steps you will take to achieve your goals. If they work, use them again. If they don't work, find out why not and revise or eliminate them. Create new affirmations. Add new techniques and tools to further your search. Make it a working document that you use on a daily basis.

You don't have time to waste time.

This all seems like a lot of work. And it is. It's difficult to force yourself to prepare your self-marketing plan because you'll feel that it's not the most productive use of your time. You most likely think that you need to be out there sending resumes to the people advertising so that you can get right back to work.

The time you take to create your job-search plan will be rewarded with more productivity later. You'll be calling on the right prospects with the proper information. You're correspondence will project the desired image. And you'll be in a better position to negotiate for a better compensation package that will maximize your take-home pay.

A simple formula for success.

This, of course, assumes that you work hard at your search and don't give up. In fact, there are only three steps in the journey to job-search success:

Step One:	Start.
Step Two:	Work Hard
Step Three:	Don't Quit.

But before you take the first step towards implementation, take the time to plan your efforts. This will make sure you're heading in the right direction. Then all your hard work will be placed on the proper tasks. Plan your work and work your plan. You will be successful.

I update my plan daily and make changes that are necessary.

Chapter Fifteen

Dear Diary

If you keep a written record of your search, you'll be able to document your actions and feelings. This will help you evaluate your progress and monitor your performance. As described in Chapter Fourteen, your job-search plan should be a working document, something that you often refer to and update. To these ends, start a Career Journal in a simple spiral-bound notebook and record your plan, your daily activities to carry it out, and your progress.

Sweat the details.

Your Career Journal will in essence become your job-search diary. In addition to the above, if you faithfully record your thoughts in it you can help yourself get through this tough period. Record all the feelings you experience. If you are having a good day, write about it; you can refer back to this entry later when you are having a bad day. And you'll find that writing down your emotions will give you some relief as well as a better understanding of them. In many cases you will come up with solutions to your concern as you write about it.

Also, describe what you did and why it did or didn't work. Later, you can try something again or come up with something new as the situation demands. Should you ever have to go through this experience a second time, recording it will serve as a reminder of what worked, as well as what didn't work for you.

Most importantly your Career Journal will be the device that holds your plan. It will assist you when you refer to it if you are trying to figure out what to do on a particular day. If your plan is easily accessible, you're more likely to follow it.

In your Career Journal you can organize all your affirmations under the headings you decide on. Then choose a group each day and say them out loud as you drive to your gym or to an interview. Keep your Career Journal with you to remind you of "What's in it for me" to become re-employed more quickly.

I keep a written record of my actions, ideas and experiences.

Use downtime more effectively.

When you are driving in your car and an idea comes to mind, write it down in your Journal at a red light. Then when you arrive at your destination, you can expand on the idea, and if it's usable, you can begin to work it into your plan. Or, if it's more convenient, use a tape recorder and transcribe and develop your idea while you are driving.

When you are keyed up, a traffic jam can make you feel even more under stress. Instead of allowing your feelings to take a negative direction under these circumstances, read your Journal entries and utilize this downtime. You may even come to look forward to traffic jams because they give you a chance to record your entries or re-read other pertinent entries.

Do your homework.

Give yourself assignments to do each day and write your answers in your Journal. At the top of a separate page, write a sentence that will stimulate answers. Then down the left hand column write the numbers 1 through 20 or 25 and begin to list answers to your question. Suggested topics could include these:

In how many ways could I increase my income to the point that I am making $X0,000 per month by X/X/9X? (This could stimulate ideas for a new career as well as other short-term, income-producing opportunities.)

In what other places could I look for prospective employers?

In what ways could I improve my cover letter and resume?

Use this technique to generate ideas for whatever you can improve. Your Career Journal becomes the perfect medium for recording and later acting on these ideas. And use it for both plans and records of activities. Also, use your Journal to stimulate new plans. It's a great brainstorming resource. If something is worth doing, it's worth recording.

I use my Career Journal to make my downtime more productive.

Chapter Sixteen

From Expensive to Expansive

The pressures and uncertainties of your job search may lead you to behave differently than you have in the past. You may find yourself acting more quietly at parties or snapping at your family and friends, when before you had a more understanding personality. These changes are borne of the mental anguish you are experiencing. If you are aware of what is occurring, you may be able to take the appropriate action to help yourself.

Certain attitudes are expensive to have. If they continue to control your actions you are more likely to experience an extended period of unemployment. They will cost you in terms of self-esteem, money, happiness and even relationships.

On the other hand there are expansive attitudes that will help you deal positively with your feelings. These allow you to grow and deal with your predicament and succeed in your search. But first you must recognize what is happening and take control of yourself. You can figuratively turn your hourglass upside down to restore your earlier self-confidence.

Instead of a feeling of futility, develop the belief that you can succeed.

You may begin to think "Why bother sending a letter to that company. They'll never hire me," or "I already applied to them and they didn't hire me." Your thoughts then dwell on the extremes of the situation. When in the past you probably saw a glimmer of hope, perhaps all you see now is uselessness and ineffectiveness.

You must *believe* a job will soon be forthcoming. If you can trust yourself to resolve your situation, you will develop a sense of hope and optimism. For example, if you prospect for potential employers, you're more likely to uncover the one destined for you. Everyday, the job market changes. Somewhere, people retire, quit or are promoted. New products are invented. Companies expand and create new positions. And the fact that a company turned you down in the past has no bearing on their future action. Perhaps the person who rejected you earlier has

---

I know that uncertainty creates opportunity.

left the company. Or maybe a new, unassociated position has become available. This should provide a sense of solace and hope.

> **Action:** Go to the library and ask for a directory that is different from the one you used in the past. Then call the newspapers at a nearby city and ask them to send you a week's worth of newspapers. Or go through your local paper again for new ideas. What new employment agencies could you contact? Review your records and Career Journal for the names of companies you contacted in the past. Write them another letter explaining how your skills have improved and expanded since you last talked. Pledge to yourself to do something positive today to uncover one new job opportunity.

Instead of a feeling of inadequacy, develop a sense of self-worth.

If you begin to believe that your jobless state is all your fault, you may blame yourself for poor results in other parts of your life. These might include your competitive activities (golf, tennis, etc) and personal relationships. An accumulated loss of accomplishment can cause an overall feeling of inadequacy.

A job does not always go to the best qualified candidate. It goes to the one who can convince the interviewer that he is the best person for the job. Therefore, you must believe that you are the best person for the position before you can convince someone else. The fact that you weren't chosen only means you need to work on your interviewing skills more.

> **Action:** Have someone interview you at home and tape it with a video camera. Ask and answer the questions as you would if you were actually on an interview. If a video camera is not readily available you can use a cassette recorder. Evaluate your body language and listen to your voice. Do you look and sound sincere and confident? Correct your actions accordingly.

Instead of feeling lonely, develop your sociability.

As your relationships become more tense and you spend more time evading social events, a feeling of being alone may envelop you. This could permeate into your family life and you could end up isolating yourself from those who are most supportive of you.

Given your unemployed status, it's no wonder that you don't feel like socializing with other people. But you should force yourself to do it.

––––––––––

I project confidence and enthusiasm in my voice and body language.

If there are no upcoming parties, have a BYO (Bring Your Own snacks and drinks) event yourself. Make an effort to spend time with every guest. Don't corner them with tales of woe about your status. Instead, find a positive topic to discuss with each person.

> **Action:** Network with unemployed people. They have their "ears to the ground" and are more likely to be aware of an open position then would somebody who's employed and not looking for a job.

Instead of feeling uncertain about your future, take this opportunity to make something good happen in your life.

Some uncertainty can't be denied, given your situation. There is no time limit on your job search. You have funds to last a given amount of time, but there is no guarantee when that point arrives you will have a job.

On the other hand, uncertainty creates opportunity. If you weren't unemployed you might not have taken this chance to seek a new direction in your life. And if you aren't sure what is going to happen, you have to work hard to make sure *something right* happens for you.

> **Action:** Perform self-analysis and research to investigate possible new careers. Have you always wanted to start your own business or buy an existing one? Now is the time to make new decisions about your career direction.

Instead of feeling resentment, become a cheerleader for others.

When your friends find employment, it destroys your theory that "nobody is being hired in today's economy." This removes one of your excuses defending your lack of success, so you may resent the fact that they have succeeded when you couldn't.

Instead, when you hear that an unemployed friend has found a job, call to congratulate him. Praise of others helps you feel good about yourself. Congratulate him for persisting and succeeding in his search. And while you're on the phone, ask what he did to get the position. Try to learn a new tactic you can use.

> **Action:** Call somebody that you know who recently found a job. Congratulate him and ask what special techniques he applied and think about how you can utilize that tactic in your search.

I live my life with passion.

Instead of feeling self-pity, develop a sense of self-appreciation.

All your negative emotions could combine themselves to create a feeling that it's "you against the world," and that everybody is out to get you. You might even dwell on the negative aspects of your life, which will only lead you further into the depths of negative thinking.

Instead, review the positive aspects of your circumstances. Are you a male or female? What are the positive points of your gender? How old are you? What are the positive aspects of your age? Do you have children? What are the positive considerations of parenthood? What about your home? Your car? Your education? Your experience? What positive things can you think of about each of these?

> **Action:** At the top of a page in your Career Journal, write one comment about yourself (age, gender, etc.) in terms of a question, i.e., "What are all the good things about being X years old?" Then down the left-hand column of each page, write the numbers 1 through 20. Start with number one and fill in the remaining blanks with ideas that are good about your topic. Then go to the next page and write another fact about your life and follow the same steps.

Instead of feeling angry, become happy with your life.

Often, casual conversations can deteriorate into an argument. As your emotions enter the discussion, you might interpret comments negatively and respond in an angry manner. You may even end up arguing just to intimidate the other person by making points that have nothing to do with your original position.

As long as you have no positive outlet for your anger, it will continue to build until it "explodes." This will most likely occur over little provocation because it's not the event itself that causes the outbreak of anger, but the cumulative effects of the constant, negative barrage on your ego.

Being happy is relative at this point. Total happiness is an elusive quality that will most likely not be yours until you are re-employed. But in the meantime, seek the optimistic interpretation when something happens. Don't feel that you have to place blame for every negative turn of events. Accept what happens to you and do the best you can to correct it. Feel satisfied that you are doing everything possible to become successful in your quest.

I smile as often as possible, at least several times a day.

Action: Look for opportunities to smile. When you hear a joke, laugh out loud. Don't snicker and try to hold your laughter inside. Whatever event occurs to you, no matter how minor, find some reason to smile about it. Then hold that feeling for as long as you can while you find something else to smile about.

Don't let expensive emotions bankrupt you emotionally. Take action that will reverse your negative feelings and help you feel better about yourself and your future.

I always create clear mental pictures of my goals.

———————————

Chapter Seventeen

Don't Talk To Me Like That

As time goes on, the sand in your attitude-hourglass continues to drain from positive to negative. Since there is no abrupt sign that this erosion is occurring, it's up to you to monitor your attitude regularly to check for indications of deterioration. The earlier you detect the erosion, the easier it will be to reverse it.

One of the most significant indications of a declining attitude is your self-talk, which includes your thoughts about your situation and your future, as well as the feedback you give yourself on any particular event or performance.

Early in your search, the feedback you give yourself will be less critical because you still have an optimistic outlook. But as you continue to experience increased rejection and its consequent frustration, your interpretation of events may become more negative, possibly causing you to berate yourself unnecessarily in your self-talk.

What you think is what you get.

Control of self-talk is vital to a successful job search because the way you talk to yourself can be both an indicator and an instigator of positive or negative thoughts. It can alert you to the fact that your attitude is deteriorating, or it can cause you to distort your perception of an event negatively.

When you ask yourself a question, you are automatically programming yourself to respond to it. Therefore, if you ask yourself, "Why do I always perform so poorly during interviews?" your mind will respond with all the reasons why you think you are not good at interviewing. This negative conjecture will only further erode your attitude. On the other hand, a question such as "How can I do better on interviews?" will direct your thinking to ways of improving your future performance.

Your mind is like a vacuum cleaner as it draws sights, sounds, ideas and feelings to itself constantly. If you don't monitor the input,

---

I trust my intuition and act accordingly.

your mind will attract undesirable information and let it sieve through your negative "filter." You must continue to think about the action you can take and avoid negative thinking. If you allow minor negativity to snowball, you can do major damage to your attitude and consequently your actions.

You are constantly thinking about something. If you don't direct your thoughts, they take on a life of their own and may focus themselves on the negative aspects of an event. They improve with the periodic positive feedback you experience (both internally and externally) and decline with negative feedback. If you listen to the automatic response your brain makes to a situation, it can give you an idea of how far your attitude has eroded. You have to tie a mental "bungee" cord on your thoughts so they only go down a certain distance before you catch them.

Self-talk in the early stage of your search.

In the early stages of your job quest, your self-talk is volatile. More than likely, the initial news of your fate was greeted with thoughts of astonishment, resentment and/or disbelief. These are soon replaced with anxiety and concern about what is going to happen to you now.

Self-discipline and control of your attitude at this point are critical. One way to do this is to immediately examine your finances and determine the amount of time you have to conduct your search. This will help you bring your self-talk from a "What will I do now?" position to a knowledge that you have more time than you thought originally. Thus some of the initial pressure you felt will dissipate as you turn your attention to planning the actions necessary to find employment.

Self-talk during your implementation phase.

As you begin your search, you become aware of all the favorable circumstances in the marketplace. The newspapers contain hundreds of help-wanted ads every week, and you're confident that one of them will be perfect for you. Similarly, the directories are packed with additional opportunities, and you become selective about those you apply to.

Given this abundance of optimism, your self-talk at this point might sound like, *"There's really a lot of opportunity out there. I know I can get a job before my deadline."* Therefore, a good attitude is based upon your opinion of the opportunities that are available, and maintaining it requires a constant influx of potential employers. Concentrate your activities on uncovering sources of possible jobs, and you'll find it much

---

I succeed because I perform to the best of my ability.

easier to sustain positive self-talk and subsequently a good attitude.

Self-talk when the rejection starts.

As you apply for the available positions and begin to experience rejection or a lack of any response, your attitude could falter. Compounding this frustration is the fact that when you go to the bank to withdraw more from savings, the balance is less than you planned.

At this point you may start to doubt yourself. It's the first indication that your attitude is draining and that you must do something to "turn your hourglass over" and restore your initial confidence. Here are several examples of self-talk that demonstrate the need to make some adjustments in the way you think about your situation:

"They probably won't ..."

This is an early signal that something is amiss. You may begin to eliminate yourself from the competition before you submit your resume because "they probably won't hire someone of my age" or some other excuse you have developed. If you don't apply for a position because of some limitation in your mind, you will reduce your chances of success.

When you insert the word "probably" into your job-search vocabulary, it should point out that you don't truly *know* their thoughts and you are substituting what you *think* is the case. Given your diminished self-concept, it's unlikely that you will give yourself the benefit of the doubt while you are in a frustrated state of mind. Learn to recognize the "trigger" words that normally start you off on a negative track, and take action immediately to re-direct your thinking in a more positive direction.

Variations of this self-talk include:

"I don't meet all their criteria for the position so there's no use wasting a stamp responding to that ad."

"I've already applied to that company and was rejected. There's no need to write to them again."

"I'm sure they'd rather hire a local person so they don't have to pay for relocation."

The Terrible Toos.

A "they probably won't, because..." statement is followed by a "reason why" statement. This is generally an expression of your self-concept as being "too old, young, experienced, inexperienced, poor or *too anything*." These are what I call the "Terrible Toos" because they

---

I perform a Reality Check to help control my thinking.

restrict your thoughts and actions. They limit your ability to find employment.

"But what if it doesn't?"

Another sign of deteriorating self-confidence is to follow positive self-talk with a negative question. An example would be a thought such as "I'm sure this opportunity will turn out to be the job for me," followed by "But what if it doesn't?" Similarly, "I know I'll have a job by next month" may be followed by "But what if I don't?"

"What if ..."

Closely associated with "But what if it doesn't?" is the phrase "what if" followed by a negative consequence. Thoughts such as "What if I don't have a job in three months? I won't be able to pay my mortgage and I'll lose my home" and "What if I have to lower my salary request. How will I be able to feed my family?" will direct your thinking to the worst possibilities. They can develop into self-fulfilling prophecies. The outcome becomes a "when" instead of an "if" in your mind.

Increasingly negative self-talk.

If you begin to dwell on the negative possibilities about what might happen, you could begin to place additional pressure on yourself, causing your thoughts to move more swiftly toward that possibility. If you think about the potentially catastrophic outcomes of your situation, your thoughts will move in that direction. As Viktor Frankl said, "It is a characteristic of fear that it produces precisely that of which the patient is afraid." Here are several examples of possible self-talk as your frustration turns into dejection:

"It's all my fault."

Once you begin to blame yourself for your lack of results you'll start <u>criticizing</u> your actions instead of <u>evaluating</u> them. You may subjectively question your own abilities instead of objectively evaluating and correcting your performance, causing you to blame the <u>performer</u> rather than the <u>performance</u> and placing the focus of your frustration on <u>yourself</u>.

"I wish somebody ...."

This is a perfect example of relinquishing control of your future. It's a sign of the sense of futility that's beginning to encroach upon your thoughts. Once you "wish" something will happen you eliminate the

---

I do all that I must do, and I am successful, too.

desire to make it happen. And the reference to "somebody" indicates that you're now willing to take any job which will allow you to take home some money to your family.

"... or else."

Few things in your job search will add as much pressure as telling yourself that something must be done "or else." For example, if you go into an interview thinking "I'd better do well and get this job or else I'll go to the poor-house," you are creating unnecessary pressure and will be less likely to relax and perform at your best.

"How could I have been so stupid?"

Perhaps you've said this to yourself following a particularly poor performance. If you begin your analysis with this statement, it's hard to review your performance objectively, and you will only increase your negative feelings about yourself. You'll stop evaluating the validity of the question and react to it without thinking. For example, someone could say to you, "Does it bother you that nobody is hiring anybody in today's economy?" In your dejected frame of mind your brain might stop evaluating the condition of "today's economy" and start thinking about how much it bothers you that "nobody is hiring anybody."

"Jud" is not a four-letter word.

I recall thinking negatively about myself and my future. My feelings of early confidence soon turned into concern, which led to feelings of self-doubt and anguish. My self-talk rapidly eroded, and I worried more and more about the probable consequences of my future.

Even my usually-reliable affirming tapes were not helpful, when in the past I found solace and motivation in them. While listening to them I found myself thinking, "That all sounds good and is probably true, but what do I tell my creditors?" I once heard a speaker say, "Happiness is found in the pursuit of a goal, not in its attainment." My first thought was, "This guy has never been unemployed." And my thoughts moved to a stronger denial of the power of positive thinking as I asked the speakers, "How would you feel if you had only one month to go before you ran out of money? I'll bet you wouldn't feel so positive then." Luckily I was able to recognize this self-talk and turn it around.

Stay out of "Never-Never Land."

After a few months, your self-talk will begin to reflect the

Negative self-talk is an indication that I must restore my positive thinking.

increased pressure you've placed upon yourself by dwelling on the worst possible outcomes. Now there is no question in your mind that the worst possible consequences are about to occur. Your self-talk uses unconditional qualifiers such as "always or never" and includes phrases such as "It can't be done."

Thinking in absolutes.

At this stage the word "probably" is replaced by more extreme qualifiers. Self-talk such as, "They'll never hire me because I'm too old" or "Nobody can find a job in today's economy" will cause you to cease taking the action necessary to find a job. These phrases can show up in other parts of your life, too. For instance, if you hear yourself saying "Why do these things always happen to me?" you'll know that your negative job-search attitude is overflowing. Of course, with an objective review you'd know this isn't the case, but at this point you don't want to hear any such rationale.

It's time to take action.

If you think any of these or similar self-limiting thoughts, it's time to take corrective action. It's unlikely that you're attitude will return to the heights of the earlier stages of your search, but it doesn't have to. It's time to recognize that you are entering a downward spiral and take steps to reverse it. You have to stop the erosion of your self-confidence, and then build upon that.

Once you surrender, there is no opportunity for success. Therefore, quitting is not an alternative. Listen to your self-talk only as an indicator that something is wrong, rather than as a statement of fact. Take steps to make the appropriate changes happen. Or if you feel that you need professional assistance, by all means seek it. Do what you must to maintain your grip on your life and revitalize your search for employment.

Begin an exorcise program.

You could be experiencing any combination of the self-talk given above. But regardless of whether you feel things can get better or not, you can always improve your attitude. Rid yourself of the "demons" of negative thinking and turn your hourglass over to restore your earlier job-search confidence.

———————

I am outstanding in everything that I do.

Do all that you must do, and you will be successful, too.

It's up to you to take control of yourself. Incorporate the strategies suggested in <u>Coping With Unemployment</u> into your plan and your life, and your self-concept and self-talk will improve. You'll place yourself back on the road to success. It will take hard work, commitment and courage to regain control of your life, but you can do it.

Instead of talking to yourself, listen to yourself.

As you begin your program to reverse your deteriorating attitude, listen to your "gut feeling," your intuition. Your inner sense of survival will tell you what you need to do and when you should do it.

From now on, carefully listen to the words you use to describe a situation or event. If you hear yourself saying sentences such as, "Why does this always happen to me? What else could go wrong? I'll never get a job at this rate," rephrase them to sound like "Sometimes things go wrong but I know that's not the norm. What else could go <u>right</u>? I'd better pick up the pace and work harder."

Listen to the way you explain an event. For example, there's a big difference between describing a temperate April day as "late Winter" or "early Spring." One description has a sense of gloomy, cold and blustery days while the other hints of growth and new beginnings. Change the way you think about yourself, people and events, and you'll turn your attitude around.

What was your first thought when you read that last sentence? If it was "That's easier said then done. I've tried everything and it's just no use" or "My situation is different and there's nothing I can do about it," you should immediately recognize that you are experiencing despair and need to take control of your attitude. All is not lost and there <u>is</u> something you can do about it if you only try.

From now on, carefully listen as you think of answers to your self-talk. If you hear a negative reply, interrupt your thinking and create a more positive response. If you start to think, "I can't...," ask yourself these questions:

> - Why can't I? Is it because A) it can't be done, or B) I can't do it?

> - If A): Why can't it be done? Hasn't anybody done it before? Is it because the task physically can't be done?

I control my destiny through total commitment to success.

Just because something has never been done before doesn't mean it can't be done. People thought a human could never run a four-minute mile until Roger Banister did it.

- If B): Why can't I do it? Because I haven't done it before? Could somebody else do it? How would <u>they</u> go about doing it? What would happen if I tried those same techniques? What one step could I take right now that could lead to success? Then what could I do next?

Once you have listed all the steps to take, start performing them.

Perform a reality check.

Refer to Chapter One and give yourself another reality check. Force yourself to evaluate your present circumstances realistically and respond accordingly. Unfortunately, when you're in a depressed state of mind, your perception of what is realistic becomes skewed. Tell the members of your Brain Trust about the way you feel and ask them for ideas on how you can turn your thinking around.

Separate fact from fiction. As shown below, write down all the feelings you have about your present circumstances in one column of a sheet of paper. Across the page from each, write a statement that reflects what you would have said about it earlier in your search. Bring yourself back to an objective analysis of your predicament gradually, and then make a decision.

Self talk	Fact
"I've been through all the papers and there are no new ads listed."	Every week there are new ads listed.
	Every day there are new articles, leads, new opportunities that are hidden from all the other people in your position.
"What difference does it make how hard I try. There are too many people out there looking for too few jobs."	Since your competitors are looking only in the help-wanted ads, you can find opportunities in other places.
"The country's in a recession and nobody is hiring anybody."	There are people being hired every day. You can read about them in your paper, too. The nation's <u>employment</u> rate is about 93%,

I feel successful today.

which means there are many more
opportunities for jobs than if the
rate was much lower.

Do you see what is true, or what seems true to you?

People don't always act upon what's real. They act upon their *percep-tion* of reality, which is different for everybody. This perception is too often clouded by the immediate environment. For example, many people say how "rotten" a day is because it's raining outside. There is another perspective on a rainy day. If you take off in an airplane from a nearby airport, you could rise above the clouds and have a beautiful view of a sunny day. A few thousand feet above the people who are complaining about the bad weather is a sun-filled panorama. All you have to do is look up and remind yourself that nearby, things are better than they appear to be in your immediate surroundings.

It's not whether you win or lose, but where you place the responsibility.

An important part of your mental well-being is to take responsibility for your actions. Circumstances may have been beyond your control, but don't *blame* other people for them. Evaluate your circumstances objec-tively, and then look for ways to change them. Placing blame only causes you to dwell on a negative interpretation of the past. If someone *was* responsible for you losing your job, you face the difficult, necessary task of forgiving him.

If your present condition is the result of your own actions, don't blame yourself either. Simply review what you did and apply the same constructive analysis that you use after an interview. Don't play "The Blame Game," even if your unemployment was caused by conditions outside of your control. Analyze where you are, where you want to go and what you have to do to get there.

Apply "responsibility" thinking.

The simple act of blaming something or someone takes your focus off possible solutions. Instead of saying "It's his fault!" say "A mistake was made. What can I do to correct it?" This perspective immediately does three things. It neutralizes blame. It encourages you to take action and to think of more than one approach to a solution. And it places the responsibility on <u>you</u> to diagnose the malady and then prescribe the remedy.

I know that my actions are controlled by my thoughts.

Don't let a problem become an excuse.

Everybody has problems. That's a fact of life. The challenge is for you to rise above them, not allowing them to create a list of Terrible Toos. As Michaelangelo said, "Inside every block of stone there lurks a perfect form." Look inside your stumbling blocks and find the perfect forms that lurk there. Look for reasons to succeed instead of excuses to fail.

What gets measured gets done.

While you were employed, you had periodic reviews. These were relatively objective critiques during which your performance was appraised and new standards set. Now you have to set your own goals and review your own performance. You must similarly evaluate your relative progress and give yourself feedback on how you can do better.

You must maintain the ability to <u>evaluate</u> your progress, not <u>judge</u> it. So you need objective written standards against which you can measure your relative success. Your self-marketing plan provides the means for recording your goal, strategies and tactics. Use this information to create checklists against which you can measure your progress.

Evaluate what you did, not what you are.

Use of checklists makes an objective review possible. They will direct your attention to a critique of the facets of your performance. You can maintain your self-esteem by recognizing that although you may have failed in certain aspects of this performance, you are not a failure. Failure is an event, not a person. As long as you try to improve, you are in the process of succeeding.

It's to be expected that things will go wrong. It will happen to you every day. But it's not wise to allow things to go wrong without learning from them. You're an evolving person who has yet to reach your maximum competency. Let your challenges excite and motivate, not overwhelm you.

Don't sanction personal incompetence.

Set high standards for yourself. Stretch to do better when you try something another time. Compete with yourself to improve, and avoid the self-talk "That's good enough." Something is never good enough if you have doubts about the results you expect to achieve. When you complete a task think to yourself, "Is this the best I can do?" If so, go on

---

My attitude is positive and enthusiastic.

to the next activity. If not, work on it until you have an affirmative answer to that question.

One thought pattern that could prevent you from doing your best is becoming too critical of yourself. Similarly, you can't allow others to criticize you in a destructive manner. Seek and accept *constructive* criticism that is accompanied by recommendations for improvement.

Attack your "mountains" with all your effort, with high standards for success. They can't get any bigger, but you can. Consciously develop yourself by feeding your mind constructive self-talk.

Maintain your values.

As you can see, it's important to set high standards for yourself. But it's also vital to maintain high moral and ethical standards. Don't allow your standard for thinking to decline any more than you would your standard for performance. Don't misrepresent yourself on paper or in person. Tell the truth about yourself.

The "you" that you decree,
Is the "you" that you will be.

Create high standards of performance and seek to exceed them. Don't overestimate the challenge facing you or underestimate your ability to handle it. As you experience frustration or dejection, keep giving yourself positive feedback. Then project the best "you" you can be.

Smoke the peace pipe with yourself.

Peace of mind is an elusive quality during your quest. But if you can achieve it, you attain relative freedom from fear, anger and guilt. If you're at peace with yourself, if you know that you're doing what's right by your standards, you'll be better able to withstand attacks on your self-esteem.

Resign yourself.

It's time to quit. Quit being negative. Quit complaining. Quit allowing others to "rain on your parade." Resign yourself to do all that you can, ethically and morally, to succeed in your search. You'll end up with a better job and more positive self-talk. Keep your integrity intact, and the feeling of self-respect you'll have will compensate for all the negative feedback you experience.

I feel better about myself today than I did yesterday.

Look to the future, not the past.

You're going to spend the rest of your life in the future, so you might as well use the bulk of your time to make it better. The future is made up of a series of days, each with the same number of hours, for every person on earth. Use your time to think about what you can do today to make your tomorrows worth working for.

Deadline or goal line.

One of the first things most people do is determine the date at which their funds will run out, when they must begin to sell their fixed assets to meet their obligations. This has been called the "go-to-Hell date," the "drop-dead date" as well as the "deadline." These terms have an ominous ring to them; they describe a destination to be looked at with dread instead of optimism.

With a twist of perspective, it can now be your "goal line." A goal line is something you strive to reach. It's the point that you must attain in order to score. The terms "objective, goal line, life line and opportunity line" help you think in less ominous terms about that date.

Deja Due: get what's coming to you.

Any time you think about what will happen in the future, you're making an assumption based upon your feelings about your past and present. If you feel badly about these now, your predictions about the future will reflect that viewpoint. On the other hand, if you currently feel good about yourself, your forecast will improve dramatically. If your future _looks_ more inviting, you're more likely to commit yourself to reaching it.

Deja Do: Look to the past but act in the present.

You don't have time to think back to when things were better, to events when you might have done things differently. Look to the past for lessons that can be learned and applied in the present. Look to the future with positive expectation and take actions today that ensure your revised forecast will occur tomorrow.

Change the way you talk to yourself.

Your self-talk should have improved dramatically if you've followed the general directions given so far. You've performed a reality check to discover a more objective view of your world. You've accepted

---

There is good in everything that happens to me and it's up to me to find it.

responsibility for what you do and have created high standards for performance. Now it's time to get into the specifics of what you can do to improve the way you talk to yourself.

Concentrate on changing your self-talk so you give yourself positive input. Don't ignore negative feedback, because it is crucial to making an effective evaluation. But evaluate the input you receive and respond to it in a responsible manner.

GIGO: Garbage In, Garbage Out.

The Computer Age made the acronym "GIGO" famous. According to this principle, a computer is only as good as the input it is given. If something is wrong with the output, it must be the fault of the programmer.

This same principle applies to your personal computer: your mind, for which you are the programmer. It will accept any input you give it and make decisions on it. For example, if you continuously tell yourself you're not qualified, you'll begin to accept these statements as true and habitually react to an opportunity with this new (but false) opinion of yourself.

PIPO: Positive In, Positive Out.

Give yourself realistic, positive feedback on a regular basis. Evaluate maturely and you will begin to act with this new definition of yourself in mind. So the first thing you must do is to change the nature of your input from GIGO to PIPO: Positive In, Positive Out.

For example, assume that you recently left an interview and felt that you performed terribly. You may have thought, "I certainly ruined that opportunity. There's no reason to send a thank-you note so they can have another laugh at my expense." And you won't need to call back next week to learn of their decision, will you? You're too embarrassed to talk to the interviewer again anyway.

If you think this way you're convincing yourself that they'd never hire someone who could have done those things, and you dwell on the reasons why they won't hire you. Do you see how this negative self-talk can destroy your job-search progress?

Another disastrous side effect is that these thoughts will prepare you for future interviews by focusing on what not to do, reinforcing the low opinion of yourself. Since you tend to become what you visualize yourself to be, your thoughts of how poorly you <u>think</u> you performed

---

I always get what I think about most.

will lead you to inferior performance in the future. Remember that you don't react to what actually happened but to your *perception of what happened.*

In his audio cassette program The Psychology of Winning, Denis Waitley said, "It's not what you think you are that holds you back; it's what you think you are not." If you think you're not qualified for a position, then most likely you won't try for it. Thinking "what you are not" will lead you to dwell on the negative consequences of your situation. Look internally to find the good in yourself and bring that to the forefront of your thoughts. Dwell on what you can do about your current status and then take the appropriate action.

Be a winner, not a whiner.

Each instance of negative self-talk can be turned into positive self talk. If you hear yourself beginning to think negative thoughts, use the following techniques to restore your confidence.

"But what if it does?"

When you're thinking about a possible job opportunity, concentrate on what you will do if it does work out rather than if it doesn't. Describe to yourself in detail the career position of your dreams and write down what you will do to find or create it. This is not an exercise in fantasy-thinking. It creates the vision in your mind that directs your thoughts and actions, and motivates you.

It also serves another important function. When the interviewer asks you if you have any questions, describe your vision and ask if the potential job will fulfill it. Doing so will impress the interviewer, since it demonstrates that you have thought about the job, are creative and are committed to finding a career position with the company. Make the interviewer feel that in five years from now he will be proud to say that he was the one who had the insight to hire you in the first place.

"What if...."

Questions beginning with "What if..." can take either a positive or negative direction. Make sure you aim them in a positive one. You can make them powerful, idea-generating questions. They can be even more productive when followed by a "In how many ways..." question.

For example, if you asked yourself a questions such as "What if there was no postal system? In how many other ways could I deliver my resume to a prospective employer?" Thus you might think of using a

---

I am invincible.

facsimile machine, overnight mail service, personal delivery or a mail-gram. As long as you are using your talents in a constructive way, they are less likely to lead you to pending doom and gloom.

"They probably...."

In a less-than-optimistic state of mind, a statement beginning with the words "They probably" will lead you to think of reasons why the potential employer would not hire you. The result will be that you won't apply for the position.

Instead, re-phrase the statement to <u>make you want</u> to apply. If you think "They are probably waiting for someone with my qualifications to apply for this position," you'll send your resume and cover letter. This positive expectation will also come through in the words you use to describe your accomplishments. In addition, it will remind you to follow up on every letter you write. If you think "They probably didn't respond because they lost my resume or misplaced it in some other file." Then you could write a first, second and third follow-up letter to remind them to inform you of the status of your candidacy.

Never say never.

If you sense yourself describing events in terms of absolutes, force yourself to describe them more accurately. If you think "There aren't any jobs available today," just pick up a copy of your local paper and look in the help-wanted ads, or look in the <u>National Business Employment Weekly</u> and <u>Employment Review</u> at the hundreds of opportunities that are listed.

Remind yourself that these represent only about 10% of the total possibilities available. That means for every ad listed in the paper there could be ten potential jobs that are waiting to be discovered. If you follow through on this thought, you've just increased your potential for success by 1000%.

Or you may hear yourself say "I'll never find a job," which is not true by any means. You can get a job today by walking into a business and telling the manager that you will work one month for free if at the end of that time they will hire you if you demonstrate that you are capable of doing the job. This application of the marketing technique "sampling" works.

Use the "absolute" terms in your favor. Instead of saying "I'll try to ..." say "I will ...." The former is not motivating. It evokes a sense of futility and does not stimulate your commitment to resolving your

---

I am proud of myself.

situation. Talk to yourself with words that demonstrate your determination and motivate you to find a new job.

The Terrific Toos.

You can have a lot of fun with this concept. Instead of thinking that you are "too old, young, etc.," say that you're "too much." Use this technique to remind yourself to keep your sights on a challenging position rather than lowering your standards. Think that you're "too good" or "worth too much" to take a lower paying job rather than hold out for the one that you want (assuming of course that you have the financial resources to do so).

Don't think about what you're bad at doing; think about what you're good at doing. You have enough negative feedback in a job search without adding your own to it. Look to your strengths and work on those areas in more need of development.

Profit from your experience.

Instead of learning to become a "good loser," become a "smart future winner." The word "loser" has a connotation of finality to it. You can't afford to lose too many times in your job-search. But if you can learn to evaluate your performance so you analyze what went wrong, you're more likely to correct the mistake and perform more effectively the next time. Don't look at what you have lost; look at what you have left.

Ask yourself the right questions.

Some questions you will never know the real answer to. For example, you can't honestly answer the question "Why didn't they choose me?" You don't know and may never know the reason you weren't offered the job. But if you start to fill in the blanks negatively, you'll berate yourself unnecessarily, leading to further erosion of your attitude.

Some questions can be legitimate but devastating, depending on the attitude you have when asking the question. For example, "How will I survive?" can be a logical question, but could lead to a negative response because of the emotion behind it. Instead, change it to ask yourself, "In how many ways can I get around this obstacle?"

And don't ask yourself a question with a preconceived notion about the answer. For example, "I wonder how long I can survive before going into bankruptcy?" presupposes that you are going into bankruptcy. It assumes that in some length of time you will run out of funds, and the only question is "when," not "if."

I always follow the words, "But what if ..." with a positive statement.

Turn your questions into a more productive activity with a positive goal in mind. Utilize the "Twenty Responses" technique (Chapter One) to find answers to questions that will help you repair your frame of mind and get on with the business at hand:

- How can I elicit the support of my Brain Trust in better ways?
- What's good in my life right now?
- What could be good in my life right now?
- What am I most proud of in my life?
- What other techniques can I try today to find a new job?
- What have I done in the past that made me feel successful? What can I do today to rejuvenate those feelings?

How do you talk to others?

The way you ask questions of others provides insight into your thoughts and level of confidence. If, for instance, when prospecting you asked a potential employer a question such as "You aren't hiring anybody today, are you?" he would probably answer "No." He would feel relieved because he wouldn't be hurting your feelings by agreeing with your preconceived notion.

Another barometer of self-worth is your ability to give and receive compliments. If you feel good about yourself, then you can feel good about others. People with positive self-esteem can offer words of praise to others. Conversely, a negative attitude about yourself will inhibit you from praising others. The progression usually goes from 1) complimenting others, to 2) not complimenting others to 3) belittling others to make yourself feel better.

Similarly, a simple "thank you" is all that is necessary in response to a kind word from someone else. Don't demean yourself. If someone says, "That's a pretty outfit you are wearing," respond with "Thank you," not with an apology that you would have looked better if you had only remembered to take it to the cleaners last week.

Listen to the way you reply to other peoples' questions. When they ask how you are feeling, do you respond with "fine" or do you answer "Not too bad" or "Not bad for a Monday?" Do you define your current status with a word such as "problem" or "predicament?" instead of "challenge" or "situation?" Your words describe and reinforce your thoughts. Talk to others in a positive way and your self-talk will follow similarly.

I use positive self-talk to reinforce my self-esteem.

Start your day off right.

Self-talk happens at all hours of the day and during all stages of consciousness. But there is one time of the day when your thoughts may be particularly negative, during that hazy period between when the alarm goes off and when you finally get out of bed. All the reasons you had for getting up early when you set the clock the night before somehow don't make sense anymore. You can easily talk yourself into just a few more minutes of rest.

For some reason, as you lie there in this state of semi-wakefulness you'll think about all the things that could go wrong during the day. To combat this, set up an important reason for getting up early in the morning. Then as soon as your alarm clock goes off, get up immediately and begin taking control of your thoughts. Say your morning credo and repeat your affirmations.

Which came first...

The next time you're feeling dejected, get up and do something. Go out and take a walk with large steps; swing your arms and charge up the hills. Practice speaking more loudly and with more authority. Adjust your posture, your smile and your body language to express a more confident, self-assured individual. You'll begin to feel like one. A psychologist addressed this phenomenon when he said, "We don't sing because we're happy; we're happy because we sing."

Physical action has an invigorating effect on your attitude and on your self-talk. For example, if you sit up straight with your shoulders back you'll begin to feel better, too. Add a smile to this and your attitude will improve. Go ahead and try doing this right now.

Did you try it? If not, why not? Don't you want to be happy? None of the techniques described in Coping With Unemployment will work unless you do. The only reason you won't succeed in your quest is if you don't try to. If you want to feel better and remove yourself from your present circumstances, you have to work at it.

Perform all these activities with the right attitude. Don't start off by thinking, "I have to work at feeling good today." Instead, affirm to yourself, "I want to feel good today," and then have some fun doing it. Take it one step at a time and just begin with a smile.

Success in the job-search game is not necessarily gaining something (a job, income, etc). It's more a matter of *freeing yourself* of something, i.e., the self-doubt and worry that occurs during your search. The more of

----

My thoughts and my self-talk are confident and optimistic.

these negative feelings you can release during the search, the easier you will be to live with (from your own perspective and that of your family). With an early-warning system that activates a corrective response, you can manage your internal feedback and self-talk so you can proceed with your search in an optimistic a frame of mind as possible.

I speak to myself enthusiastically and only in positive terms.

Chapter Eighteen

You Can Change the Past

There is a technique associated with visualization that can help you maintain a more positive and constructive frame of mind. It's based on the theory that your subconscious mind cannot distinguish between an actual event and an imagined event. Therefore, if you reinforce an actual positive event or change a past negative event so you recall it positively, your subconscious will respond to the positive image.

Reinforce the positive.

Begin by thinking about past events during which you performed successfully. Retrace your life to find what you consider to be your major achievements. They may be your graduation from college, surviving hard times or meeting the emotional needs of your family. They don't have to be monumental successes in order to be considered. It's more important they be something you accomplished on your own and which you feel good about.

Then recreate that performance in your mind. When you review this scene from your past, picture yourself as actually being there again. Recall the emotions you felt, and the sounds and sights you experienced. Begin to feel good about yourself by re-living the times in your life when you performed effortlessly or exceptionally well.

You could think of these events as you would files on your mental computer disk. When you want to retrieve them, you simply do so by calling up that file containing intense descriptions of the sights, sounds, smells, tastes and feelings you experienced. Vividly recreate the event so you can vividly "see" the sights, "hear" the sounds, "smell" the smells, "savor" the tastes and experience the feelings you felt at that moment. This technique is fun, invigorating, and it works to help you improve your mental attitude.

Create your own success files.

It's been said that you can't change the past. However, you can use a variation of this technique to change the way you recall past events

_____

I see myself performing successfully.

in your mind. For example, if you performed poorly at something in the past, it was filed in your mental computer. Now, recall the event and replay that file in your mind. But this time correct your actions and visualize yourself performing successfully in the same situation.

This time see yourself doing everything perfectly. For example, recall an interview in which you performed poorly and change it so this time you ask and answer the questions properly, and close the sale. Of course, you now get the offer.

The interesting fact is when you recall that same "disk" again in the future, you won't remember performing as poorly as you may have thought you originally had. Eventually, you'll remember the event happening as you re-created it. This is not denial, because by re-creating the file, you're performing the actions as you know they should. It becomes a learning experience.

Look to the past only for the lesson to be learned. Don't dwell there, replaying all your old failures and mistakes. You're not trying to change what really happened, but only your recollection of what happened so you can prevent it from occurring again. Think of the change as you would buying a new pair of glasses that give you a better view of your past.

Back from the future.

I read a newspaper article that helped me do this better. The article described how a person solved an ancient chess puzzle. Until this discovery, a final position in which a king, a rook and a bishop met a king and two knights was considered a draw. This person solved the problem by starting with a checkmate position. Then, using computer simulation he worked back until the initial enigma was encountered. The computer, using "retrograde analysis," actually considered 100 billion moves, moving backward from a winning position.

You don't have time to consider 100 billion "moves" you could make to win in your job search. But the theory is important. For instance, picture yourself at your new job with the calendar proclaiming your goal-line date. Then feel satisfaction that all your work had finally paid off. Experience peace of mind as a result of achieving your long-sought objective.

Once you have this image in your mental file, back-track and record the actions you took to achieve your goal. By associating dates with each event, you can create interim goals that will lead you to your

---

I think about the actions that lead me to my goal.

ultimate objective. At each point, savor the feelings you experience so it becomes a new success file. Close your eyes and think back to your original event and relive the experience.

Describe the situation into a cassette recorder. Provide as much detail and emotion as you can summon up. *Re-experience* the pride and increased self-esteem you had when the event first occurred. Then as you begin to feel your attitude eroding under the forces of frustration and dejection, you can relive your success files and re-create your positive emotions.

You can have fun with this exercise while restoring your waning attitude. Practice changing your mental files and re-playing them with the new information. You'll begin to feel better while performing at your top level. You can make the results exactly as you want them to be, and you'll feel like a winner.

I develop my talents at every opportunity.

———————

Chapter Nineteen

I'm In No Shape To Exercise!

A regular physical-conditioning program is vital to your job-search success. In addition to providing a positive outlet for tension, it can provide a pleasurable way to network and find new career opportunities. And there are many other benefits of exercise that will help you through this difficult period in your life.

It's not necessary to begin a rigorous exercise program immediately, nor is it required that you join a gym. Your goal at this point does not have to be a strenuous workout to build up your muscles. It should be to release pent-up emotions and relieve stress. A side benefit is that you will improve your health and muscle tone, and subsequently look and feel better.

With this definition, physical conditioning can be as simple as stretching while you're waiting at a red light or taking a brisk walk through a shopping mall. It gives you a new perspective on mowing your lawn, shovelling snow or washing your car. Seek ways to stay active physically, and you will find yourself more mentally aware, too.

You can perform your exercises at almost any time. But the most important time to do them is right now. A prolonged period of unemployment can cause lethargy, which will lead to further inactivity. But if you regularly set aside time for a physical conditioning program, you'll want to be more active in your job hunt.

The January 3, 1992 edition of the local Sunday newspaper contained a brief article about the importance of physical conditioning from (then) President Bush's perspective. The major benefit of exercise for a commander-in-chief, he said, is a better attitude. "I'm finding on this job that if you get out and exercise, you can do your job better and you get things in better perspective," he said. If it helps someone in that position deal with the pressures associated with the presidency, it can help you.

Physical conditioning doesn't have to be "against" someone in order for it to be effective. As discussed earlier, competition with yourself is often the most productive and positive way for you to improve.

I feel healthy, happy and productive.

Most of the techniques mentioned here are solo events which you can perform by yourself in your home or outside. There are benefits to exercising with others, but it's certainly not necessary to do so.

Why you should exercise.

A program of regular exercise has advantages in all phases of your job search. Early in your search, it provides you with the energy to take advantage of your confidence and pursue all the options available to you. As you continue on your quest, your conditioning program will help you release some of the stress associated with a prolonged period of unemployment. Consequently, you'll experience these benefits:

1) Reduced stress.

There is nothing quite like hitting a tennis ball, taking a brisk walk or riding a bicycle to help you release some of the tension that has built. Similarly, a simple professional massage can work wonders in helping you relax. The type of action itself is not as important as the fact that it helps you unwind and take your mind off the tensions of the day.

Therefore, you should seek opportunities to exercise often, daily if possible. For example, you could exercise while driving in your car on the way to an interview. Sit up straight and take deep breaths. Try to align your shoulders over your hips and "keep your chin up." This will open your breathing passage and allow you to "breathe easier." As you do this, roll your shoulders and your neck. One of the simplest ways I have found to relieve tension is to relax my jaw muscles. I seem to tense these up when I'm under pressure.

When you finish relaxing your muscles, try some voice exercises to relax your vocal cords. These will help you lower your resonance and speak with a more confident voice. Say all of the vowels, each one with a lower voice. Then add the letter "M" to each and say them again (MA, ME, MI, MO, MU). Then "hum" the scales (DO, RE, ME, FA, SO, LA, TE, DO) higher and lower. You'll be surprised how these simple exercises can help you relax and perform better while on your interview.

2) Increased creativity.

As little as 20 minutes of regular aerobic exercise, such as running or cycling, releases in the brain a natural opiate known as belaendorphin, which produces a dulled sense of pain and a feeling of euphoria, sometimes referred to as "runner's high." In addition to making you feel better, it helps you become more creative in your thinking

---

I take some action every day to reduce stress.

because it relaxes your mind.

You'll find that an idea or solution will come to you while you're taking a walk or gardening. The answer to a challenge which has eluded you for weeks will suddenly "pop" into your mind while you are doing something unrelated to solving it. Let your mind wander to positive thoughts and images. Think about these as you are exercising. And keep a pencil and paper with you while you are performing these activities so you can record your ideas.

3) Networking.

The locker room is a great place to hold casual conversations. Those who know you well will ask you how the "battle" is going. Others will chime in with ideas or names of people they know who can help you. Create a networking card (a business card with your name, address and telephone number on one side and a brief resume on the other) and keep several with you. Hand them to anyone who seems remotely interested in your situation.

The gym also serves as a source of camaraderie which will give you a lift. As the theme song for the television show "Cheers" states, "Sometimes it's nice to go where everybody knows your name." The gym can provide that place. The same effect is gained when you meet the regular group of friends you walk with each morning or evening. Talk with them about your search or anything that helps you feel better.

4) Increased energy level.

Have you ever seen one of the space shuttles being launched? As it sits on the pad, ready for take-off, it is perched on top of an enormous tank of fuel. After a matter of minutes of flight this entire fuel system is jettisoned because it's empty. A tremendous amount of energy is required to get it off the pad and into its initial flight. Once it is free of the "negative forces" of gravity, very little power is necessary and only minor adjustments are required to make corrections in its flight path.

You should apply sufficient power to get yourself moving and into orbit. Don't allow the negative forces of the environment pull you down by reminding you of all the jobs that are being lost and about the bleak outlook for prosperity. Don't think about the averages, think about how you can improve your own situation in the shortest amount of time. Then energetically pursue each idea to its conclusion.

Energy and vitality are welcome attributes in any employee. A potential employer will rate your apparent level of energy and compare it

---

I look, feel, think and act better after exercising.

to that which he thinks is required on the job. You may also be required to interview with people all day and then go out to dinner with the decision maker in the evening. Your devotion to your conditioning program will reward you again by providing you with the stamina to perform at your best even after an arduous day. If you can exude energy through body language and good posture, you'll make a better and more lasting impression.

5) Increased length of your productive day.

A job search requires that you devote long hours over many days to prospecting, sending letters and making telephone calls. Again your stamina will reward you by making the late evening hours as productive as the morning hours.

If your increased energy allows you to add one productive hour to your schedule per day, that's the equivalent of seven hours per week or almost one extra work-day per week. How much more effective could you be with one extra day per week? So take care of yourself and you can literally add weeks to your allotted time for finding employment.

6) Get more sleep.

It matters less how many hours you have to work at your search than it does how productive you are during that time. A good night's sleep will help you make your time more productive. However, uninterrupted sleep and a job-search don't necessarily go hand in hand. You may find yourself waking up at all hours of the night, pacing the hallways trying to think of something else to do.

Exercise will help you get a full night's rest after an action-packed day searching for work. It's a good, healthy sleep, not induced by pills or alcohol. You'll go to bed at night with a feeling of accomplishment and wake up invigorated after a restful night. You'll be more creative, energetic and productive during your waking hours.

7) Look healthier.

When you are energetic and rested, you'll have a confident glow about you. Your posture will be more erect and your complexion will be improved through a combined program of physical conditioning and nutritious eating. Your clothes will also fit better, which improves your overall bearing. Lack of exercise could cause you to gain weight, which will make your blouse or suit fit tighter. Conversely, exercise will help you control your weight and maintain the image you want to convey to the interviewer.

I am more creative and energetic after exercising.

8) Take control of yourself.

There are few things over which you have total control in your search, and your exercise program is one of them. Only <u>you</u> suffer from lack of exercise and only <u>you</u> benefit from getting it. It's one thing you can do, on your own, to take charge of your life.

If you feel that you're overweight, set a realistic objective and work to achieve it. On the other hand, you may be underweight and need to gain a few more pounds to look your best. As you approach your goal in either case, you'll feel better about yourself. You'll have more self-respect and feel more confident that you are in control of your life.

What to do.

Your physical conditioning program does not have to be a vigorous tennis match every day. It should be an activity that you enjoy doing and that can help you take your mind off problems and experience all the benefits stated above. You compete with yourself, not with others (unless you so choose) and therefore you can't lose. Joining a gym may not be in your budget, but there are still many activities you can join that cost nothing.

You may choose to exercise alone or engage your neighbors in joining you. People in your unemployment support group may be willing to exercise with you, as may your family members or significant other. The choice is yours. Do what you feel comfortable doing with whom you feel comfortable doing it and you're more likely to adopt physical conditioning as part of your daily ritual.

If you choose an outside activity, have several in mind that you can do during all seasons. Vary your routine so you can exercise indoors when you can't exercise outdoors and vice versa. Try these programs if nothing else comes to mind:

1) Bicycling.

Clean up that old bicycle which has been lying dormant in your garage. Fix the tires, give it a safety check and then take it for a spin. Don't overdo it the first few times, but each day try to go one block further than you did the previous day. Vary your routes so that you can view different scenery each day.

If you have a stationary bike, use that during the unseasonable months or if you live in a city where it's more difficult to ride a bike. You don't even need a bicycle to benefit from this exercise. Lie on your back and pump your legs as if you were on a bicycle.

I get a good night's sleep and am more productive as a result.

2) Shopping.

When you go shopping, don't park near the store or mall. Park at the far end of the lot and walk briskly to the shopping center. This has the added advantage of eliminating tension caused by fighting among others for the limited number of parking places close to the mall.

Once you are inside the mall, engage in aerobic window shopping. In addition to taking your mind off your job search, you can walk without interference from dogs or the elements outside. It's not required to stop and buy something, but only to walk the full length of the mall. If you're shopping in a multi-floor mall or store, walk up and down the stairs instead of taking the escalator. On nice days you could even shop/walk outside, down the main street of your town.

3) Chores.

The word "chores" has negative connotations, but you can make a game out of doing them. Time yourself when mowing the lawn or shovelling snow. Then next time you do these tasks, try to beat your last time and set a new record (of course, you shouldn't push yourself if you're not in good shape or just starting your program). I usually break my lawn down into segments so I get a feeling of accomplishment after completing each section. As another example, when my kids were younger, one would mow the front while I mowed the back. We would each take a tennis ball and sneak up on the other and toss it at him. A game like this one lengthens the time it takes to get a job done, but it is immeasurably more fun to mix play with work.

When washing your car, painting the walls, working in your garden or working at any of your home/apartment-improving jobs, make it enjoyable as well as energizing. Listen to motivational tapes as you work. Think about new approaches to your search. Try to invent other ways to answer tough interview questions. Always try to improve your performance and you will improve your chances of finding a new position.

4) Stretching.

There are few exercises as rewarding and invigorating as a simple stretch. When combined with a big yawn, it's almost Nirvana. When sitting at your desk or driving your car (of course, with safety in mind), perform the muscle-relaxing exercises described earlier. Alternately tense and relax your muscles. Stretch your arms out as far as they will go and hold then there for a few seconds before relaxing. When you find yourself stationary, take the opportunity to do something that will reduce tension.

I enjoy myself while I exercise with my friends.

5) Hobbies.

What did you do in your spare time before you became unemployed? Is there a way you can continue doing what you enjoy? It will be relaxing, and you may be able to turn your hobby into something lucrative. You may even find it has potential as employment.

6) Hugging.

Hugging is one of the most beneficial mental and physical activities that you can do. It improves your attitude and at the same time it helps you stretch. An additional benefit of hugging is that it's the universal sign of forgiveness. If you're having a disagreement with your spouse, significant other or good friend, a simple hug will let the other person know you still care for him of her even if you can't bring yourself to say it at the time.

7) Sports.

If you have the desire to compete with others in athletic events, you can work at improving your mind as well as your body at the same time. Participate in competitive tennis, golf, running, swimming, basketball, softball or whatever sport you enjoy. They sharpen your desire to win as well as provide positive feedback when you do well.

8) Other activities.

You don't have to compete against others in order to succeed in your physical conditioning program. You can swim, walk, run, cycle, shoot baskets, ride horses, join an aerobics class, go to the golf-driving range or do anything you like as long as it takes your mind off your search and invigorates your body.

Where there's smoke, there's fire.

Some people use this period in their lives as an excuse not to quit, or actually to *begin* smoking. They feel that the tension-relieving benefits of a cigarette outweigh the negative risks to their health. You can pick up any magazine or newspaper and read about the dangers of first- and second-hand smoke, so these facts will not be repeated here. If you don't smoke now, don't start. If you do smoke, try to use this time to quit.

It's not a moral issue, but a factual one. At some point in time you will aggravate a non-smoking interviewer with your habit. You could also have a cigarette roll off an ashtray and onto an interviewer's desk. And more than one interviewer has been heard to say that they

---

I am full of enthusiasm and vitality.

seriously question the judgement of a person who smokes given the known facts about the ill-effects of smoking.

These same warnings apply to any other substance abuse. With the increased time on your hands, you may be tempted to start the cocktail hour a little earlier each day. An important consideration at any point in your job search is not to relieve tension through alcohol, drugs or over-eating. For example, if you go to a restaurant for lunch on a rainy afternoon, you may fall into the trap of sitting at the bar for one last glass of wine. Doing so will decrease your productivity for the remainder of the day and cause health problems in the long run. It will not help your search in any way.

Be your own bodyguard.

If you choose to begin a strenuous physical-conditioning program, consult your physician to help you plan one right for you. Then take time every day to perform some relaxing or challenging physical activity. Get your heart "pumping" in your target range and keep it there for at least twenty minutes. You'll look, feel, think and act better for your efforts.

The ball's in your court.

Just for today, do one thing to get you started on a physical-conditioning program. Walk to a neighbor's house and ask him to join you in a longer walk. If he declines, at least you've had the exercise walking there, and you may want to continue on your own. Do some stretching exercises. Call several gyms to find out if they have any membership specials available. Walk up and down the stairs in your home several times. Do something today, and tomorrow do it for a little longer time. You'll begin to feel better and more productive immediately.

I take care of myself mentally and physically.

Chapter Twenty

What's Your Best Level of Tension?

The concept of tension management is important to understand because many people think tension is always bad. Some tension is actually necessary to keep you performing at your best. The right amount will keep you motivated and working toward the successful attainment of your goals. Yet it seems that the longer you are unemployed, the greater the pressure is to get a job. Negative tension could surface and hamper your search.

Consider the analogy of tension to a piano wire. If the wire is stretched to the right tension, it creates a fine sound. If tuned so that it is too loose or tight, the result is not good. Job-search strain is similar. If you are too "keyed up," you won't perform at your best. But under a healthy amount of tension you will perform more efficiently and effectively, and thus be successful.

Your task is to maintain a healthy amount of tension to keep you performing at your best. The emotional roller coaster you find yourself on creates tension. If handled well, this tension can be motivating. It's important for you not to eliminate tension, but to manage it so that you perform effectively.

A curse disguised as a blessing.

I experienced this quandary during one job search. After being released from one position, I was given a four-month severance package. However, a former customer of mine said that if I found nothing else during my search that he would hire me at the end of that period. This may sound like a fairly good deal to you, and it did to me at the time, too.

This knowledge was a blessing because in the back of my mind, I knew that even if I couldn't find something else, I would have a job to go to. I would still be able to take care of my family and financial obligations. But it was also a curse because I didn't push myself as hard as I might have. I didn't put forth the extra effort that a successful job search requires.

———————

I control tension to keep myself working productively toward my goal.

During this period of looking for a job with one in my "back pocket," I went through the motions but didn't have the real commitment to go to all the lengths I could have. I didn't have the tension required for peak performance and wasn't aggressive enough to keep searching for the best job.

Keep the faith (and lose the fear).

In an extended job search, there are two forces pulling at you, the forces of faith and fear. You want to believe that there is a light at the end of the tunnel, but you aren't sure you'll survive until you get there. Undaunted faith is a positive, reinforcing feeling that occurs when you really <u>know</u> inside that you can do it. Trust in your abilities, tenacity and determination that you will make something work out for you. And believe it or not, it will.

For example, during one search I was within a month of being completely out of money. I received a telephone call from an employment agent whom I hadn't contacted since my last search. He described an opportunity and asked if I'd be interested in pursuing it. I interviewed with his client and actually turned down the position. But during the negotiations the client and I agreed to my accepting a temporary position where I would work for him two days a week on a retainer that at least met my expenses.

I can't promise that something will come along at the last minute to "save" you. But the likelihood of that happening is much greater if you keep working to make it happen. Your faith in yourself will see to it. And the greater that faith, the less fear will encroach upon your thoughts.

How to control your tension.

Don't procrastinate now, do it later.

One major cause of tension is procrastination. You may find yourself delaying doing the things you need to do but don't like doing. For example, you may not like knocking on the doors of people you don't know, but you have to make contact with them in order to develop more prospects. To overcome procrastinating, create and prioritize a list of people to contact and then pursue them in the order in which you listed them. Set aside time in the morning to do this so you get it out of the way early. You'll "get it over with" mentally and you won't have it on your mind all day, affecting your performance of other duties.

I create my own luck through hard work and persistence.

Do whatever is necessary to be successful, even if you are reluctant to do it. Push yourself to do what you don't like doing, even though it may create tension. It will create more tension if you know something must be done and you don't do it. Procrastination only fosters anxiety.

When you finally get around to making a previously-delayed phone call and find out that the decision was made in someone else's favor yesterday, you'll have learned too late that procrastination can be deadly in a job search. You have to force yourself to do today what must be done today in order to reach your goals.

As the adage goes, <u>don't put off until tomorrow what you can do today</u>. Make your daily plan and follow it, doing each task in order of its importance until it is completed to your satisfaction. Call the people you need to call to perform your prospecting activities. Do the requisite follow-up to tie up all loose ends. Use every available moment of your time for productive activity and you will succeed.

Constant activity also has a soothing effect on your attitude. If you are busy working your plan, you won't have the time to feel negative. And as you reflect back on what you did each day, you'll experience a feeling of satisfaction that you did everything you could to further your cause.

Don't be an extremist.

One way to manage your tension is not to use "either/or" thinking when you are approaching a task. If you only look at the extremes, you're missing potential solutions and opportunities. For example, you could say to yourself "by X/1/9X I'd better have a job or I'll go bankrupt." This will create unnecessary tension and worry. Instead, look at other possibilities that could occur, ways that you could extend your goal line. Look at the gray areas between the "black and white" extremes.

Your level of tension will move along a continuum over time. The two extremes of this range are shown below. If you don't care whether you find a job or not, you won't be motivated to go out and find one. On the other hand, if you try too hard you won't perform well. Find the right place for you on this continuum and do what you can to stay there.

	Don't
Don't	Perform
Care	Well

|—————————————————————————————|

I take responsibility for my actions and my results.

Prepare for unexpected downtime.

How many times have you been delayed while waiting for something or someone and felt as if you were wasting time in the process? It may be an uncontrollable delay due to traffic ahead of you. It could be waiting in the doctor's office or perhaps for your child to finish a practice session. These delays and interruptions to your schedule seem to increase the level of tension because they appear to be a waste of time.

A technique that helps you use your time during periods of delay involves keeping a pad and pen with you in your purse, glove compartment and/or briefcase. Have them readily available when you want to write down ideas as they come to mind and thus utilize your time while waiting.

There is another way to utilize your time. As you listen to the positive tapes and read the motivating books, write on 3" x 5" cards the affirmations and phrases that have particular meaning for you. Keep these cards with you and re-read them when you are delayed. As you read them, make notes in your Career Journal about ideas that come to mind for ways to advance your job search.

Don't fix the blame, fix the problem.

Once you take responsibility for your actions, you take responsibility for the results. If something goes wrong, it's because of what you did or did not do. On the other hand, when things go right, you can take full credit. The indisputable fact is that you created the results. You did all the work to succeed and nobody can take that feeling from you. It's worth all the effort, frustration and anxiety you have gone through to know deep down in your heart that you "came through" when the pressure was on.

Don't blame other people for lack of success in your job search. You could blame your previous employer for putting you in this situation. You might blame your family members for not understanding your situation and spending too much money when they should be restraining themselves. You could blame prospective employers for not taking the time to review your superior experience and skills adequately. You might even blame the postal system for losing your mail, secretaries for losing your correspondence, directories for not sufficiently updating the list of names, your parents for not paying for your college education, the government for its policies that depress the economy and even your typewriter for misspelling all those words.

But if you do any of these, you're not accepting responsibility for your circumstances and your actions. All things considered, the

---

I am in control of myself and my future.

sooner you take control of your actions and your attitude, the sooner you'll get a job. It's up to you to discipline yourself to get done what needs to get done.

When something goes wrong, look for creative ways to keep it from happening again. Re-commit yourself and <u>make</u> something occur. If the results are favorable, do more of that action. If the results are unfavorable, find out why and correct it.

Motion begets emotion.

Your attitude erodes at a slow-but-steady rate. Similarly, you have to work at restoring it one day at a time, one step at a time. A major step you can take in that direction is to remain active in your life. If you are an action-oriented "doer," you're more likely to maintain a realistic outlook. Continuous, productive motion will help you control tension while it keeps your mind off the negative consequences of joblessness.

Examples of how to keep active are moving your arms in wide arcs, relaxing your jaw and shoulders and walking more quickly. Stand up when you can, rather than sit down. Read the newspaper while you are riding your stationary bicycle, or take a walk around the block as you think of different places to look for prospective employers the next day.

Similarly, lack of motion can lead to depression. If you don't do something to direct your attention away from negative possibilities, your thoughts will dwell on them. According to the laws of physics, a body in motion stays in motion, and a body at rest stays at rest. You won't become employed unless your body and mind are in motion.

Maintain control.

The feeling that you are losing control of your search can increase the tension you feel. Therefore, you have to regain control in order to manage that tension. A fast way to do this is to create a new plan for organizing your search. Go back to Chapter Four to review the essence of control and think of ways to design a new system that will get you back in charge of your search.

If you can learn to use tension as a motivating, positive force in your life, you're well on your way to finding that elusive job. Maintain a healthy level of stress that will keep you actively doing what's necessary, even if you don't want to do it. Tension management will help you combine courage and commitment, which will take you to your goal.

I manage my tension so I am more productive.

———————

Chapter Twenty One

Reach Out and Talk to Someone

In today's difficult times there are many people who have found themselves unemployed. The fact that many people are unemployed does not in itself offer you much solace, but it does provide you with an excellent opportunity to meet with them. Support groups for the unemployed (also known as job-transition networks) provide this forum.

A support group is an informal association of people who are looking for work. The members may be unemployed or under-employed people seeking to improve their situation. Support groups are sponsored by churches or other organizations seeking to assist people in finding a job and coping emotionally with unemployment. They are also sponsored by public libraries, private service agencies and union halls.

There are four different types of groups: 1) emotional, 2) educational 3) networking and 4) combinations. An emotional support group tends to be small in size and rarely exceeds ten members. The number is limited so that everyone gets the chance to share their ideas and feelings if they so desire. The second type is educational in the sense that it will have speakers and/or specific topics for the group to address. These groups tend to be larger and may have sixty or more members who attend meetings on a regular basis. Even larger groups provide the opportunity for their members to network at each meeting. Most groups offer some combination of these activities.

You should attend meetings of different groups to find the best combination that meets your needs. Most offer weekly or bi-weekly gatherings for their members to discuss their latest ideas and challenges and provide time for speakers to address specific topics of interest. These range from the standard presentations on interviewing and writing resumes to creative self-marketing techniques and methods for dealing with the emotional strains of prolonged unemployment.

The meetings are not necessarily therapy sessions but opportunities for each member to help him or herself, through interaction with other people in a similar situation. You'll normally be given the opportunity to introduce yourself and describe your background and goals. After

---

I attend group meetings for new ideas and emotional support.

presentations and coffee, you'll also have the opportunity to network with other members and share information you have about positions that are available.

Support groups are generally open to anyone looking for work, regardless of his or her age, race, sex, creed, religion or former occupation. However, if you so desire, there are groups that are open only to specific populations such as men, women, Hispanics, those over 55 years old, spouses of the unemployed, union employees and specific trades/professions. The meetings are free of charge and run by people who are either unemployed or employed, generally on a volunteer basis. If there is not one in your area, you could consider starting one yourself.

One of the greatest benefits of a support group is you'll have the chance to meet with people in a situation similar to yours and exchange ideas on coping. You can network and learn new techniques for writing resumes and cover letters, interviewing, prospecting and all the other activities necessary for job-search success. The leaders are generally protective of their group's members' feelings and will not employ speakers with a commercial message. The speakers donate their time to provide you with a variety of perspectives for improving your job-search skills. The goal of everyone involved is to help every member find a new position.

Support groups tend to take on personalities of their own, reflecting the members' attitudes. Be careful that you don't get caught up in a negative "Why me?" group, whose members commiserate with, instead of support each other. A positive, supportive group offers an excellent opportunity for you to feel better about yourself and at the same time offer help to others who need and value your input. Join and actively participate in one of these groups and you'll be much better off for it.

I feel good about myself.

Chapter Twenty Two

Dealing With Job-Search Rejection

It's unfortunate, but you'll be rejected by 99% of the people you contact in your job search. Rejection could demoralize you more than any other attack on your early confidence. You must find ways to deal with rejection and maintain your self-esteem.

You'll feel rejection by n̲o̲t̲ hearing from a prospective employer a̲n̲d̲ b̲y̲ hearing from them via a letter notifying you of their negative decision on your candidacy. You may even begin to think it's a lose/lose situation. This, of course, is not true, but your mind can play strange tricks on you.

Rejoicing follows rejection even in the dictionary.

If you keep working at your search even while the rejection letters continue to pummel you, you'll experience greater elation once you get a job. Persistence will win out and you will eventually find employment i̲f̲ y̲o̲u̲ d̲o̲n̲'t̲ g̲i̲v̲e̲ u̲p̲. Deal with the lack of acceptance and recognition and become greater for it. You will eventually be rewarded with a job as well as greater self-respect.

Rejection is most likely to occur in four ways. The first is hearing nothing from a prospective employer which you have contacted. The second is receiving a rejection letter in the mail before you even go on an interview. The next is experiencing rejection during the interview itself. And the last is being rejected after the interview, probably the most devastating one because you had the chance to give it your best shot and they still didn't want you. Each of these will be discussed in more detail.

A) Handling rejection caused by being ignored.

As a rule of thumb, approximately 80% of the people you apply to will ignore your first attempt to contact them. And the percentage may be higher among those whom you cold call. Yet there are techniques that you can use to deal with these people while helping yourself cope mentally with their lack of response.

---

know that rejection is only an indication that I am progressing toward my goal.

No news is bad news.

Nobody likes being ignored. The lack of response translates into a feeling that the recipient didn't think you were <u>worthy</u> enough to take the time to send you a reply. If you begin to believe this yourself, it diminishes your self-esteem and causes you to become more despondent.

An important action you can take to deal with not hearing from the prospective employer is to keep good records and continue to follow up on every letter until you hear from them in one way or an other. Doing so will result in several positive things for your job search.

First, following up will ensure your correspondence communicated the information you wanted it to convey. For instance, a help-wanted ad in a competitive economy may draw one thousand or more responses. Most employers will read each looking for a reason to disqualify the applicant. As soon as it is found, that person is eliminated from contention. A misunderstanding about your experience may cause the reader to misinterpret your words and subsequently dismiss your application. So your follow-up telephone call will allow you to clear up any misunderstanding.

Second, it will prove that you really want the job. In many cases, a determined employee will out-perform one with more impressive credentials. If you can demonstrate to the interviewer that you have the wherewithal to succeed, you may be reconsidered. Your repeated attempts to get through will demonstrate that you are serious about working for the company. This repetition will attract the interviewer's attention in a positive way and cause him to review your new approaches with greater interest.

Next, your consistent follow up will demonstrate your tenacity. In my estimation, 99% of <u>applicants</u> do not follow up on their initial correspondence. If they don't hear from a company, they simply cross that one off their list of current prospects and go on to the others. But if you send a follow-up letter informing your contact that you haven't heard from him and that you are still interested, you're demonstrating that you really do want to work for the company and that you are not going to give up until you do.

And finally, your follow-up will prove that you are a well-organized person. In your first follow-up letter, let the reader know that you haven't yet received a response to your first letter and that you are still interested in working for the company. And in your second and third follow-up letters, refer back to the dates of the previous letters to prove your

---

I have a plan in place to deal with rejection.

record-keeping ability. An organized individual is valuable to a company.

Keep in mind that people don't like to admit they were wrong when they made a decision. If you ask the decision maker to take another look at your resume without providing a face-saving "out," you're asking him to admit he was incorrect. A person needs a reason to change his mind, which you can offer by providing new information. Each time you write or call the person you should convey something new or different from that which you included the last time you approached him.

Begin each new contact by letting the interviewer feel that he made the right decision to eliminate you b<u>ased</u> <u>on</u> <u>the</u> <u>information</u> <u>he had</u> <u>at</u> <u>the</u> <u>time</u>. Let him know that you now have additional information that sheds new light on your candidacy. Make him think that if he changes his mind, it's only because initially he didn't have sufficient information, not because he was somehow at fault by overlooking some important data. And since he won't remember what was on your first resume, he'll read your new correspondence with greater care.

Therefore, your follow-up letters should always provide some fresh piece of information about you. This could be a recent award you received, the volunteer or temporary work that you have performed or anything that will give you the chance to re-tell your story. Lead off with this new information and then go into your complete presentation.

As a final note, don't allow your later follow-up letters to indicate increasing frustration, which you may easily feel if you see the same ad you applied to still running a month after you responded to it. Simply notify the company that you haven't learned of their decision and that you are still interested. And, of course, alert them to the new piece of information that has come up since the last time you wrote.

Reach out and remind someone.

Your mail is not the only thing that will be ignored during your search. Your telephone calls will rarely be returned, especially if you are making an unsolicited cold call. If the person doesn't recognize your name or why it will benefit him to return your call, he won't.

If you are repeatedly transferred into voice mail, take the option normally given to speak with a human being. If the person you are trying to contact is on vacation or travelling for a few weeks, you don't want to have ten or more of your messages on his voice mail upon his return. And many times a person will respond if he knows that someone else in his company is aware of the message. But if your target continues to

---

I am committed to succeeding in my job search.

ignore you, leave a message containing some information as to why it will benefit him to return your call.

Careful, methodical and consistent follow-up will make you appear to be a well-organized professional. It will also help you deal with the frustration of being ignored. You will feel more in control and more professional than the company you applied to.

Don't think of yourself, think about yourself.

If your correspondence is regularly ignored, it should be a good indication that you need to revise your cover letter and/or your resume. If you continue to focus on improving your correspondence, it will keep you from becoming too frustrated.

Test different approaches, "buzz words" (i.e. jargon; words familiar to people in a specific industry) and layouts with each of your follow-up letters. See which techniques generate a positive response and then regularly use them on future applications. Always look for ways to improve the presentation of your skills and accomplishments.

B) Handling rejection caused by receiving negative responses.

Approximately 16% of the people you communicate with will reply to your correspondence with a letter informing you of their decision not to proceed on your behalf. At times, knowing is better than not knowing. But receiving too many of these is another cause of job-search frustration.

Experience defeat.

In "Catch-22" fashion, the more you prospect, the more rejection letters you will receive. So your repeated actions will only provoke a greater number of these negative responses. Since continuing your prospecting is critical, you must find ways to deal with the increased rejection.

When you encounter a defeat, **experience** it. Pass through your frustration and disappointment so that you have the clarity of mind to look at what happened. Don't continue making the same mistake over and over again. Analyze it. Evaluate it. Learn from it. Then you can move on. Experiment with different ways to deal with rejection so that your feelings of self-worth are not diminished.

———————

My habits are productive and good.

Don't take it personally.

The prospective employers are not rejecting you as an individual, and they are not even insinuating that your qualifications are insufficient. All they are saying is that your background and experience (as you communicated them) do not make the best fit given the competition and the circumstances surrounding this specific position.

Many of the reasons for which you could be rejected have nothing to do with your ability to perform on the job. Perhaps your letter was damaged in transit and parts of it were unreadable. The boss's relative may have applied for the job. The ad you responded to may have contained inaccurate information about the position. It could even have been out of your field. Give yourself the benefit of the doubt without making up excuses or refusing to accept responsibility for your action.

Always follow up.

One technique that I have used with excellent results is to send a thank-you note following the rejection letter. You obviously don't want to thank them for rejecting you, but you do want to thank them for having the courtesy to make you aware of their decision. Let them know that you recognize their professionalism and leave the door open for a future opportunity.

You could also ask for a referral, i.e., some other person the interviewer knows who might be looking for someone with your skills. Be specific when you ask for a referral. The person may not be able to readily come up with an idea if the realm of choices is too broad.

For example, don't ask, "Do you know of anybody looking for someone with my background and skills?" Instead, help him narrow down his list of potential opportunities by asking if another division in the corporation has an opening. Then you could ask if one of their customers or suppliers has a vacant position. If he doesn't know, ask for the names of people you could contact there and add them to your prospect list.

Also ask the ex-prospective employer to offer you ways to improve the appearance and content of your resume and cover letter. If he says he doesn't remember your correspondence, ask if you could send another package for him to critique. About half the people will do this, and now that you have a better idea of what they are looking for you can customize your letter to show them your "new" skills. Enclose a postage-paid reply card for their use in replying to you.

I succeed because I believe in myself.

Create your own "ego wall."

My son found a unique way to deal with his rejection letters. At the top of one wall in his bedroom he placed a sign that read "Companies that don't recognize talent." Below that he placed all the rejection letters he received. This helped him deal with one company that sent him three computer-generated letters in as many days, all informing him that he was no longer being considered for the same position.

Find some way to learn from and deal with rejection. Try to stay on top of the situation by having "the last word," even though you're the only one who knows it. In one frustrated moment, I crumpled up one of my resumes and wrote on the top of it, "Please don't throw this away again." I felt that if the recipient saw this he might think I had gone through his waste basket to retrieve my resume. I never sent this, but it does demonstrate one way you can have some fun with your feelings and by doing so make it a little easier on yourself.

Use your creativity to turn adversity onto opportunity. Don't look at a rejection letter as an attack on you personally but as an indication that you are performing the activities that you must in order to become re-employed. If you did nothing to find a new job you would never receive a rejection letter. When you learn to deal with the negative in a positive way, you will have gone a long way toward becoming re-employed.

C) Dealing with rejection during the interview

About 4% of all your inquiries, applications and cold calls will result in the opportunity for an interview. The telephone call inviting you for that event creates within you a wonderful (and well deserved) feeling of success. But this is only the next step in the process and is by no means the final one.

You are being interviewed because the company's representative felt that your background (as expressed in your resume) seemed to be close to the requirements sought in a candidate. Since there may be ten or more people in that category, they are all invited to come in for closer scrutiny. At any point during the interview, the interviewer may make the decision that you are not going to be one of the finalists.

There are many indications that this decision has been reached, and most frequently they will be exhibited in the form of objections to something in your education or experience. Therefore, you must learn how to handle these objections and turn them into reasons for hiring you.

The height of my success depends on the depth of my commitment.

D) Dealing with rejection following an interview.

Rejection following an interview can be emotionally devastating. Rejection before the interview is easier to handle because you were rejected without having had the chance to tell your story in person. Now that you have had that opportunity and are still rejected, you feel there's nobody to blame but yourself. If you do that, it will cause more damage to your self-esteem than almost any other part of the job search.

The first thing you should do is let the interviewer know that while you are disappointed with his decision, you hope that you will be considered for future job openings. Do so with a thank-you note or a personal telephone call, depending on how much rapport you established during the interview. If you call, be sure to find out why you were not chosen for the position.

Then find out what you could do differently in the future in order to correct it. If you feel comfortable contacting the interviewer personally, ask him what you could do to improve your interviewing skills. Then practice these skills using a video camera or audio cassette recorder.

Create a post-interview checklist (such as the one found in Chapter Nine) that will help you objectively evaluate your performance and learn new techniques to improve your interviewing skills. It will also prevent you from dwelling on the possible negative aspects of your interview performance. Don't look at what you did wrong, but look at what you did right. Then look at the things you could do differently next time. Regular evaluation will keep you from practicing bad habits. Make sure you are reinforcing positive techniques in your practice sessions.

Rejection during a job search is to be expected. Just remember that the company is not rejecting you personally. They are rejecting the fit between your background and skills and the qualifications being sought for the position at this time. Keep good records and always follow up. Be persistent, learn from your mistakes and you'll find your new position more quickly than you ever imagined.

Everything I do and the way I feel express my self-confidence and enthusiasm.

Chapter Twenty Three

Dealing With Rescinded Offers

A rescinded job offer is one that is revoked after it is made and before you begin working. More than likely, this occurs for reasons beyond your control. The department head might have exceeded his authority by making the offer. The company may have been purchased and all hiring decisions suspended. Political infighting may be the culprit.

There could be numerous factors leading to the recision that have nothing to do with your skills, so don't blame yourself for the event. It's difficult to deal with this circumstance emotionally during the best of times, but at this point in your life, it can be devastating.

The impact of a rescinded offer on your job search could be disastrous because when you initially received the job offer, you probably ceased all your searching efforts and told those people who were considering you that you accepted employment elsewhere. Now you are back out on the street, beginning your search anew, feeling demoralized.

Don't count your chickens before they're hatched.

Without lying to any company, keep all your other opportunities in place until you actually start on the new job. Delay decisions for as long as you possibly can without antagonizing or deceiving the other potential employers. It's not necessary to continue your prospecting or networking activities, but keep as many options "on hold" for as long as you can legitimately. Then if an offer is rescinded, you'll be able to maintain the momentum of your search.

When the offer is rescinded: a personal example.

If you understand that an offer may be rescinded, you can be better prepared to deal with it. The important point is to continue working at your search and at shoring up your attitude. During one three-month period, I had two offers rescinded, neither due to my own fault.

The first occurred one month into my search. I was offered a position with a nearby company and accepted immediately. I felt the "weight of the world" removed from my shoulders. I began to believe in

---

I maintain my composure because I know there's always a way to succeed.

myself again and exalted in the fact that there was an end to my anxiety about the future.

However, my elation was short-lived. The president of the company called me the next morning and asked if I could meet with him for lunch that afternoon. We met and he explained to me that his accountant had just finished preparing the financial statements from last year and he could not afford to hire me. He then rescinded the offer.

I was devastated. I hadn't prepared for this eventuality and wasn't quite sure how to deal with it. So I went through all the arguments you would expect me to make at that point, and during the discussion an idea came to my mind which I broached with him.

I recalled the marketing technique of "sampling" and quickly adapted it. I asked if he would agree to take me on, at a reduced salary, for two days a week over two months. During that time I would prepare and begin to put a complete marketing plan into motion. If he saw value in retaining my work, I could be employed on a month-to-month basis after that. We discussed the details, and he agreed to a one-month temporary assignment.

A temporary position with a company is an excellent way to work for them for a limited time. You'll benefit by having some income while at the same time being given an opportunity to demonstrate your skills. You'll also have the chance to see what the company is really like. Perhaps most important is the positive impact this will have on your attitude.

"There's always a way."

Another fact you should keep in mind is the importance of not giving up. In my example, I sensed the desire on the president's part to try and work out some sort of win/win situation. He didn't want to rescind the offer any more than I wanted to have it rescinded. All he needed was a logical out for himself so he could do the right thing by his conscience while doing good business.

The idea of "sampling" came to me while I was quickly going through a list of strategies to convince him to change his mind. Had I just given up and accepted his decision as final, I wouldn't have had this idea. As Tony Robbins says, "There's always a way," and you have to keep looking for it. You must truly believe that there is an opportunity "waiting out there somewhere" for you and all you need to do is keep working until you find it.

I have a plan in place to deal with rescinded job offers.

I felt good about myself after that meeting. I needed that job and the income it represented to maintain my emotional stability and to take the pressure off my financial situation. I remembered that as we were talking, I kept thinking of new ways to keep him from <u>finally</u> saying "no." For every idea that he turned down, I thought of another one simply by continuing to <u>think</u> about how to win in that situation and not giving up. I didn't think, "What <u>else</u> could go wrong in my life?" I thought "What other argument could I use that would convince him to keep me on?" And that difference in my thinking process changed a negative situation into a positive one.

Deja Vu.

About one month later I received a telephone response to one of my unsolicited cold-calling letters. We spoke for an hour about my background and the position that he had in mind. He then asked me to come in for an interview. On the appointed day, I arrived at his office and we had a very pleasant and productive discussion. I also met with several other people, including the president of the company.

I was asked to return in a week or two for a second round of interviews. When that occurred, the situation seemed more relaxed. We went to the cafeteria for coffee and on a plant tour. During this interview he explained that a major investor was leaving the company but that it shouldn't upset this *offer*. I heard that word and tried to contain my enthusiasm. He did make me an offer and said that we would discuss compensation later. I accepted on that contingency and left.

However, he called me the next day to tell me the political situation was deteriorating. The investor was making some major waves upon his departure, and although the offer wasn't rescinded, it was put on hold. Although I was still his first choice, he had no idea how long this upheaval would continue. He wanted me to hold off as long as possible, but he knew that I had to do what was right for myself and my family. I eventually took another position, but it was a good idea I continued prospecting. One year later, he had still not filled the position.

Implement a damage-control process immediately.

If this does happen to you, find out right away why the decision was made. The company has a moral obligation to be perfectly frank with you. If the decision was made based on an inaccurate reference or credit check, you have the right to challenge it. Determine the reason behind the recision and try to salvage what you can.

I interpret events with a positive frame of mind.

There's still more to do.

Time, dwindling financial resources, continued rejection and a lack of interviews all take their toll on your attitude. Without constant attention to all that conspires to erode your self-esteem, you will gradually move into a state of dejection or depression, which results in a continuing downward spiral of your confidence and feelings of self-worth.

At no time is your situation ever hopeless, regardless of what you think. You must continue to work at rekindling the confidence you held earlier. Remember, you don't have to be 100% positive all the time. You need only to deal with the attacks on your confidence effectively and maintain the feeling that if your troubles are to be resolved, it's up to you to resolve them.

Continue to work hard at making that happen. Try new approaches, evaluate their results and make changes as necessary. If you stay busy doing that, you won't have time to let your mind wander to the negative consequences of what might happen some day. But if these thoughts persist, there are still other techniques you can use to combat the erosion of your confidence.

A rescinded offer represents one of the uncontrollable elements of the job search. Since you can't control the event itself you must be able to control your response to it. Don't blame yourself if you're not at fault. Negotiate from a position of strength to make the most of the obstacle. Keep your other options open until you actually start on the job and you'll maintain the momentum of your search. Never give up and never give in.

I live in a world of abundance.

Chapter Twenty Four

Learn To Laugh With Yourself

The ability to smile and laugh is vital to maintaining a good attitude during your search. I don't mean that you should always tell jokes and be the life of the party. I mean that if you "lighten up," you'll be able to see the brighter side of things.

Smiling stimulates creativity.

During the past few months, have you heard someone tell a funny story? You're first reaction may have been to stifle a laugh because you had convinced yourself that you weren't happy. If so, you're at a point in your life now where you have to let go of the constraints you have imposed on your ability to enjoy yourself. Let yourself smile more often and see how good it feels.

Develop the ability to release negative feelings that prevent you from enjoying life (at least as much as you can, given your circumstances). You'll find that you'll be more creative at the same time. In addition, you'll appear more enthusiastic, and you will actually perform better during an interview.

Creativity requires an open mind in order to be most effective. Your renewed sense of humor will enable you to look into a situation and create a new idea. When you hear someone say, "Can you imagine what would happen if ...," you'll automatically start imagining what positive event could occur. And so you may come up with ideas for new prospects or career opportunities. Years from now you may look back on your thriving business venture and think, "This all started out as a joke."

Become a BAG Person.

Your revitalized sense of humor can help you turn your life around. For example, you may have had thoughts that you will end up on the street, without a home or food, left to beg for your very substance. If you think about this enough, it could become a subliminal goal for you and your actions could set in motion a self-fulfilling prophecy. Take this opportunity to turn around your thinking about the BAG-Person concept and creatively form a new acronym:

I start every day optimistically.

Benefits: Think about all you have achieved in your life and what this means to you. It's comforting to know that no matter what happens, these will remain. If you worked hard to put yourself through night school and still graduated with honors, your pride doesn't have to diminish. What other experiences did you have that helped shape you into the good person you really are? What do you have to offer a prospective employer that nobody else can? Write these down and focus your attention on communicating them in your future correspondence.

Attitudes: What can you do just for today to improve your attitude? What steps can you take right now to improve you chances of finding a job? How will it make you feel if you accomplish that? What new affirmations can you prepare that will help lead you to a stronger mental foundation?

Goals: Write down a simple goal that will direct you back on the track toward restoring your earlier attitude. Make a plan to fully utilize your time just for the next week. Set the goal that you will find and respond to one new job opportunity each day for the next seven days. Don't set an enormous goal that you are unlikely to be able to achieve over the next few days. Start with an attainable objective that will motivate you to take some action.

As you look on the lighter side of your predicament you'll stimulate your enthusiasm. Soon you'll transfer your zest for life into action, and then you'll be back on the road to finding a new job.

Don't get even, get mad.

A good first step toward the passion for success is to get angry. Get angry for taking all the abuse you have for the past few months without a fight. Re-kindle your self-esteem and your ability to take control of your life. You don't have to take the rejection and frustration "sitting down." Get up and fight back. The best way to do this is to remain productive in the face of adversity.

I feel good about myself.

Remember the song "Whistle While You Work?" Actually whistle or smile as you perform your job-search tasks and you'll perform them more ardently and with greater devotion. You'll feel better about yourself and you'll be more successful in finding another position.

A smile is the universal symbol of confidence and contentment. If you can laugh, your attitude will take a turn for the better. You feel an improvement in your mood with a broad smile, and others will take a more immediate liking to you. So smile as you exercise, talk on the telephone, look in the mirror and talk with people.

Give yourself a wake-up call.

Did you ever wake up late on a morning that you had an important event to attend? What did you do? You probably jumped up immediately and ran to the shower to begin an abbreviated sequence of steps to get ready and leave.

You should start every day with this spirit. Tonight, set your alarm clock for the time you normally awoke when you went to work. Resolve to get up then. When the alarm goes off, immediately get out of bed and start your day. Say your morning credo, and say it **out loud.** It's not necessary to scream but revitalize yourself by saying it with enthusiasm.

Have some fun with this process and begin your day on a lighter note. If you have fun you will improve your attitude even a little bit. But that's all you need at this point. You aren't going to quickly reverse your attitude to a feeling of "This is going to be a great day." Remember how the sand representing your initial positive attitude slowly drained out of your hourglass. When you take the initiative to turn your hourglass back over, your attitude is renewed slowly but surely. Give it time to work and you'll feel better about yourself and your future.

Find some time every day to "play." Relax with your favorite book or read a novel written by somebody previously unknown to you. Create a table and chairs from scratch. Buy some new material and make a dress for yourself. Make time every day to do whatever it is that makes you happy.

You'll feel better about yourself, and you'll come across better in an interview. You'll appear to be a more confident person. If you make a blunder, make a light comment that will relieve the immediate tension felt by both parties. Don't demean yourself with sarcasm. Respond to a gaffe in such a way that your humor is remembered and not the cause of your remark.

I am a happy person.

Humor can also help you answer a potentially negative question in a positive way. For example, an interviewer inquired into the ages of my children. I told him that I had twin sons who were (at that time) twenty one years old. He said "You don't look old enough to have children that age. How old are you?" I could have responded by saying that he's not allowed to ask me that question. In that case I would have won the battle but quite possibly have lost the war.

Or I could have responded by telling him my age, which was forty two. But at the time I was sensitive about my age and thought that it might have disqualified me from receiving an offer. So I responded by saying ,"I'm in the generation that thinks a CD is a certificate of deposit, not a compact disc." This generated a chuckle and the age question never came up again.

Your ability to perceive, enjoy and express the humor of an event or situation will help you maintain a more positive attitude during your period of unemployment. You'll be more creative, enthusiastic and successful and you'll have more fun. You don't have to respond to every minor comment with a belly-laugh, but you can smile and enjoy yourself more often. Your family relationship will improve as will your self-esteem. Try it. The only thing you have to lose is your frown.

I enjoy my life.

Chapter Twenty Five

Perfect Practice Makes Perfect

Practicing your job-search skills will help you develop and maintain each of the seven necessary attributes of a realistic attitude. You can practice your control and self-discipline by creating your daily plan. You can stimulate your commitment by confidently concentrating on your objective. And you practice your courage by making telephone calls when you dread doing it.

Practice is also closely linked with self-competition. For example, you should periodically evaluate your relative progress. As your feedback tells you that you need to make adjustments in your implementation techniques, you can make the necessary changes, practice these new tactics and try again. Subsequently your actions are always directed toward accomplishing something.

But practice has a negative side. That is, if you continue practicing bad habits, they become even more ingrained into your performance. Updated plans, based on regular evaluation, will help you practice only the positive and productive portions of your repertoire. It's been said that practice makes perfect. But as coach Vince Lombardi stated, practice makes permanent. Only perfect practice makes perfect.

Fear of performing any action can cause tension. If you practice doing what you are afraid of, you can minimize that stress. So prepare for the event when there is no pressure on you to perform perfectly.

You can practice formally and informally. Formal practice might include having someone interview you while being taped with a video camera. Or you could go on informational interviews and practice your skills. Informally, you could practice your voice exercises while driving to an interview or speaking into a cassette recorder asking and answering questions.

If you feel at ease with yourself and your ability to perform properly, your attitude about yourself will improve and you'll come across better in an interview. Your first and lasting impression will be one of confidence and preparation, a person who would be a credit to any organization. Your spontaneity will impress the interviewer and help you

---

I practice my job-search skills to eliminate fear and tension.

form a positive image of yourself in his mind and yours. If you believe in yourself, you'll also act the part of the perfect employee.

In addition to making you more effective, practice can actually improve your self-confidence. If you prepare a list of questions interviewers could ask you, and possible responses, you'll handle yourself more comfortably while under the pressure of the interview itself. Similarly, if you plan the questions you could ask an interviewer, you'll come across as a polished candidate who is more likely to get an offer over an unprepared competitor.

As Bobby Knight once said, "The will to win is not as important as the will to <u>practice</u> to win." Creatively approach your search and practice each technique. The more you feel at ease with what you have to do, the more confident and effective you'll be in your search.

I practice perfect performance.

Chapter Twenty Six

Some Assembly Required

Have you ever tried riding, or watched someone ride a unicycle? If so, you've noticed something important happening. That is, if you're not moving ahead, you have to work the wheel back and forth to stay in place or else lean on something or somebody to remain upright. Leaning on others will help you through some difficult times while you are unemployed. Learn to rely on friends, family and professionals for emotional support and logistical help.

You need the support and assistance of other people in all stages of your job search if you are to be successful. From the initial discussion with your family and friends to the celebration after you receive the job offer, you'll find that it's much easier, productive and more fun when you take time to talk to other people.

Get by with a little help from your friends.

Carefully select a group of friends and colleagues who can provide you with an objective evaluation of your attitude, correspondence and efforts during your job search. I call this group of people your Brain Trust. They should become your personal support group you can rely on for a source of feedback, assistance and emotional support. Be sure to choose people who think enough of you to be empathetic <u>and</u> honest.

Beginning early in your search, your Brain Trust members can help you with your plan. Once you've set your ultimate objective, they can assist you in developing your strategies and tactics. If they know you well, they can offer advice on the best way to present your unique benefits in your correspondence. And they can perform "mock" interviews with you, asking questions and helping you critique your performance.

Many people seek agreement with their excuses for their lack of job-search success. When you tell people outside your Brain Trust how bad things are "out there" and that "nobody's hiring anybody," they will tend to agree with you rather than disagree and make you feel worse. In their desire to comfort you, they may place a metaphoric arm around

---

I seek the opinions of people who know me well.

your shoulders and say, "You're right. It's not your fault that you're not finding a job. After all, just look at these statistics that show help-wanted ads at their lowest point in forty years." Then you both lower your eyes and shake your heads in commiserating agreement.

You don't need commiseration at this point, and you may not need a lot of advice. What you do need is a resource to help you to think problems through for yourself. Sometimes it's comforting just to have someone listen while you play Devil's Advocate (or Angel's Advocate) with your own thoughts. Your Brain Trust serves as this sounding board for new ideas and a source of opinions.

Be creative when seeking assistance.

You may not think of your previous supervisors as part of your Brain Trust, but they could become one of your most valuable assets. If you left your previous employer on relatively good terms, contact your supervisor and ask him or her for an "exit interview." Neither of you has much to lose by being open and candid, and you can gain a great deal of insight into what you might have done differently during your tenure with that company. You may even be surprised how other people viewed you and your actions in a way that was different from your perspective and intentions.

For example, when you thought of your behavior as aggressive, others may have viewed it as intimidating. On the other hand, what you thought of as introspection, others may have read as shyness or introversion. Find out how your image was actually interpreted. Your previous employer may be in the best position to point this out to you.

Family members may be "too close" to you to be of much benefit. Although they know you better than others, they may not want to be as frank with you as is necessary. Similarly, you may be less willing to hear what they think since they are so close. If arguments regularly arise, the chances that they will be frank are reduced. Also, they may be distressed under the tension of hard times and thus less available than a good friend.

Choose your Brain Trust members carefully and then utilize them liberally. The group doesn't have to be large; in fact it could be made up of only one person. If you choose to invite others to join, make sure only to include people who know you well and are willing to tell you what you need to hear, not necessarily what you want to hear. Find people who will help you when you need it and cheer for you when you experience successes.

I associate with positive, supportive people.

But be careful when choosing your cheerleaders. They have an awesome responsibility to you. If they give you a pat on the back when you both know it's undeserved, they're diminishing their credibility. Choose cheerleaders who will tell you when your performance is not up to your usually high level of competence. They'll tell you your performance is not good enough because they **know** you're capable of doing better. It's this type of constructive criticism that can give you a jump-start back on the road to success.

You can't allow your Brain Trust members to try to do your work for you. They should only supply their *opinion* of your actions. Take it as such and meld it into your plan as you see fit. People are more willing to help people who help themselves. It's still up to you to get the work done, but you don't have to do be alone while you're doing it.

Utilize all your human resources.

Professionals are also available to assist you at every stage of your journey. Career counselors will give you tests to help you determine your career direction. Therapists help you emotionally, and family counselors provide assistance in keeping your relationships intact. And financial planners will help you organize payment schedules and suggest ways to use your limited funds to best advantage.

Social insecurity.

Many unemployed people decline party invitations because they are either ashamed of their status or too frustrated and dejected by their lack of progress. Don't avoid doing something because you're unemployed. If you stay home and feel lonely, you'll just reinforce your dejection. Be a "joiner" and get involved with community activities. Go to parties and seek opportunities to relax and forget about your troubles.

Social events are beneficial in many ways. In addition to helping you feel better, they provide an excellent opportunity to meet new people for networking purposes. Try to circulate in new groups. Meet strangers and talk with them. Ask questions of them to practice your interviewing skills.

Giving yourself a break from your troubles is difficult to do during the holidays at the end of the year. I recall going to parties, finding everyone else in a party mood. I had to work hard at not being the "wet blanket" and usually ended up having a good time, feeling better about myself.

I attend social functions to give myself a mental break.

You can't choose your relatives, but you can choose your friends.

Carefully choose the people with whom you spend the bulk of your time. Associate only with positive people at this time. You may have friends that tend to be negative and that's their choice. But for the time being, try not to spend a great deal of time with them.

You don't need a Devil's Advocate at this point. You need constructive criticism, but not from someone who's going to tear you down. Seek out the *Angel's Advocate* who will offer his opinion as to why your proposal is not good (from his point of view) but who then suggests ways to improve upon it. Then you can decide whether or not you will incorporate his suggestions into the next version of your correspondence.

Is there a hitch in your get-along?

Try very hard not to let your job-search frustration take over your personality. This task may be the most difficult one before you in your period of unemployment. I found myself becoming less gregarious and preoccupied while I was between jobs. I had difficulty making eye communication during conversations and spoke in a more quiet tone of voice. Many people pointed this out to me and I finally took the hint and worked on my social skills. I found when I acted as if I were in a happier frame of mind, I actually felt better.

Seek and use the resources at your disposal. These include your family, friends, relatives, local librarian, employment agents, bankers, insurance agents, previous employers, unemployed friends, role models, support group members, professional counselors, spiritual leaders, previous teachers, pets, motivational books/cassettes, self-help books, job-search books and anything or anybody else that can provide you with mental, physical and spiritual assistance.

Associate with positive people who will provide emotional and social support when you need it most. You'll be surprised how willing people are to be helpful to you if you seek their assistance. Treat them right and they'll do the same for you. Treat yourself right and you'll get through all this in a better frame of mind.

I utilize all the resources available to me.

Chapter Twenty Seven

Time to 'Fess Up

There comes the time when you have to tell your good friends and loved ones about what happened. Although you'll feel apprehensive about opening up to them, certain people in your life should be made aware of your circumstances. Most people, especially children, assume the worst if left to their own imagination and interpretation of your changed mood.

With more complete information, people will understand the situation better. Share your feelings and plans with your family and friends and draw upon their support. Then keep them updated on your activities, especially reports on the success you are experiencing.

The following are examples of how to relate feelings and plans to a spouse and family. However, the comments about communication and discussion apply to dealings you have with anybody who is important to you. Those without a family have the same apprehension as those who have one. It's as difficult to express your emotions to friends and relatives as it is to your spouse. If you're not married, you'll want to apply these suggestions to whomever is significant to you.

Techniques that make it easier on everyone.

The best thing you can do during your period of unemployment is communicate openly. Talk about what your plans are, and express your feelings and anxieties to those who want to listen and help. When your family and friends know what is going on, they'll be in a better position to offer you assistance. Communication acts like a pressure-relief valve because it allows feelings to be expressed, rather than held in until they explode.

United we stand.

Your approach to dealing with your family should be to develop unity and togetherness. Take them into your confidence and share what you plan to do and what you are doing already. Then meet regularly to evaluate your progress in the job search and controlling expenses.

I communicate with my family and friends openly and honestly.

A second helping of PIE.

You should approach this situation as you did your entire job search. First you Prepare what you are going to do; then you Implement your plan and Evaluate your results and make corrections.

General guidelines for communicating with your family.

Before you meet with your spouse and family, you should do your preparation. Go through your monthly expenditures to see where you are currently spending your money and in what amounts (see Chapter Thirty Five). Then you should have a rough idea of what your new monthly expenses should be. The objective of your meeting with your family should be to decide <u>together</u> where and how cuts can be made.

If you work up a plan together, each person becomes *involved* in the decision process and is more likely to be cooperative. A person is more motivated to carry out a decision that he has participated in making than he is a decision that has been imposed upon him by another. The result is that less enforcement is necessary.

Understanding the details of your current circumstances before you meet with the others will inspire confidence. During the meeting they are bound to come up with questions about what's going to happen. If you answer "I don't know" too frequently, they're more likely to worry about the future.

Maintain control through active listening.

If you listen more than you talk, you will encourage everyone to participate. By so doing, you retain the position as final arbitrator while everyone has the chance to become involved in the process. Keep the conversation moving forward. New ideas are bound to come up and recognizing them as they do will bring you all closer together.

Ask one- or two-word questions to keep the other people talking. Probes such as "Oh, really?" and "No fooling?" (without sounding sarcastic) tend to keep people talking since they feel that you are listening to and interested in what they are saying. If they are reluctant to speak, make short statements to get them started. Phrases such as, "Tell me about it. Tell me more. That's a good point; please explain it. Let's hear what you have to say" will get others talking, particularly the children.

I talk with my family and friends in a positive tone.

Maintain a positive attitude.

Make sure you maintain some optimism. Describe the situation objectively. Your voice should project seriousness but not urgency at this point (unless things are critical). Speak calmly and with confidence. Don't allow your voice to become sarcastic or frustrated.

Your family will take their direction from you, so be as open and honest as you can. Admit that your concerned about the future. Doing so will make everyone realize that the discussion will be open, frank, compassionate and realistic.

Keep the conversation headed in a positive direction. Don't get defensive and don't blame your previous employer, your family members for their lack of thrift in the past, the economy or anything else. Be responsible in accepting your current status and create a budget which you can live with as comfortably as possible, given the circumstances.

Be willing to compromise.

The sacrifice can't be on the part of one person alone (or perceived to be on the part of one person). Try to make a win/win rather than a win/lose agreement where one side feels he or she got the short end of the stick.

Give it a rest.

Temporarily give up your unnecessary rituals, expenses and pastimes (i.e., golf every week, alcohol, dinners out). Plan low- and no-cost activities that you can all do together. Go to parades, outdoor concerts, beaches, lakes, for walks or whatever will keep you together and enjoying yourselves.

Have a pre-summit meeting.

If you have a family, meet with your spouse first, and so create a unified front before the rest of the family is brought in. You don't have to agree on every point, but you should agree on the ultimate objective and share the commitment to get through this with a minimum amount of disruption to your lives.

Don't worry. Be happy.

Once you and your spouse agree on the general direction, have a meeting of the entire family. Obviously, the ages of your children will

---

I express my feelings when I communicate with people.

dictate the extent of their involvement, but for the purpose of this discussion we'll assume they're at an age when they can contribute.

Choose a convenient time when nobody is in a rush to go to a party, school, work, practice or whatever. Have the meeting where you normally hold family discussions, like the kitchen, living room or the car on a ride in the country. The physical setting is not as important as the emotional tone, but it should be comfortable and familiar.

Your position in the family meeting is that of facilitator. Ask their advice about where money can be conserved. Be realistic but don't impose your ideas on them unless the process gets out of hand. As facilitator, you're the ultimate decision maker when agreement cannot be reached. But don't begin with, "Here's my plan and this is what you are going to do." If you want cooperation, seek their input.

Manage the meeting, not the people. Allow free, positive discussion without trying to satisfy your ego needs at the expense of the others. Your self-esteem is fairly low at this point, and asserting yourself now could be interpreted as an attempt to recoup it. This tightrope is difficult to walk, but work diligently to control yourself and the tone of the conversation.

Begin by describing objectively what has happened to you. Tell them about your plans to find a new job and the time frame within which this should occur. Then explain that during this time, they should reduce expenditures as much as is reasonably possible. Present your ideas as a starting point and then open it up to discussion.

At each phase, ask them questions in order to see what they understand or misinterpret. Discuss what you feel could happen and solicit their feelings and recommendations. Don't assume you know what they're feeling. For example, your statement "We have a very difficult time ahead of us" could be interpreted in different ways, from "They think it's all my fault" to "I wonder if we'll have enough food to eat?"

Be understanding and honest. Create a unified plan that you will act upon together. Each person should leave with an assigned area or task for which he has responsibility. Set a date for a follow-up meeting so everyone knows his contributions will be shared and applauded.

Follow-up meetings.

When you get together in the future to assess the progress everyone is making, maintain a constructive atmosphere. Begin by

---

I seek the advice of family members to get them involved in all decisions.

telling everyone about what you are doing in your search and what you have accomplished so far.

Next, recap your agreement from the previous meeting. Analyze the results of each person's efforts. Support and applaud those which have been successful and probe into why others were not. Ask for (don't *demand*) an explanation for why the goal was not achieved, and what can be done differently to achieve it.

Reassure and console where necessary. Don't allow the discussion to deteriorate into condemnation and don't moralize, threaten, ridicule or lecture. You're all in this together and you'll get through it as a family unit. But you have to work arm-in-arm to make that happen.

Conflict is not necessarily bad, but the way it's handled could be. Cope with it and resolve it constructively. Your objective is not to impose your will but to facilitate.

Communicate continuously.

Don't communicate with family members only during your formal meetings. Take time regularly to talk informally with one another about your progress. You're so close to your plan that you may not be able to see other options. Seek ideas from your spouse and friends about what you might do differently.

Take time out to relax with your family without discussing your search or your finances. Remain as upbeat as possible without being phoney about your feelings. It's difficult to fool those who know you best, and any attempt to do so will tell them you are hiding something.

As you feel frustration setting in (as indicated by your self-talk) you unknowingly have a testy edge in your voice that is immediately picked up on by your family members. They may initiate conversations less often if they experience irritability in your responses.

When the frustration begins to enter your communication.

The "Catch-22" involved in communicating with your family is the more you tell them about all the letters you are sending, the harder time you'll have facing them with your lack of job-search progress. If you begin to interpret their looks to mean "maybe you're not as good as you think you are," you could start to believe this yourself.

I take time to relax with people without discussing finances.

Maybe we should start to worry a little bit.

The time comes when you must begin to impose greater restrictions on your family's spending and ask them to start economizing more. It's a difficult time in any unemployed person's life, so take care that your new controls are not delivered with impatience or exasperation

As your time unemployed is extended, you could begin to get more abrupt with others as the things they buy seem less necessary than they should. As you try to reiterate the need for everyone to cut back on purchases, it will become harder to be patient.

As the pressure continues to mount, it might become more difficult to understand why they can't empathize with you. Conversations become heated and all parties begin to blame each other for the deteriorating condition of your family's finances.

The unfortunate part is that your irascibility is fueled by the financial attack on your ego. In the past you may have had no trouble contributing to your family's security or handling it all on your own. Now you feel their diminished standard of living is the direct result of your unemployed status.

If you begin to place more of the blame on yourself for your difficulties, you'll become more touchy. The comments that before were taken in jest are now seen as attacks an your ability to take care of your family. You attach negative interpretations to innocent remarks that heretofore caused you all to laugh.

The sooner you recognize that you are feeling defensive the sooner you'll be able to get the support you need. Listen for the changes in the words and the tone you use to communicate your feelings. If you notice your conversations deteriorating into arguments, express your feelings to a trusted friend instead of holding them inside. Then you'll be able to share them with your family in a more controlled manner. It's tough enough getting through this period. Don't alienate those who are closest to you in the process.

How can you be so happy when I'm worrying so much?

As time passes and the pressure you have placed upon yourself builds, your remarks could become more resentful. You may feel that you are carrying a heavy burden on your shoulders and others don't understand that fact. Too many people blame their family for their predicament, assuming that if it weren't for them, the unemployed party wouldn't have all these bills to pay and consequently all the pressure to bear.

I interpret remarks positively without reading in hidden meanings.

Over time you may find yourselves giving each other the silent treatment. Enough irretrievable words have been said that the parties involved no longer even try to have civil conversations. You have to recognize what has happened to you and talk to your family as openly about your feelings as possible. Family therapy may be the right thing, in spite of the added expense, to hold you all together.

It's not their fault anymore than it's your fault. There is no blame to be placed. Instead, express your <u>feelings</u> about the way you interpret the outside events. If you say "I feel extremely frustrated about the fact that I can't pay the bills on time the way I used to. How do you feel about it?" These words do not place blame on anyone and subsequently do not force them to take an immediately defensive stance.

Your relationship with your family may be in jeopardy and you must <u>all</u> work to keep whole. Talk with each other. Express feelings, concerns and needs. Don't say things you'll regret later. If you get too angry, take a walk or do some other exercise to blow off steam and then come back to talk. In order for the family to be functional, there has to be room for everyone's feelings and needs, and these have to be negotiated and shared.

One of the benefits of unemployment is that when you get through it, you'll all be more conscious of the impact of your words and actions on the others. And you'll be a stronger and closer family as a result.

I have a strong relationship with my family.

———————

Chapter Twenty Eight

Time: Your Most Precious Resource

Once you set your goal line for obtaining a job, you've placed a limit on one of your most critical assets: time. This can create pressure and affect your attitude if you approach it without a new position in sight. You have a specific number of hours available, and you must make the most of them. It's how you use this precious resource that determines your success in finding new employment and releases the pressure building up inside you.

Managing your time effectively has an exhilarating effect on your attitude. As long as you are working diligently to find a new position, you will tend to feel hopeful. In addition, if you keep busy on your search you won't have the "free" time available to worry about what might happen to you if you don't get a job.

You only have 16 productive hours per day, if you plan on getting eight hours of sleep. The key is to spend as much of that time as possible either with a prospective employer or trying to set up a meeting with one. Don't allow yourself the "luxury" of getting out of bed late, lingering over your breakfast and morning coffee, and then getting to your search mid-day.

Time management is <u>self-discipline</u>. Until now, you have probably had someone else tell you when to be at work and when you could leave. In many instances even the content of your day was directed by someone else who gave you projects to complete. All that has now changed. It's up to you to determine when you get up, go to sleep and plan for what occurs between those two events.

If you want to get back to work in the shortest amount of time, you have to get up early, go to bed late (yet still allowing for enough sleep) and pack into your waking hours as much purposeful activity as you can. This should occur seven days a week until you receive an offer.

I create and use monthly, weekly and daily plans.

Manage your time to maximize your results.

Time can be your best ally or dreaded enemy. The difference depends on how you utilize and control it. Ask yourself one question as you plan your month's, week's and day's actions: "Will this activity bring me closer to my goal?" If your answer is "yes," do it. If your answer is "No," find and perform a different activity that will take you closer to your objective.

The most effective planning technique you can utilize is to plan your day. Every evening, plan the following day's activities by taking a sheet of paper and dividing it evenly into two columns. At the top of the left hand column, write the word "Do." At the top of the right hand column write the word "Call." Then list everything that you should do the next day in order of priority and everyone you should call. Go through you old business cards and list the people with whom you could network. Add their names to the list.

Prioritize your activities and calls so that you are sure to do the most important items first. Divide the columns into sections labeled A, B and C and write the actions you must take tomorrow in section A. Those that you should do tomorrow, but that are not critical, are then added in section B. Those which would be nice to get to are then added to section C. Remember that a B-priority item (or even a C-priority item) could become an A priority a few days hence if you don't get to it by then.

You can customize your daily plan by adding a section to keep track of your expenses, record mileage, show the specific appointments you have and actions you can take in the evening after the day-time work is completed. During a job search it's important to plan your time so that during typical non-business periods (weekends and after 5:00 pm on weekdays), you can do the things that don't involve contact with other people.

I highly recommend that you use some calendar system to record actions to take in future weeks and months. The Pocket Day-Timer is such a device that you'll find helpful. A complete catalog of planning aids is available through Day-Timers, Inc., One Day-Timer Plaza, Allentown, PA 18195-1551.

Shown below is an example of a customized daily plan taken from the book Job-Search 101 and may be duplicated for your use. You may choose to use this system to plan and control your time informally. The best technique is the one that helps you use your time effectively.

Managing my time has a motivating effect on my attitude.

SAMPLE DAILY PLAN

Things to do today: (Date)

DO	CALL	
A Priority	**Person**	**Number**
1.	1.	
2.	2.	
3.	3.	
4.	4.	
5	5.	
6.	6.	
7.	7.	
8.	8.	
9.	9.	
10.	10.	
11.	11.	
12.	12.	
13.	13.	
14.	14.	
15.	15.	
B Priority	**Follow up necessary:**	
1.		
2.		
3.		
4.		
5.		
6.	**Expenses:**	
7.		
8.		
9.		
10.		
C Priority	**Appointments:**	
1.	**Time**	**Person**	**Place**
2.		
3.		
4.		
5.		
To do this evening:	**To do this weekend:**	

I prioritize my actions to do the most important things first.

If you don't have specific names of people to contact or things to do, block out periods of time for certain events to occur. For example, you could arrange your weekday to look like this:

Morning

6:00 to 8:00	Daily credo; morning exercise; read paper
8:00 to 10:00	Respond to ads/articles/leads found in the paper
10:00 to 11:00	Telephone networking or cold-calling
11:00 to Noon	Letters to follow up on telephone calls

Afternoon/Evening

Noon to 12:30	Lunch break
12:30 to 2:30	Visit the library to review directories; call companies to find the name (and proper spelling) of the person to send your correspondence
2:30 to 5:00	Write and send 20 cold-call letters
5:00 to 6:00	Dinner break
6:00 to 8:00	Calls to earlier time zones, if you live on the East coast (those on the West coast could call the East coast from 5:00 am to 7:00 am)
8:00 to 9:30	Analyze today's events and make changes; plan tomorrow; Career Journal entry
9:30 to 10:30	Reading for enjoyment/relaxation

Once your prospecting and other activities become successful, your schedule needs to be adjusted to accommodate more specific time periods. For example, your plans for days later in your search might look like this:

Mornings

6:00 to 8:00	Daily credo; morning exercise; read paper
8:00 to 9:00	Respond to ads/articles/leads found in the paper
9:00 to 11:00	Telephone calls and follow up
11:00 to 12:30	Review information for your interview; practice interviewing techniques

I use my time for good, gain and success.

Afternoon/Evening

12:30 to 1:00	Lunch break
1:00 to 1:40	Drive to interview; voice exercises; anticipate questions and objections
1:40 to 2:00	Wait in office; review questions and company data; complete the application
2:00 to 3:30	Interview
3:30 to 5:00	Personal cold-calls on nearby companies
5:00 to 5:30	Drive home; critique your performance on the interview
5:30 to 6:30	Dinner break
6:30 to 8:00	Send thank-you notes; calls to earlier time zones
8:00 to 9:30	Analyze today's events and make changes; plan tomorrow's activities; Career Journal entry
9:30 to 10:30	Reading for enjoyment/relaxation

Make sure you schedule time for relaxing and for quality time with you family and friends. Allocate a few hours on the weekend to review the Sunday papers, but spend at least a couple of hours performing some activity that you enjoy doing. Take your mind off your search and you'll come back to it more motivated and invigorated.

If you control your time carefully and methodically, you'll generate the self-discipline that will keep you from becoming lethargic and unproductive. You don't have time to waste, and if you keep busy, you'll spend less time worrying about what <u>might</u> happen. Instead, you'll be spending your time <u>making</u> things happen.

If you get up early and fill your day with productive activities, you'll find a job much more quickly. If you create a plan each month and translate that into a series of weekly and daily plans, you'll surprise yourself with the amount of work you can accomplish in a short period of time.

Plan for the unexpected.

The job search is replete with "minor malfunctions." You'll find that appointments will be cancelled or delayed. You'll be stuck in your

---

I spend my time making things happen.

car in traffic or in planes circling the field due to air-traffic delays. At many times in your search you'll have unplanned down-time, and you'll be more productive if you plan something to do when it occurs.

If you're able to adapt to these situations, you'll find your attitude will remain more calm. You can almost feel your blood-pressure build when you are sitting in traffic with nothing to do. On the other hand, this event won't bother you as much if you have something to keep you busy while you are waiting. A specific activity will keep your mind off the feeling of "impending doom."

Always leave enough time to arrive at your interview early. You'll find that it's better to wait out in your car and arrive in the office exactly at the appointed time than it is to sit fuming in traffic as the time for the interview rapidly approaches (and passes). There is no excuse for being late for an interview. If you travel a great distance to it, fly or drive in the evening before. When driving, allow sufficient time for traffic delays. Always keep something to do with you and you will be able to use your downtime well.

Don't forget the PIPO principle.

If you spend a lot of time in your car driving to and from interviews, the library or elsewhere, use your time wisely. Don't just listen to your radio or gaze unproductively out the window. Buy and listen to motivational tapes. Put positive and useful thoughts into your mind and you you'll be less tempted to think negatively. You can borrow tapes from the library, but I recommend that you buy your own so that you can listen to them over and over again.

If your car doesn't have a tape player built in, bring a battery-operated unit with you. Take notes if you can safely do so, or pull over to the side and write down the words you want to remember. Or, use a cassette recorder. Remember the PIPO principle and fill your mind with good, positive and enthusiastic thoughts.

By listening to these tapes you can avoid the sometimes depressing music you can hear on the radio. "Elevator music" can be relaxing or depressing, depending on your mood. Don't allow your emotions to be affected negatively by a minor outside event. Control what goes into your mind and you can control what comes out of it in terms of positive self-talk and creative ideas.

My thoughts focus on what I can do today to be successful tomorrow.

Start your day off right.

The way you start your day sets the tone for the remainder of it. Don't linger in bed. Set your alarm clock for a specific time and get up immediately. Don't press the "snooze alarm" while you debate with yourself whether or not to get up. When you can, set early-morning appointments to make sure you get up on time. If you have a full day of activity planned, it's much easier to start your day early.

Once you're up, use your time wisely. Start immediately to take control of your attitude. A good way to do this is to ask yourself a series of questions that help you to think about your day positively. For example, here are five questions you can ask yourself every morning to get your day off to a good start:

1) What is there good about today, or what *might* be good about today?

2) In how many ways can I find a job today?

3) What is my objective for today?

4) What's one *new* reason for me to keep searching for a job?

5) When I go to bed tonight and review this day, what accomplishment will I be most proud of?

Make a decision right now to commit yourself to managing your time more effectively. What can you do at this very moment to begin this new regimen? Here are some ideas:

1) Set your alarm clock for a specific time.

2) Call someone to work out (walk, etc) with you early tomorrow morning.

4) Prepare an affirmation saying that you are an effective time manager and you utilize your time productively.

5) Tell your spouse/friends that you are going to begin planning your time more efficiently from now on.

In the past, you knew you had to get up at a certain time to go to work. Once you were there you had a certain hour for lunch and a definite time that you could leave for home. Your evening and weekend hours were probably regimented with specific activities and times, perhaps dictated by the programs on the television.

I succeed by making the most productive use of my time every day.

Now all your rituals are thrown into disarray. It's up to you to decide what you are going to do, when you are going to do it and if you are going to do it at all. More importantly, you now determine the standards for successful completion of every task you undertake. Commit yourself to taking control of your life again. You can do that through effective time management and self-discipline.

I plan my work and work my plan.

Chapter Twenty Nine

Finding Hidden Job Opportunities

Most people define a job search as responding to the help-wanted ads in a newspaper and calling their friends to network. But after a few weeks, the newspapers seem to repeat the previous ads and there are no more new people to network with, causing many people to lose their initial confidence in a successful job hunt. Pessimism reigns.

Searching for prospective employers maintains your early optimism. Once you have contacted a company, it remains a possible employer until you hear differently. Therefore, the more contacts you make, the more opportunities you will have and the longer you'll keep a positive attitude about your ability to find a new job.

Prospecting for the names of people to contact is as much a source of mental energy as it is a fountain of potential employers. As you locate a different directory, a new list of trade shows or a new career opportunity, the rush of energy will sustain and motivate you. As long as you continue your search for additional people to contact, you'll always have hope for your future. And you won't have time to worry about what might happen to you later, as long as your are purposefully moving toward your objective.

PROSPECTING

Prospecting is the act of looking for people to contact about possible employment opportunities. Many places to seek opportunities exist other than those listed in the newspapers. And the search for those hidden possibilities will take up a significant part of your time. Prospecting is beneficial to your search and your attitude because:

1) A continuously renewed list of people to contact is reassuring.

Every time you uncover a new suspect, you feel "this will be the one" who will eventually hire you. A suspect is the name of a potential employer before you have evaluated that company to determine if it

---

I constantly seek new sources of potential employers.

meets your needs. Once you have found this to be the case, the company becomes a prospect for you.

As long as you have several prospects in the offing, you feel optimistic. While you have open inquiries (those which have not been rejected), you feel hopeful that one of them will hire you. You find yourself regularly thinking about these potential offers and about how you will perform when finally on the job.

2) The act of pursuing names of people to contact will keep you busy.

If nothing else, pursuing prospects will keep your mind off other concerns. But uncovering new opportunities has an energizing effect. You'll feel better working on some positive step that will enhance your chances of finding a new position.

As long as you still have other directories to review and new sources of names, you feel as if things can work out for you. On the other hand, once you begin to deplete the names of potential employers, you're attitude could erode.

But even in this case, opportunities still exist. People who rejected you in the past may have moved to other companies or to new positions, reopening your candidacy with the new incumbent. Or perhaps a different division in the same company has a position open. Continuous prospecting will alert you to changes in *former* prospects before your competitors know about them. If a company or person rejected you once, you shouldn't write them off completely in the future.

3) Prospecting gives you a chance to develop your creativity.

If you seek names of people to contact where others just see billboards, signs on the sides of trucks, ads in a magazine or newspaper articles, you can get a head start on them. And as you develop your innate creative powers you can apply them in many other ways.

4) Continuous prospecting will enable you to create opportunities where none existed previously.

Prospecting for a job is analogous to prospecting for gold. If you search where everyone else is looking, you will find only tapped-out veins and many competitors. You'll be more successful if you look where others aren't and find the hidden opportunities before they become general knowledge.

When you find a company that might need your skills and benefits, you can contact them to discuss possible opportunities. You'll

---

I know there's a job "out there" for me and it's up to me to find it.

be able to generate offers from companies that didn't even advertise a position. So you have another way to eliminate your competition for a specific position.

5) The responses you receive will help renew your faith in the system.

More often than not, your unsolicited application will earn a personal letter in response. Consequently, your information is kept on file (at least in their minds) longer than others. You'll find you'll receive inquiries up to one year later from these people wanting to know if you are still interested in working for their company.

What goes up must come down.

Prospecting in these hidden sources requires you to find the names of the department head for your particularly specialty and contact him with the objective of creating a job that may not be available presently. Your overture must demonstrate that if they were ever considering a position such as the one you describe, now is the best time to create it and you are the best person for it.

The negative side effect of prospecting for positions that have not yet been created is you will receive a significantly higher percentage of rejections. This is not a consequence of your prospecting skills but a result of the fact that these companies are not looking to hire someone.

You can minimize rejections by narrowing down the companies you contact. Qualify them against your specific standards for employment by creating a list of criteria for your ultimate company and job. Then compare prospective employers against this list prior to contacting them. Therefore, you will call only on those who meet your criteria. Successful prospecting is not just a matter of the number of doors on which you knock. It is more a matter of the quality of the doors and how and when you choose to knock on them.

The amount of time you have available for your search will determine the extent to which you "weed out" the prospective employers as well as the effort you place on prospecting. If you don't have a great deal of time before your funds are depleted, you will have to generate a large number of suspects in a short period of time. Doing so may require you to use direct mail and telephone calls to contact more people in a shorter time.

But if you have sufficient funds to last a year or more, you will probably be more selective in your prospecting and qualifying activities. You won't need to send out five hundred letters in a brief period, but

---

I am totally dedicated to resolving my present situation.

your quest will be extended or shortened to reflect the effort you put into it in the time allotted.

Vary your attack.

You can look for employment prospects in many places. Newspapers provide the most obvious and frequently used lists and therefore will have the most competition for a given position. Your objective should be to find the opportunities that are not as obvious so you can minimize or eliminate your competition for a job opening.

Below is a brief summary of prospecting techniques you can use to find potential employers. At this point your emphasis should be on contacting all available sources and creating new ways to find names of people to contact.

1) Newspapers.

In addition to looking in the help-wanted ads, look in other sections of the paper. Read articles for information about companies and their plans. Look for companies' ads for information about their products and services.

Stay in the paper for a while longer. Look at the business and franchise opportunities that are available. Also look in other sections of the paper. For example, the **Week In Review** section of the Sunday New York Times lists healthcare and educational positions that are not found among the general employment ads.

When you're finished with one paper, go to the next and the next. Find a store that sells newspapers from around the country. Some will ask you to prepay for the paper a week in advance but many do not. If you know the city to which you would like to move, subscribe to its local paper and have it delivered to you.

> Creative approach: If you read about people who have been promoted, write to congratulate them and offer your services to assist them. In addition, write to their company to apply for the position that was vacated as a result of the promotion.

2) Networking.

Networking is the traditional means of contacting everyone you know and telling them about your availability and goals. Contact colleagues, schoolmates, friends and people at church, PTA meetings, your gym and even at parties. The objective of networking is not to ask the

---

I improve my chances of employment by contacting more people.

person for a job but to gather information and have them spread the word that you are available for employment. By doing so, that person acts as a "reference" for you as he tells others about your skills.

Call a friend in need.

"Reverse networking" is a call to someone who is out of work, just to see if there is anything you can do to help. If you know of someone in this position, give him or her a call even though you too are unemployed. If nothing else, you can exchange leads and ideas about prospecting, interviewing or anything else that could help you both be more successful.

> Creative approach: Although most of the people you contact will be sincerely interested in helping you, they may forget what you told them about your background and goals. As a simple reminder, have a business card printed with your name, address, phone number and career objective listed on one side. One the other side show a brief list of your skills and accomplishments. Hand these out as a reminder of what you are seeking.

3) Cold calling.

Cold calling is different from networking. In cold calling, you contact people you don't know and ask them for a job. A position may or may not exist, but you call on them to find out if there is a possible match between their future needs and your skills.

There are three ways to do this: by telephone, mail and personal contact. Obviously the *quantity* of people you can contact is greatest with mail and least with personal visits. But the *quality* of contact is just the reverse.

A) Telephone cold calling. If you have little time available, or are performing your search in a restricted specialty, you could call the person directly. You should also make this call before sending a letter to any company to make sure you have the right person and the correct spelling of his name.

> Creative approach: Utilize time zones effectively and increase your productive day by three hours. If you live on the East coast, make your calls to the earlier time zones after 5:00 pm. This will also save you money. You could also FAX your letter with the notation that you will call

---

I evaluate and respond to every event in a positive way.

later to follow up. Those of you on the West coast can begin your calls to the East at 5:00 am.

B) Direct-mail cold calling. Cold calling by direct mail entails sending a letter to the department head for your particular specialty. Your letter should describe the one or two major benefits that you can offer that company and request a personal meeting to discuss the possibilities.

> Creative approach: Include a business reply card that has the return postage pre-paid. On the other side, offer several positive options for the recipient to check off.

C) Personal cold calling. This approach increases the quality of the call but reduces the quantity of contacts you can make. However, if you have a highly qualified list of prospects, you should call on each personally.

> Creative approach: Don't ask to see the decision maker the first time. Ask the receptionist for the name of the appropriate person to contact (and the proper spelling and pronunciation). Also ask for information on the company, such as product literature, the company newsletter or annual report. You may even be able to make an appointment for a later meeting.

4) Personal observation.

Every ad, tee-shirt, business card and bumper sticker can hold the name of your future employer. Look at your world with a new sense of awareness. Find opportunity where others just see the names of companies or products on a shelf.

> Creative approach: Contact your prospect's suppliers, distributors and customers for ideas on how you can help your target company be more successful in its sales efforts. Then call your prospect and make an appointment to discuss the results of your "research."

5) Job fairs.

Periodically, many companies will get together to present opportunities available in their companies. Much like a trade show, they set up booths and interview candidates right on the spot.

> Creative approach: Eliminate your competition by simulating a job fair. Find out when and where a major trade show will be held in your industry. Go to it and cold call on the people exhibiting there.

6) Miscellaneous sources.

I think, feel and act confidently when contacting prospects.

There are many other areas in which you can look for employment opportunities. One such place is your school's career placement office. The library is another excellent source of information during a job search. You can find directories containing information on companies and their officers. They also provide information on the company's sales, products, regional offices and other details. You can use this data for your letter-writing campaigns or for background information prior to the interview.

One very important resource that can provide you with a tremendous amount of support, solace and leads for job opportunities is a local unemployment-support group. In many cases these are church-sponsored, so you could contact your local church for more information. If there are none available nearby, you might consider starting one, which in itself may make you feel better.

Another group-oriented tactic is to join associations, a good way to improve your attitude as well as increase the circle of people you network with. These include the Rotary Club, a lead-finding organization for local businesses or your town's Chamber of Commerce. Their meetings provide a great way to meet new people and spread the word about your availability. These associations generally have a members' list, which you can obtain as a source of new names to contact.

Similarly, you should also review magazines related to your field of interest. The local library has many suitable magazines, and you can subscribe to others. Read these as you would a newspaper, sending letters to companies mentioned in the articles, to the authors of articles and also respond to the employment ads listed in many of the magazines. The library also has directories with the names of other magazines that could provide suitable information.

The positive effect of all these activities on your attitude will be increased if you perform them often. You'll find that when you think of a new way to uncover an opportunity, you will improve your attitude toward yourself.

But what if you're shy?

Many people consider themselves shy and unable or unwilling to prospect personally. If this is true for you, you must find other means of uncovering and contacting suitable names of prospective employers. Some of techniques are no less effective than those listed above, but they may extend the time of your search.

I only contact prospective employers that meet my criteria for success.

You could stress the impersonal ways to prospect, which include responding to newspaper ads and cold-calling by direct mail. Joining a support group would be ideal for you, since these are run by knowledgeable and empathetic people who are there to help you be successful. A job fair would be equally suitable to your needs, since the attendees are all there for the same reason and the interviewing process is conducted in a routine and friendly fashion.

In addition, you could place an ad in the newspapers announcing your availability. The National Business Employment Weekly regularly has a section they call **Talent For Hire** and it is specifically designed for people to advertise their skills and objectives. The Employment Review has a similar section. Or you could place more emphasis on using employment agencies to make the initial contact with the employer.

Case History.

Perhaps a discussion of one of my prospecting "adventures" will demonstrate the need for creativity, flexibility and a good attitude while prospecting at any stage of your quest. This sequence of events actually occurred to me after being unemployed for about four months. It revolves around my efforts to prospect for employment opportunities at a major trade show (convention) in the healthcare industry.

Trade shows in general offer an excellent way to meet decision makers. Companies usually send their top executives to the largest conventions, so prospecting at them is an effective way to by-pass the personnel department and meet the decision makers for the type of job you are looking for.

The show I went to was held in Houston, Texas, the largest healthcare convention of the year. I decided to go there, contact the exhibitors and talk to them about the chance of employment with their companies. I planned for several weeks to make this trip effective since I was travelling from my home in Connecticut at my own expense.

I had worked at many of these shows in the past and I knew that there were several "givens" that I could count on:

- Companies wouldn't ordinarily fly me to their location for an interview if an equally-qualified candidate was nearby, but they would talk to me if it didn't cost them anything to do so.

- While at trade shows, executives like to be booked for

I actively pursue every employment opportunity.

breakfast, lunch and dinner meetings and they don't like to "work" the booth.

- Most executives walk around, viewing the other exhibits and otherwise maintaining their "executive" status. Consequently, I knew that I had to set up specific appointments whenever I could, to meet them before and after the show.
- There is usually an exhibitor's lounge, and the people working the exhibit like to take breaks, particularly near the end of the show hours.
- Those at the booth wouldn't have a great deal of time to talk with me so I had to have a quick way to gain their attention and provide information to leave with them.
- There is a sense of "neutrality" at a trade show. Neither party has the "home-field" advantage, and people seem to be more congenial than they otherwise might be back in their office.

With these thoughts in mind I worked out my strategy. I acquired the list of exhibitors and cross-matched it with my directory to get the names of the people to contact at each of my target companies. I sent them each a personal letter notifying them that I would be there and would like to meet with them for an interview.

I had made up regular business envelopes with the words "Marketing Manager" printed on them. In each, I placed a letter with large and brief "bullets" proclaiming my accomplishments. Included on this page was my hotel telephone number along with the hours I would be there for personal contact. I planned to leave one of these on each booth at the convention the night before the show started.

Tell me quick and tell me true, or else my friend the heck with you.

Knowing that I had little time to meet with people while they were at their booth, and that their attention span would be minimal, I needed something that would quickly get and maintain their attention. The device also had to communicate my benefits quickly, be easy to carry and informative. With these criteria in mind, I created the idea for the two-sided business (networking) card discussed earlier.

Every day I make ten new contacts with potential employers.

An unconventional convention.

I spent the two weeks before the show personally calling people to arrange appointments. I set up meetings to occur before, during and after the show hours. The time finally came to leave for the show and I flew to Houston the day before the convention started.

I knew the companies I wanted to contact and their booth numbers. So the night before the show opened, I went to every exhibit and placed on each the envelope addressed to the Marketing Manager with my letter inside of it. I knew there would be about 500 prospects there, so I made extra copies to use as reminders and to hang in the exhibitors' lounge.

The next morning was the opening day for the show. I left for the convention hall. Since the exhibitors were permitted to arrive early in order to make final preparations, many of them would have already seen my letter. As I walked in, I glanced around looking for people reading my letters. But after a short time I realized that there were no letters anywhere. I later found out that it was against show rules to prospect for employment there, and someone had come around the night before and picked up every letter. I was disheartened to say the least ("crushed" was more appropriate).

I had invested too much time, money, effort and emotion in this project and I wasn't going to let this setback defeat me. I still had my networking card with me, in addition to extra copies of the handout. The night before, I had mapped out my "routing" around the exhibit hall, so I began to make my rounds. When people at my target companies were not busy, I would walk up to them and explain myself. Then I would make an appointment for an interview, a time to come back to meet with the decision-maker or cross them off my list.

I did this for four hours until the exhibit hall closed for the day. Then I went to a local print shop and had more copies of the poster made. There wasn't time to have the envelopes printed, so I bought blank envelopes and carefully printed the title **Marketing Manager** on them after I returned to my room. I spent that evening addressing and stuffing envelopes while waiting for the telephone to ring.

During the remainder of the show I made all the contacts I had planned to make, and ended up with six interviews. One of those eventually concluded in an offer several weeks later. It was also an excellent networking opportunity since I saw many of my old associates whom I worked with or met over the years in the business.

I am creative in finding new ways around obstacles placed in my path.

A successful job search takes a great deal of hard work and there is very little positive feedback. It's up to you to fill every hour of your day with results-oriented, goal-seeking activity and keep your mind off the negative consequences of what <u>might</u> happen to you if you should fail.

You'll experience days when you feel as if nothing can go wrong, and you'll experience days when you feel nothing can go right. But every day without a job takes something out of you. The sand will continue draining out of the positive upper chamber in your hourglass unless you reach down for the strength to turn it over.

You must perform you're own damage-control function and minimize the effects of the negative environment. Without constant attention to the barrage of rejection, you could begin your slide into increasing levels of frustration. Prospecting can help you avoid the depths of dejection and depression. Use your time wisely and productively, and you'll find a job more quickly and maintain a more positive attitude longer.

I create my own circumstances.

Chapter Thirty

Realistic vs. Positive Thinking

Positive thinking is an important part of your job-search attitude. Look to optimistic possibilities rather than potentially bad consequences. But if you get too carried away with positive thinking and ignore warning signals, then positive thinking alone ceases to be beneficial.

A more realistic job-search attitude is to always look for the good, but keep in mind some negative and uncontrollable events may occur. When they do, you must have the confidence, commitment and courage to handle them. And there you have a definition of *realistic* thinking. It's positive thinking translated into positive action based upon the understanding that problems will be associated with your search but that you can overcome them.

"Steady as she goes."

Realistic thinking combines positive thinking with an awareness that life doesn't always deal from the top of the deck. Level off your emotional ups and downs. If you must err, err toward the positive but recognize that your commitment will regularly be tested. Just keep in mind that you can deal successfully with whatever happens.

Manipulate your thinking. Resolve your mental conflicts. Control the direction of your attitudes. Manage your defenses against the negative attacks of rejection and frustration. Recognize that <u>rejection</u> is an external force and <u>frustration</u> is your response to it. When you learn to respond to external forces in a more positive way, you've come a long way in managing your emotions.

When you acknowledge that you will be rejected 99% of the time, you'll be able to <u>respond</u> to the feelings of rejection rather than <u>react</u> to them. If you understand what is happening to you and what is causing it to occur, you're more likely to take the appropriate action.

On the path of least resistance.

Your attitude seems to have a "mind of its own," and left to wander, it can be good, bad or neutral. If you don't exert control over the

---

I control my response to external events I cannot control.

direction you want it to take, it will proceed along the path of least resistance. In your existing frame of mind this will be toward the potential negative consequences of your circumstances, further fueling your spiral into frustration, dejection and eventual surrender.

Sustaining and defending an attitude of absolute certainty that you will have a new job by your goal-line date is difficult. Too many forces are pulling your attitude away from this position. But hard work, concentration and commitment protect your attitude from becoming negative. If you understand that not being 100% positive all the time is OK, you'll be able to deal with the challenges with which you'll be confronted on a daily basis more objectively.

Your well-meaning friends will tell you to "stay positive and everything will eventually work out for the best." But after hearing this message too many times, it can have the opposite effect by reminding you that you <u>have been</u> thinking positive thoughts and things haven't worked out yet.

Let's be realistic.

Instead of seeking that elusive state of Nirvana (i.e., a 100% positive attitude), your goal should be to recognize and deal with the forces attempting to erode your attitude. This more realistic approach will help you balance your desire for a solution with your awareness of the potential hazards that could occur if you don't take control.

A good solution to minimizing the conflict of these polarized forces is the application of realistic thinking *in addition to* positive thinking. A sense of realism will enable you to evaluate your situation objectively. You can then take action without over-correcting your mistake or overreacting to an obstacle.

Even the ultimate high of the words "I'd like to make you an offer" needs to be tempered with realism. Before you allow yourself to become too elated, make sure you've nailed down every element of the offer. Agree on the compensation program, benefit package, starting date, job responsibilities, potential rewards and any other details that are specific to your negotiations. Remember that the possibility that the offer will be rescinded still exists.

I'm not suggesting that you temper all your thoughts and enthusiasm with negative possibilities. It's not in my nature to do that. I am suggesting that you manage your emotional state realistically. Rarely does everything go smoothly without any problems or irritations. If you

---

I combine positive thinking with realism to reduce frustration.

are aware of a possibility that something could go wrong, you will be better prepared to anticipate alternate solutions.

Employ strategic action with positive thinking.

Positive thinking and futility are not the only two choices you have. If you can maintain the feeling that you are in control of your circumstances and can deal with anything that may happen, you'll be able to keep a grasp on your commitment and confidence.

Recognize the difficulty that confronts you, evaluate it, correct it, learn from what you do and try again. Continue this process with different circumstances as they arise. Your goal is to make sure any significant error doesn't happen again. If you challenge yourself to prevent the repetition of mistakes, there should be fewer of them, and you'll have greater resources to handle them.

Failure is in the eyes of the beholder.

The word "realistic" may be defined as negative by some people. Your guard should immediately go up when you hear someone say, "Let's be realistic about this and give up." People define what happens top them in terms of their perspective, their notions of what is possible based on their observations given their own capabilities, not *yours*. Realistic thinking is a positive alternative to feelings of futility and follows an objective assessment of the challenge from *your* point of view with a clear understanding of *your* capabilities and limitations.

Common sense is so uncommon.

Common sense is an example of realistic thinking. It's the art of knowing what the right thing to do is, at the right place and time. It is innate, but not everybody who has that inner voice listens to what it says. Common sense is not only knowing what is right, but *doing* what is right.

Everybody has common sense, but some people listen to it more than others. Common sense tells you that you have to get up early and spend the day making contacts with prospective employers. Your inner voice tells you what is right and wrong. Here, feelings of guilt begin, inspired by not doing what you know is right or by doing what you know is wrong. You are responsible for what you do and what you fail to do.

I use common sense when faced with unfamiliar circumstances.

If you do what you always did, you'll get what you always got.

Common sense tells you that if you disliked your previous job you're setting yourself up for failure again if you seek another position just like it. But because you have experience in that field, getting a job in it should be easier. The right action to take in this case is to investigate other career alternatives and try something else. If you're first reaction is "I'm too old to start a new career" you should realize that you are entering your Terrible Toos and corrective action is necessary.

Whenever you're faced with a challenge, listen to your immediate reaction. It tells you what you truly think. That voice should serve as one of the "red flags" that indicate the direction your thinking is taking. Listen to it and honor it by taking action on it.

Success is a manner of speaking.

Common sense tells you what your mother told you years ago: "Watch your manners." You may wonder how such advice applies to your job search, but your manners say a great deal about you. Courtesy in your speech and actions will show the interviewer that you have class, which could be what makes him choose you over an otherwise equally-talented competitor.

The words "please and thank you" seem easy enough to say but your reduced self-esteem may keep you from uttering them. Use them liberally in your correspondence and personal meetings and you'll be surprised at the response you'll receive. Practice saying these and other words that demonstrate common courtesy and they'll become more natural in your interviews.

Take the path of most resistance.

Common sense tells you to discipline yourself to do what you must in order to succeed. When you make the choice to take one action you make the choice not to take another action. For example, when you discipline yourself to get up at 5:30 PST and make telephone calls to the East coast, you're choosing not to take the easier path of sleeping later. Success in your job search requires you make tough choices, leading you toward the attainment of your objective most quickly.

Increase your response-ability.

The discipline to take action that will help you achieve your goal will cause an increase in tension. Since you're telling yourself and the

---

I assess my challenges with a clear understanding of my abilities.

world that you're doing everything you can to get a job, you're not making it easier for others to excuse your lack of progress.

With commitment to your search, you give up the chance to blame your lack of success on the economy, your age, experience or another excuse. You're taking responsibility, and you're on your way to success.

Positive thinking is part of realistic thinking, as are common sense, commitment, courage and confidence. You need all these attributes in order to deal with the trials and tribulations of an extended job search. Always expect positive responses to your actions. But understand that less-than-positive circumstances may occur and you have the ability to overcome the obstacles, learn from them and eventually succeed.

I make the tough choices that enhance my search.

Chapter Thirty One

Listen to What Others Have to Say

There are many sources of positive input that are available via books, video tape programs and audio cassettes. These can provide techniques you can use to maintain a more constructive attitude about yourself and your future.

Purchasing these books and programs can be expensive, but the money is well-spent. I bought the <u>Personal Power</u> tape program produced by Tony Robbins for over $300 at a time when I was already living off credit-card cash advances. However, I listened to it over and over again and performed all the exercises he recommended. It was worth much more than $300 to me in terms of ideas, comfort and direction.

There are many excellent speakers and authors available to you. Among those that have been particularly helpful to me are Zig Ziglar, Tony Robbins, Robert Schuller, Denis Waitley, Earl Nightingale, Brian Tracey, Wayne Dyer, Napolean Hill, Maxwell Maltz and Norman Vincent Peale. You can find them in book stores and libraries near you.

Use this literature to form and stimulate your thinking. Translate their positive thoughts into action you can take to improve your success ratio. For example, when you hear Robert Schuller say, "The inner self you project determines how others will treat you," you should be reminded to convey a feeling of confidence to an interviewer through your posture, eye communication and voice so that you'll be treated respectfully.

Several lessons will help you get the most out of the speakers and authors you select. These points will assist you in more quickly assimilating and applying the valuable lessons of these modern-day prophets:

- Positive thinking alone will not make you succeed.
  You must translate these thoughts into actions that are
  directed toward achieving a worthwhile objective. It

I use the motivational words of others to stimulate my thinking.

takes hard work to succeed in your job search, but you'll find it will be accomplished more effectively with a good frame of mind.

- A positive approach to a job search doesn't mean that setbacks won't occur. But when they do, you can deal with them and not allow them to diminish your self-confidence.

- A positive attitude is an important ally during a job search. It will help you deal better with anything that happens and will provide greater solace than a negative attitude.

- Unless you believe in yourself, positive thinking by itself will not make you perform better. It's been said that in order for you to perform better during an important meeting (i.e., interview) you should repeat the words: "I'm the best." But this won't be effective until you are first able to build up your self-image enough so that you accept that as true. Positive input (including affirmations) won't properly function if it is not accompanied by your own feelings of self-esteem.

- When you hear a particularly appropriate quotation, write it down and keep it with you. Brian Tracey said, "If it's to be, it's up to me," and Tony Robbins said, "There's always a way." Both of these people said many other motivating and sustaining comments, but these two had special meaning for me, and I wrote them down to refer to them.

Take notes while listening to the speakers. Write down their comments, leaving enough space between them to add your own thoughts and action plan for each. Don't just listen to the tapes and read the books. Get <u>involved</u> with them. Allow them to become part of your life. Taking notes which you review will increase what you remember. Without review you will forget 80% of what you read or hear within two weeks.

Your attitude about yourself will determine the extent to which these people will motivate you. Don't let <u>your</u> negative frame of mind skew your interpretation of what you learn about helping yourself. Listen and read with an open mind and you will get a great deal of motivation and strength from these people.

I translate positive input into productive action.

The words you glean from each tape and book are not as important as the ideas that will flow into your mind. When you are confronted with a new challenge, re-listen to or re-read the messages and seek specific advice for resolving your situation. It's amazing, but you will hear something new that you'll swear wasn't there before. New ideas will come to you and you'll create actions that will enable you to reach a new solution to your predicament.

It's not always necessary to purchase motivational books and tapes to feel better about yourself. If you have a VCR, rent a funny movie and spend an evening at home watching it. This can make you laugh and forget your troubles even if only for an hour or two. And when *It's A Wonderful Life* comes on the television, don't miss it.

I take notes while listening to inspirational messages.

Chapter Thirty Two

You Can Teach An Old Dog New Tricks

In today's job market, you must update your skills to stay current with the rapidly changing body of knowledge. The time that you have available now provides an excellent opportunity to continue your education. By taking evening courses or through less-formal means, you can maintain your mental acuity as you improve your skills in your present field and/or learn the skills necessary to compete in an entirely new field.

As you learn, you'll be more competitive with recent college graduates. These people bring with them the most current data available. You have to demonstrate to an interviewer that you are up-to-date too, and that you have the experience, honed through years of trial and error, to apply these latest theories most effectively.

This knowledge will also help you perform better during an interview. You'll be able to converse with the interviewer about the current trends and articles in the business journals. In this instance, it will also behoove you to learn about other specialties. That way you can discuss, for example, the impact of your anticipated marketing decisions on production, stock dividends and personnel.

That's why you should be well-rounded. As you devour the daily newspapers looking for prospects, you can also pick up vital information about world events, local happenings and yesterday's winners in sports events. These facts will help you open the interview more effectively as well as provide ammunition for your discussion in the latter stages of the interview.

As you continue your education, you'll also keep your mind active. You'll discover and respond to opportunities that remain unknown to your less-resourceful competitors. And you'll be more likely to maintain a realistic attitude that will carry your through these tough times.

Your unfolding education can be as formal or informal as you wish. There are evening courses offered by high schools and colleges in

---

I improve myself at every opportunity.

addition to those offered by special-interest groups. And you can go to a nearby (public or college) library and read books on an almost endless list of topics. Here you'll also find the latest periodicals and newspapers from around the country.

Seek to improve yourself by adding to your knowledge base. You'll feel more self-respect and self-esteem. You'll perform better on interviews and shorten the length of your search. You can learn new hobbies, improve your skills or prepare for a new career. There is literally no end to the resources you can find that will make you a more marketable product.

Your self-education need not be all career oriented. Try to improve yourself by learning more about yourself and simply by reading more. There are many self-help books in the book stores and libraries. They provide theories and examples of techniques you can use to improve your lot in life. Learn more about the mechanics of self-esteem and strategies you can use to generate greater self-confidence. You'll be better able to face yourself, your family and your daily routine with equanimity. Companies such as Successful Self Management (Hartford, CT) offer seminars on improving self-esteem and on ways to create a life that you love. Take advantage of the resources available to help you feel better about yourself.

You could also take time out to read fiction and other non-fiction books. Doing so will help you relax as you also learn from them. They'll also give you ideas for ways to "break the ice" when you go on an interview.

The next time you find yourself with nothing to do, go to the library instead of watching soap operas. Improve yourself every chance you get. Then practice using that knowledge in your conversations with others; not to impress them with your intelligence but to practice being more conversant in a broader range of topics.

I am current in my specialty, as well as knowledgeable in others.

Chapter Thirty Three

The Employer's Viewpoint

You know that you are a good person with excellent skills and that you would make a good employee. Your resume lists every function you have performed and shows a steady progression of increasing responsibility and competence. So why aren't the recipients calling you immediately upon receipt of your letter and resume? An understanding of the decision-making process from the employer's point of view will help you understand the possible causes for the delay in responding.

Why is this happening?

Although of little comfort to you, delays are to be expected. For instance, a company may receive one thousand or more responses to a help-wanted advertisement placed in a large newspaper. If each is comprised of a cover letter and a two-page resume, then the potential employer has three thousand or more pieces of correspondence to review, in addition to the normal activity required to perform his every-day functions. More often than not, travel schedules, meetings, vacations and other unforeseen events conspire to delay the first pass through the pile of responses to the ad.

The employer will wait a week or so to make sure most of the responses have arrived and then perhaps take them home for the week-end to peruse. Good intentions notwithstanding, he rarely does his homework and thus takes another week to go through them. The reader will dispose quickly of those that are not qualified and narrow down the list of the remaining resumes until about twenty potential candidates remain (2% of the initial 1000 responses) .

As time passes and pressure builds on the decision maker to hire someone, he becomes more selective and more likely to eliminate those with good but relatively marginal qualifications for this position. These applicants are weeded out and placed in a separate pile of those who will not be considered. Remember that a job offer does not always go to the best-qualified candidate. It usually goes to the candidate who can best sell himself in non-personal and personal communication.

I follow up on every action I take.

The decision maker will eventually send the remaining cover letter/resume packages around to his associates for feedback, since a person will rarely make the hiring decision on his own. This step may take another week or more, depending on how many interruptions the people who are contributing to the decision have. At this point, it could be about one month from the time you originally sent your letter.

Once their opinions are given and the number of candidates further reduced, the original recipient will decide to either telephone the remaining candidates for an initial interview (if, for example, it's a national search) or invite them to come in for a personal interview.

It may take two weeks to arrange and perform the first interviews, and another two weeks to narrow down the list further and invite the finalists back. It could then take these people a few additional weeks meeting with other people and waiting for the decision to be made. These final events might occur about two to three months from when you first responded. If the personnel department initiated the search, the initial response will usually take less time, but the interviewing process is extended because they will perform the initial screening interviews.

Waste not, want not.

Most of your activities will be wasted if you don't follow up on them. If you don't hear from a prospective employer within two weeks after sending your resume, send a follow-up letter or call to reiterate your interest in the position. And people will rarely heed your first unsolicited inquiry into a job. You must take the initiative to maintain the connection once you establish it. You can waste hours of time, many dollars and reams of paper just by ignoring the follow-up portion of your search. Keep all the loose ends under control and you will be more successful in less time as a result.

You must follow up on every contact you make. This may involve something as basic as a quick telephone call or hand-written note to thank someone for his assistance, or it could involve something as formal as a type-written summary of your understanding of the terms of your employment agreement. But if you are courteous enough to thank someone, your name will be remembered with positive associations.

I always evaluate my correspondence to make it more persuasive.

Form letters are a fact of life.

Some companies will respond to every inquiry with either a form letter or post card informing you that your correspondence has been received and is being evaluated. But in most cases the company will notify only the semi-finalists that they are being considered. The other 99% of the applicants will more likely than not receive nothing in return for their efforts. At best, you'll receive a form letter that looks something like the following:

> *While we are impressed with your knowledge and experience, they do not match our needs as precisely as we would like at this time. We shall continue to hold your resume in our active file and will contact you if a suitable position occurs in the near future. Thank you for your interest in ABC Company. We wish you the best of luck in your future endeavors.*

If you understand this point early in your search, it may be easier to accept. There is no excuse for the lack of common courtesy and understanding expressed by not responding to every letter. It takes time, but a simple post card alerting you of your fate will allow you to eliminate that prospect from your list and redouble your efforts on those that are more likely to include you as one of their semi-finalists.

A job search is not fair to everybody. Just because you're not selected doesn't mean that you're not a capable and qualified person. It may mean that your resume and cover letter need more attention to make them more persuasive. Keep evaluating and improving your correspondence to make it get the positive attention of the recipient; you'll be more likely to get your chance at an interview. After that, it's all up to you.

My expectations are positive and realistic.

———————

Chapter Thirty Four

A Job-Search Potpourri

During the first few months of unemployment, you'll have more than enough activities to keep you busy looking for a job. But eventually your pace will slow down as your prospects begin to diminish. At this point many people give up their search and spend their days in front of the television or in some other unproductive, energy-draining way, waiting for the phone to ring with a job offer.

There are still many options to investigate that will help you maintain a realistic and positive attitude. You can spend your time productively even though you're not actively involved in contacting prospective employers. You can do several things to provide extra income, remain productive and network while at the same time helping other people.

Volunteer your time and energy.

There are as many ways you can benefit from performing volunteer work as there are activities you can do. You can offer to help non-profit organizations in the arts, child health & welfare, drug prevention, the environment, mental health, social services and many other worthwhile causes. These agencies are always looking for assistance.

In addition, there are organizations you, along with your family, can help. These include scouting, the local YMCA/YWCA or your child's school. A great way to help yourself and at the same time help other people in your situation is to start, or assist, a local support group for unemployed people in your area.

What have you done for you lately?

Volunteering your time can actually benefit you more than it does the recipients of your efforts. When you offer your time and energy you can reduce your tension, feel better about yourself and also further your job search.

When you keep busy helping other people, you won't have time to worry about your impending deadline. You can keep you mind

---

I investigate alternative career opportunities.

focused on what you are doing and off of your problems. And when you lie down in bed at night, your final thoughts of the day will be on the good that you have done for other people.

Another benefit of volunteer work is that you will feel better about yourself. There is nothing quite so satisfying as someone giving you a hug and a heart-felt "thank you" for all that you did for them. As Zig Ziglar says, "You can get everything you want in life as long as you help enough other people get what they want." Volunteer work is rewarded not with dollars but with self-satisfaction. Therefore, the more you help others, the more psychic income you will receive, providing a much-needed boost to your self-esteem which will overflow into other areas of your life.

Volunteer work can also further your job search. It provides a way to make new contacts. As you meet a greater number of people, they'll spread the word about your ability and availability. So, you can look at volunteer work as a way of increasing the size of your network. And some of the people you meet may become life-long friends.

Furthermore, volunteer work also provides the opportunity to learn new skills or improve those you already have. Depending on the type of activity you choose, you could learn more about organization, leadership, teamwork, persuasion and making presentations. And when you add this information to your resume, it will make you appear to be a more well-rounded, capable and caring person.

You could also combine the principle of volunteer work with income production. By offering others the benefit of your knowledge at a highly-discounted price, both parties will be better off. For example, unemployed people have placed ads in a local community newspaper offering to write resumes for a nominal fee. They received some income and the recipient of their service received a resume at a fraction of the cost of a "professional" resume-writing firm.

Professional "Temping".

Temporary positions are available that could augment your income while you are searching for a permanent position. They may be secretarial positions for a few hours a day or "free-lance" executive positions. The field of professional temping is growing rapidly. Management, healthcare and even media service opportunities are available on a full-time, yet temporary basis.

I seek creative ways to augment my income.

Taking this route provides a source of income, and you can usually command a higher rate than normal because the client is saving 30% or more by not paying your benefits. At the same time, you are gathering valuable experience and making contacts that could lead to full-time employment later. And you can generally work around your own schedule, leaving time for other job-search activities.

The company also benefits by employing a candidate on a temporary basis. In addition to saving the money that would otherwise be spent on benefits, they can easily terminate the agreement if it doesn't work out. For instance, if they hired a full-time employee and later found out they had made a bad decision, it could take them months to get rid of that person equitably. The company also profits from your outside viewpoint and can more easily lay you off when demand does not require your services.

A resource for more information on this topic is the book called Professional Temping, A Guide to Bridging Career Gaps. It was written by Eve Broudy, and was published by Collier Books, Macmillan Publishing Company, 866 Third Avenue, New York, New York, 10022. A company dedicated to helping you find temporary work is Management Assistant Group, 10 North Main Street, West Hartford, CT 06107. Mr. Jack Tracey is the President of that firm and he can be reached at (203) 523 - 0000.

Part-Time Work

You can take a variety of jobs on a part-time basis. These can provide badly-needed income as well as the chance to get your mind off your immediate concerns. Some of these opportunities will provide benefits, but they all provide the chance to learn a new skill, sharpen an old one, network and keep you productively busy during the slow times in your search.

Begin a new career.

In September, 1992, Shearson Lehman Brothers released a survey that examined whether people found their work personally and financially rewarding. Only 11 percent said their careers were rewarding on both counts. It reported 45 percent said they would change careers if given the chance to start over again. But they have it all wrong: people aren't **given** the chance to start a new career. They have to **take** the chance.

I remain active and maintain a positive attitude.

If you have ever wanted to try something else in your career, this is the perfect time for you to take that chance. You could open a business, buy an existing one or purchase a franchise. You could take many different directions, but be aware that any of these choices requires a great deal of time, money, commitment and effort.

The stress involved with starting a new career may be as great as what you experienced during your period of unemployment. But it is more of a <u>positive</u> tension because you're involved in a labor of love. Investigate this opportunity while you have the chance. It's a serious commitment, but for some people it's well worth the investment.

The Great American Dream

A hobby is a good way to make productive use of your time as well as help reduce your tension. You can keep busy in your woodworking shop, model-building room or on your sofa quilting for hours without thinking about anything else but what you are working on at the time.

Doing so can free your mind to create solutions that have eluded you thus far. It's been my experience that ideas "pop" into my mind when I'm doing something unrelated to thinking about a specific topic. Thus, your time spent on your hobby can further your search as it helps you relax.

The Great American Dream is to build a hobby into a lucrative business. This could be your goal, or you might gradually move in that direction as your period of unemployment grows longer. In either case, investigate the opportunities for turning your hobby into self-employment.

If you can remain active during your search you'll maintain a better attitude. When you help other people, you help yourself as you give yourself a mental boost. Look into ways to further your emotional well being and take this opportunity to investigate new directions you could take in your career.

I have a career strategy in place to achieve financial abundance.

PART FOUR: Financial planning during unemployment

Chapter Thirty Five

Evaluating Your Current Financial Situation

Your finances will have more impact on your attitude than perhaps any other single event. Unless you have the luxury of large financial resources or family members with whom you can live, the gradual depletion of your "nest egg" will erode your self-confidence and add pressure to your daily life at an increasing rate.

One of the biggest causes of this pressure is fear of the unknown. Initially you will think of the worst possible outcome, so evaluate your position and create a program to deal with it.

After learning of your unemployed status, your first thoughts will most likely be on your financial situation. Most people who have been established in their careers have significant financial obligations. These may include a mortgage, car payments, college tuition and other debts. The easy availability of home-equity loans in the past caused many people to look at a second mortgage to finance home improvements, college education or other large purchases.

Don't begin to feel overwhelmed by these debts. Review your income and expenses. Contact those who hold your greatest obligations and inform them of your new plight. You'll be surprised at the assistance and comfort these people can provide. Use this early period to resolve your financial burden, cut back on expenditures where necessary and determine a date when you need to be re-employed without wiping out all your resources.

Start a fiscal-conditioning program.

The health of your finances has a dramatic impact on your overall attitude. Your inability to pay your bills will weigh heavily on you and affect all aspects of your job search. This pressure may make you feel increasingly irritable and thus affect how well you conduct your job search, leading to an extended time of unemployment. Therefore, assess and monitor your finances right away and as often as is warranted. Equally important is the need to communicate regularly with your family

---

I have a program in place to control my finances.

members and other people affected by your financial status. Discuss ways you can work together to conserve expenditures without creating undue hardship.

First of all, assess your expected income. It will help you get an objective picture of your current status. "Only a few thousand dollars in savings" means nothing until you determine the total amount of money at your command.

You may have a severance package that will provide regular income for a limited period. Begin immediately to reduce your expenditures to make this income last as long as possible. Then look to your savings account, checking reserve, insurance cash value, certificates of deposit, stocks, investments and tax refunds. Using these will eliminate any cushion you have, but you can go through this period without increasing your debt. If your spouse works it can take a great deal of pressure off. And if you are eligible for unemployment benefits, don't overlook that source of income.

Also think of ways to augment your income. Look into finding part-time work. Perhaps if your spouse or working-age children are not working, they could re-enter the work force to provide additional income and cover your insurance. If you discuss this opportunity, be sure to consider the net impact on your income, i.e., after you deduct the costs for child care, transportation and clothes for the new job from the expected net income. You could also consider having a garage sale, which can generate hundreds of much-needed dollars in a short period of time.

Next, review your monthly expenditures and look for ways you can minimize them. There are some that may be temporarily suspended and others that can be dramatically reduced. Look at decreasing the outlays for luxury items first, including such things as alcohol, cigarettes, memberships and subscriptions, meals in restaurants and movies. Then look to see where you can cut back on essential items. For example, food is a necessity but you can eliminate snacks and convenience items. Or perhaps you could pack school/work lunches.

Create a Monthly Expense Plan as shown below. It will help if you prepare it with your entire family so they can all see where they can play a part in reducing the total expenses. A difficult part of this is to plan for unexpected events. Try to set aside a fund for family emergencies, a broken furnace and other unpredictable occurrences. But where you can, list your actual expenses specifically, show where decreases can be made and then create an estimated plan based on the implementation of the reduction program.

———————

I always look for new ways to augment my income.

Monthly Expense Plan

	Actual	Reductions	Estimated
Shelter			
Rent/Mortgage	$	$	$
Property Taxes/Condo Fee	$	$	$
Home Owner's/Renter's Insurance	$	$	$
Household Maintenance	$	$	$
Furnishings	$	$	$
Food			
Groceries	$	$	$
Household Supplies	$	$	$
Meals Away From Home	$	$	$
Clothing			
Purchases	$	$	$
Laundry/Dry Cleaning	$	$	$
Utilities			
Gas/Heating Oil	$	$	$
Electric	$	$	$
Water	$	$	$
Sewer	$	$	$
Trash Removal	$	$	$
Telephone			
Local	$	$	$
Long Distance	$	$	$
Cable Television	$	$	$
Transportation			
Auto Payment(s)	$	$	$
Gas/Oil	$	$	$
Auto Insurance	$	$	$
Auto Maintenance	$	$	$
Parking	$	$	$
Public Transportation/Tolls	$	$	$
Taxes			
Personal	$	$	$
Property Tax	$	$	$
Income Taxes	$	$	$
(Owed or paid Quarterly)			

———————

I review my monthly expenses regularly and seek new ways to minimize them.

Savings			
Reserve/Emergency Fund	$	$	$
Other	$	$	$
Regular Savings	$	$	$
Investments	$	$	$
Family Expenses			
Vacations	$	$	$
Family Entertainment	$	$	$
Child Care	$	$	$
Tuition	$	$	$
Alimony/Child Support	$	$	$
Health			
Un-insured Medical Expenses	$	$	$
Dental	$	$	$
Optical	$	$	$
Prescriptions	$	$	$
Health Insurance	$	$	$
Life Insurance	$	$	$
Disability Insurance	$	$	$
Veterinarian	$	$	$
Gym	$	$	$
Personal			
Haircuts	$	$	$
Toiletries/Cosmetics	$	$	$
Tobacco/Alcohol	$	$	$
Gifts	$	$	$
Books/Newspapers/Magazines	$	$	$
Educational Expenses	$	$	$
Hobbies	$	$	$
Allowances	$	$	$
Membership Dues	$	$	$
Charities			
Religious Organizations	$	$	$
Other Contributions	$	$	$

Total Expenses

Calculating Your Net Worth

Your net worth is the sum of your assets minus your total liabilities. It is a snapshot of your finances at a particular point in time. If you sold all your assets and paid all your debts, the resulting amount would be your net worth.

I have a written monthly-expense plan to record my expenditures.

Knowing your net worth is important because it can help you:

- determine the reserve of assets that can be easily converted to cash to help cover your expected and unexpected outlays.

- review your debts before taking on a consolidation loan.

- make decisions about your ability to meet your obligations.

- discuss your finances with greater accuracy. Professionals such as accountants, counselors, lawyers or bankers will be able to offer better advice if they have a complete picture of your financial situation.

Net Worth Statement as of / /

Asset		Liabilities	
Cash on Hand	$	Mortgage	$
Checking Accounts	$	(balance owed)	
Savings Accounts	$	Taxes Due	$
Certificates of Deposit	$	Credit Card Balances	$
U. S. Savings Bonds	$		$
Money Others Owe You	$		$
Life Insurance (Cash value)	$		$
Furniture	$		
Stocks	$	Installment Loans:	
Appliances	$	Home Improvement	$
Bonds	$	Student	$
IRAs	$	Auto	$
Annuities	$	Other	$
Pension	$	Charitable Pledges	$
Other Retirement Accounts	$	Unpaid Bills	$
Home (market value)	$	Other Liabilities	$
Other Real Estate	$		
Business Interests	$		
Automobiles	$	**Total Liabilities**	**$**
Other Vehicles	$		
Furnishings	$		
Jewelry/Furs	$		
Antiques/Silver	$		
Artwork	$		
Other Valuables	$		
Total Assets	**$**		

Total Assets - Total Liabilities = Net Worth

My net-worth statement helps me make financial decisions.

Creating your financial plan.

Once you have a good understanding of your expected income and of your estimated expenses, it's time to put these together to get a feel for the amount of time you have to find a new position. You can use the sample cash-flow chart shown below to place this in its proper perspective.

In this chart, list your revenue on a monthly basis and deduct that month's expenditures from it. The resulting figure becomes the beginning balance for the next month. As a deficit occurs, plug in the funds gained from liquidating assets or from other sources. Be sure to include regular quarterly (or other periodic) payments for insurance or other debt.

SAMPLE CASH-FLOW ANALYSIS

	JAN	FEB	MAR	APR	MAY	JUN	JUL	AUG	SEP	OCT	NOV	DEC	TOTAL
BEGINNING		3699	2892	2052	3701	2790	1862	134	417	200	467	228	
SAVINGS	4000												4000
CHECKING	500												500
INSURANCE							1500						1500
TAX RETURN			2500										2500
UNEMPLOY	800	800	800	800	800	800							4800
HOME EQUITY											1500	1500	3000
SPOUSE	1500	1500	1500	1500	1500	1500	1500	1500	1500	1500	1500	1500	18000
CERT DEP									500	1500	2000		4000
AVAILABLE	6800	5999	5192	6852	6001	5090	3362	3634	3417	3700	3467	3228	
FIXED COSTS													
HOUSING	800	800	800	800	800	800	800	800	800	800	800	800	9600
TUITION LOAN	1000	1000	1000	1000	1000	1000	1000	1000	1000	1000	1000	1000	12000
CAR PAYMENTS	290	290	290	290	290	290	290	290	290	290	290	290	3480
CAR INSURANCE	150	150	150	150	150	150	150	150	150	150	150	150	1800
MEDICAL INSURANCE	85	85	85	85	85	85	85	85	85	85	85	85	1020
GYM	50	50	50	50	50	50	50	50	50	50	50	50	600
TOTAL FIXED COSTS	2375	2375	2375	2375	2375	2375	2375	2375	2375	2375	2375	2375	**28500**

I carefully evaluate all financial-assistance programs.

VARIABLE COSTS

SEARS	20	25	25	25	25	30	30	40	40	45	50	50	**405**
VISA	35	35	50	50	50	50	50	55	55	60	60	60	**610**
FOOD	510	490	500	500	550	550	550	525	525	525	525	525	**6275**
PHONE	25	40	45	50	55	60	60	60	60	65	65	65	**650**
UTILITIES	50	50	45	45	45	55	55	55	50	50	50	50	**600**
GAS-CAR	20	25	30	35	35	30	30	30	35	35	35	35	**375**
MISC	66	67	70	71	76	78	78	77	77	78	79	79	**896**
TOTAL VARIABLE COSTS	726	732	765	776	836	853	853	842	842	858	864	864	**9807**
TOTAL COSTS	3101	3107	3140	3151	3211	3228	3228	3217	3217	3233	3239	3239	**38307**
ENDING CASH	3699	2892	2052	3701	2790	1862	134	417	200	467	228	(11)	

If there are any additional funds remaining in your home-equity account you could extend your deadline for as long as the positive balance remains. In this example there is a one-year period before there is a need to begin selling fixed assets.

There are several notes of caution here. First, don't panic and pay off all your bills right away. And don't immediately cash in all of your stocks and CDs, etc. Work through your savings initially, and then more-liquid assets, before you cash in the other items. Delay selling your fixed assets (house, furniture or car) for as long as possible.

Second, before you find yourself getting into financial trouble, talk with the people carrying your debt. They will be much more sympathetic and willing to help you if you alert them to your situation and demonstrate that you don't want to default on your loan. In most cases they will work with you to determine a new re-payment schedule which in itself will take some of the pressure off you.

Furthermore, if you receive a large severance package, don't immediately go out and pay off all your debts. Continue making the minimum payments, but save as much as you can for essential needs: mortgage payments, food, utilities and job-search expenses. If you are eligible for a lump-sum payout from your pension or 401(k) plan, you should consider not taking it as current income. Look into the tax implications and penalties for cashing in this money early. You have sixty days (not two months) to make your decision before you must pay taxes on it.

I communicate regularly with my family.

There are several options open to you. For example, you could roll it into your next employer's pension plan. Or you could place it into a roll-over Individual Retirement Account (IRA) at a mutual fund or a bank. In addition, you could leave it with your ex-employer to manage, provided you can tap the fund as needed. A good IRA investment for the unemployed is a safe money-market mutual fund that preserves the principal while giving you ready access to cash.

Make sure you investigate all the financial assistance that may be available to you. Don't allow your pride or ego to get in the way of providing for yourself and your family. There is no shame in standing in an unemployment line, and you may find your friends waiting there with you. You and your previous employers have paid into these funds so now it's your turn to collect what's rightfully yours.

Financial Assistance Programs

1) Unemployment Compensation

Unemployment compensation is the most important program for the laid-off worker who has been actively employed for twenty weeks or more before the job loss, although the requirements vary from state to state. Workers displaced by plant shutdowns, reductions in the work force, temporary or seasonal layoffs or termination without cause usually qualify.

File an application at the state unemployment-compensation office nearest you immediately upon notification of the layoff. Bring your termination slip as well as identification, last pay stub, W-2 form, Social Security card and company identification with you when you apply. You may also want to bring a book to read since the process may take some time to complete. If you are denied benefits you should file an appeal quickly. In most states you have a limited time in which to file an appeal.

2) Trade Adjustment Act (TAA).

Under federal law you are eligible for financial assistance if your unemployment is directly attributable to foreign competition.

3) Early Retirement (Social Security).

If you are sixty-two or older, you may choose to take Social Security early-retirement benefits. If you do, you may still return to work if you are re-hired. This is a good option for temporary employment.

I communicate regularly with my creditors.

4) Aid to Families With Dependent Children (AFDC).

AFDC is the primary assistance program for low-income families with children. AFDC is funded by the federal and state governments and is commonly referred to as "welfare." AFDC is usually administrated through the state Department of Human Resources or Public Assistance.

Benefit levels, eligibility and support services vary from state to state. In most states, low income, single-parent families with children under age eighteen can qualify. In some states, a family with both parents in place is eligible. In other states, a two-parent family where one is disabled can qualify. Check eligibility requirements in your state. You may need proof of income, Social Security number, birth certificates for your children or other documentation. Call ahead to find out what you need to bring.

5) Supplemental Security Income (SSI).

Supplemental Security Income is a program of the federal Social Security Administration. SSI has very narrow eligibility requirements. In general, only those with virtually no income and who don't qualify for other assistance programs may be eligible for SSI. Apply at your local Social Security office.

6) "Union Privilege" Programs.

Union Privilege is an AFL-CIO endorsed, nonprofit corporation that provides financial services to union members through their unions. There are currently six Union Privilege programs:

- The Union Privilege Credit Card lowers the finance charges and fees paid by union members.
- A life insurance program offers affordable coverage to ensure union members' families are fully protected.
- Legal Service makes legal assistance more accessible and affordable.
- A *Health Needs Service* helps lower the cost of prescription medications.
- The UnionRATE Savings Program is designed to provide union members with a higher rate of return than regular bank passbook-savings accounts.
- The Union Privilege Travel Service helps cut the high cost of travel.

I address my daily challenges with energy and optimism.

Programs available to the injured or disabled.

These programs are available to you if your unemployment is a result of an injury, severe illness or other physical disability.

1) Workers' Compensation.

This state program is for workers injured on the job. In some circumstances an injury sustained travelling to and from work may be covered. Workers' compensation laws in most states require that the employer be responsible for all medical bills arising from an on-the-job injury and for payment of lost wages up to a certain level and for a certain length of time. Benefits vary from state to state.

2) Social Security Disability.

If you are disabled through injury or illness to an extent that will prevent you from working for at least a year or more, you can apply for Social Security disability benefits. Disability benefits provide a minimum income for Americans unable to support themselves because of disability.

It generally takes six months to a year to qualify with even the most extensive disability. Every effort will be made by Social Security to prove that your are physically able to work or that there is some kind of work that you can do with your limited physical disability.

3) Vocational Rehabilitation Services.

If an injury or disability makes it impossible for you to return to your old job, but you can recover and retrain for another kind of job, you are a candidate for vocational rehabilitation, usually provided by state governments and some nonprofit agencies such as Goodwill and Easter Seals.

Determine your Goal Line.

Evaluate your total financial program and determine the amount of time you have to locate a new position. Generally you'll find that you have more time than you thought before resorting to more drastic means of generating funds, such as selling your home or going to relatives for assistance.

Once you have this under control, begin to implement your plan. Communicate regularly with your family and creditors to keep every-

---

Adversity reveals my true nature and I like what I see.

body up to date on your financial status and job-search progress. Finding new ways to increase your revenue and decrease your expenses will have a positive impact on your goal line, thus relieving you of more pressure.

I objectively evaluate my finances and take appropriate action.

Chapter Thirty Six

Putting Your Fiscal-Control Program into Action.

Once you have your financial plan in place, you should put it into action. For some inexplicable reason, the income portion of your cash-flow chart never seems to add up to your forecast. And the expenses you so carefully analyzed earlier in your search always seem to be larger than you had planned. Unexpected car repairs, medical bills and other items will take their toll on your budget and frame of mind.

Those entering a job search for the first time will be astonished at the expenses that will be incurred in their quest. Costs for printing, telephone calls, travel, postage, clothes and miscellaneous items add up very quickly and are difficult to forecast.

Use your new tools wisely.

Your early confidence may lead you to continue spending at a rate lower than before, but not quite as low as it should be. Depending on your severance package, your income may still arrive at the same rate it did when you were employed. A severance package is good for your peace of mind, but if not properly managed, it could spell future trouble.

Use your Monthly Expense Plan as a tool for monitoring your ongoing expenditures. Create columns with headings for each month and compare your actual outlays with those you have forecast. With your family, regularly discuss your progress. Always offer accolades to those who helped conserve the most. And at the same time refrain from raising your voice to those who continue spending at the same rate. Discuss in a conversational tone the ways you have agreed upon to save and plan new ways to do so.

Dealing with creditors.

Just as you need open lines of communication with your family and significant others, you need to communicate openly with your creditors. It's best to contact them in writing since you both will then

---

I allocate sufficient funds to cover job-search expenses.

have written documentation of your proposed re-payment plan. In addition, you won't get upset or confused if the creditor tries to intimidate you verbally. You could use a letter similar to that shown below to make the initial contact with each of your creditors.

Sample Letter to a Creditor

Date

Creditor's Name

Address

Re: Your Account Number

Attention Account Services:

    I have recently become unemployed. After careful examination of my finances, I feel it is necessary to make an adjustment to the way in which I am currently paying each of my creditors. Doing so will insure that you are regularly compensated until my unemployment is ended. After drafting a strict budget for my expenses, I find that I must ask you to accept a reduced payment schedule for a period of time. Rather than my regular monthly payment of $, please accept payments of $ until I am through this emergency. You can expect my next payment on (date) and on the first day of each month after that.

    It's very important to me to meet my financial obligations. I appreciate your cooperation with my plan to restructure my payments. I am earnestly seeking new employment and will update you every 60 days on my status at that time. You can be sure that I will resume normal payments as soon as possible. If there are any changes, I will notify you of them as soon as possible. Thank you.

Sincerely,

Your Name

Address

Telephone Number

    Notify your creditors before you begin to get behind in your payments. They are easier to work with if they know ahead of time that there could be a problem. It also shows that you are sincere in your

---

I always monitor my expenses.

efforts to deal with them and that you are concerned about your debts and your intention to repay them.

Similarly, if you are making child support or alimony payments and are unable to meet them, contact the clerk of the court and explain why. Failing to notify the court of your inability to pay can result in legal problems. Also stay in touch (in writing) with your ex-spouse to avoid unnecessary legal action.

Even if you cannot pay creditors the amount they want, make your best effort to pay something regularly. Partial payments may keep your account from being turned over to a collection agency.

Maintaining shelter.

Mortgage payments.

Generally, the creditor does not want to foreclose on the mortgage. Some lenders may allow skipped payments and others may suggest partial or interest-only payments for one to six months. Your home is usually the largest single investment you have made, and it's an important part of your lifestyle. Therefore, your mortgage or rent payment should be your top priority in paying your bills each month.

When you contact your mortgage holder, you could be intimidated by terms if you are not familiar with them. You should know the definition of these terms:

- Default: a mortgage is in default when more than one payment is due but unpaid. Mortgage contracts generally allow for foreclosure to start when a default exists, although most lenders will not act that quickly.

- Equity: the value of your property minus what you still owe on it.

- Forbearance: an oral or written agreement to repay the delinquency over a period of time so that the loan payments can be brought up to date.

- Foreclosure: the process by which the lender takes over your property when you fail to meet the terms of your mortgage contract.

- Section 8: a government program providing private housing for low-income families by subsidizing rents. The amount of rent assistance is determined by your income.

I know this is a temporary condition and I triumph over it.

A variety of repayment alternatives are available to you. Seek information from qualified professionals for advice on how you can repay your debt. Some of the alternatives you could investigate include temporary forbearance, extending your loan, refinancing, selling or voluntary surrender of the property to the lender instead of foreclosure and bankruptcy.

Once foreclosure begins, you may not be able to sell your home. Voluntary surrender is sometimes a less harmful option if you have little equity in your home. You lose the equity (as you would in a foreclosure) but you avoid having a foreclosure on your credit record. Your primary motive at this point should be to avoid foreclosure and bankruptcy.

If your mortgage is federally insured (such as FHA, HUD or VA) a special provision may exist for helping families in financial trouble. This may extend the period before foreclosure or even result in the government agency buying you out.

In areas with high poverty or unemployment rates, the Federal Emergency Management Agency (FEMA) provides funding for small grants through local community agencies for one-time assistance with a rent or mortgage payment. In most communities, the United Way is the place to start. To qualify for a FEMA grant, you must meet individual agency eligibility requirements which are currently pegged to your financial status.

Rent payments. First, be familiar with the terms and conditions in your lease. Then talk with your landlord immediately. The landlord may accept partial payment for one or two months. Ask if you can do some maintenance work in place of part of your rental costs. You may want to look for less expensive housing, but be realistic and remember to include moving expenses, lease-breaking penalties, deposits and family adjustments in your calculations. If you live in public housing or a Section 8 home, notify the public housing authority about your reduction in income. Your rent may be reduced to a level in line with your new circumstances.

Dealing with a utility company.

Contact your electric or gas company immediately. Arrange a payment schedule so your bill does not continue to grow. You should also check with them to see if you are eligible for the Low-Income Home Energy Assistance Program (LIHEAP). Avoid a disconnection notice by telling them about your being recently unemployed and working out a plan to:

My fiscal responsibility is forming good habits.

- decrease your usage as much as possible.
- participate in a utility-company-sponsored weatherization program.
- enter into a budget-payment plan so your bills remain consistent throughout the year.

Dealing with the telephone company.

Telephone service is not an essential human need and may be disconnected if a bill is not paid. Yet it is vital to your job-search success, so do all that you can to keep it connected. Avoid the threat of shut-off by keeping bills to a minimum. Eliminate excess services like unlisted numbers and Total Phone. Curtail long-distance calling and keep necessary calls to a minimum.

Making automobile payments.

If you do not make payments on your car loan, it can be repossessed. In some states, the value of your vehicle (not the amount received by the sale) must be applied to your balance. However, you are liable for the "deficiency" balance owing after the value is subtracted from the amount of your loan.

Continuing payments on credit cards.

Credit card payments are usually part of your credit rating. If you are late on your payments, these facts will be reported to the credit bureau. Do not use your credit cards no matter how much you think you "need" something. And be especially careful not to get a cash advance off one credit card to pay off another bill.

Remaining insured.

There may be a grace period in making insurance payments, but check with your insurance company to make sure. If your car is paid for, you could cut the premium cost by increasing the deductible on Collision and Comprehensive. Check your state's laws about liability coverage before making any changes.

In addition, find out from your former employer if your health insurance is continued and for how long. Determine who is responsible for the premium and at what amount. The 1986 Combined Omnibus Budget Reconciliation Act (COBRA) is a federal law that provides the

---

My family and friends support me.

right for each worker (in companies with 20 or more employees) to continue their health insurance in the event of a layoff, strike or other displacement from the job at the same cost your employer was paying, plus 2%. You have 60 days to elect this option.

In some states, COBRA insurance protection lasts for up to 24 months. It may be expensive, depending on your family's size. But it offers protection to those who otherwise could not get medical insurance.

Review each of your policies and list what's covered, any deductibles (and if you have reached your deductible for the year), monthly payments and terms under which coverage ends. Call or write your insurance agent and explain your situation. Determine your minimum coverage needs and then ask your agent to suggest a different payment plan or different coverage. Perhaps you could lower your premiums by changing to a quarterly or semiannual payment plan with the same coverage, converting to term insurance and changing to more basic coverage that meets your minimum needs, or by using accrued dividends to reduce your premium.

Putting food on the table.

The need for good food does not stop just because you are unemployed. But even if you have to cut back on your food budget, you can still have nutritious meals if you plan well.

You could apply for food stamps. The U.S. Department of Agriculture distributes food stamps through state agencies. They can be used like money to purchase food only, although some states may give cash instead of stamps.

Try to stretch your shopping budget by planning a week in advance. Then make a shopping list and stick to it. Look at the food sales and even the generic items. Saving and using coupons can greatly reduce the cost of food and other retail items. Go shopping as infrequently as possible and leave the kids home if you can. Don't shop when you are hungry or hurried. Take time to compare prices and brands before making your purchasing decision.

You could also consider other shopping options. For example, you could grow your own vegetables or barter with your neighbor. Sometimes farmers let people pick their own fruit and vegetables and charge them a reduced price.

The Women and Infant Care (WIC) Program provides nutritious food for low-income women or low-income parents with newborn

---

I believe there's always a way to succeed.

infants with low body weight. If qualified, you will receive WIC vouchers that can be used at food stores like money for specific items. In most communities, the Salvation Army, charities and other nonprofit agencies, unions or churches will provide a limited supply of basic groceries to a family in need.

Debt consolidation loans.

You may benefit from consolidating some or all of your debt into one loan. The monthly payment of this new loan is normally lower than the combined monthly total of the individual payments. The advantage of this is that you can protect your credit rating by paying off your debts before they become delinquent. It is also easier to keep track of one monthly debt payment than many individual ones.

However, disadvantages to consolidation loans exist. The lower payment may tempt you to increase your debt in other areas, such as with credit cards. Moreover, consolidation loans often have higher interest rates than those of your original debts. In addition, the longer repayment period increases the amount paid in finance charges.

Home equity loans.

You can also borrow against the equity in your home to consolidate your debts. The advantage is that the interest may be deductible on your federal tax return (if the amount borrowed is $100,000 or less). In addition, the interest rate is usually lower than that on traditional debt-consolidation loans. The major disadvantage is that the loan is secured by your home. If you can't repay the loan you could lose your home.

Consumer Credit Counseling Service.

The CCCS is a nonprofit organization that helps people in financial difficulty, with approximately 500 offices around the United States. The people associated with the CCCS offer money-management counseling sessions and debt-management programs. In the latter, the CCCS arranges a repayment plan acceptable to your creditors, but realistic in light of your ability to pay. A monthly fee may apply and you are charged by them based upon your ability to pay.

Look for the red flags.

Depending on the length of time that you are unemployed, you may begin to experience the warning signs of a credit crisis, regardless of

---

I believe in myself and my ability to succeed.

your efforts to control your expenses. These indicators occur when you are at or near your limit on your credit cards, charge more each month than you make in payments, don't know how much you owe, are using cash advances from credit cards to pay other creditors, have defaulted on your rent or mortgage payment, have paid a bill with a post-dated check, have had a check returned for insufficient funds or are facing creditor lawsuits and/or repossessions.

When combined with lack of job-search success and the resulting frustration, they will have a dramatic impact on your attitude, self-talk and family relations. As early as you can, try to recognize and deal with the pressure and seek to reduce its impact on you and the other people affected by it.

Call for help.

State and federal organizations ensure that your rights are protected under the law. If you are unsure of your rights or have questions about what you should do, contact an attorney. If you cannot afford an attorney or wish to investigate your options on your own, contact the appropriate agency in your state for more information.

I persist in the face of adversity.

Chapter Thirty Seven

When You're in Financial Trouble

As your period of unemployment is extended beyond your initial plans, your financial resources will become depleted. Most likely your unemployment benefits have run out. And as your savings account is closed and your home-equity balance is at its maximum, there seem to be few places to turn for assistance.

Your debtors may begin to call more frequently, and as you run out of excuses for them, you could become increasingly depressed. Your family members making what appear to you as unnecessary purchases also affects your relationship with them. The extra desserts, alcohol, golf games and other nonessential items now become the objects of contention. If your spouse continues to pay for these over your protestations, you could easily lose your fragile self-control and vent your anger in ways that could cause damage to your relationship.

If you do nothing to reverse the effects of the pressure placed upon you by your deteriorating finances, you could end up in bankruptcy and/or divorce court. Bankruptcy may be the most attractive alternative for some people, but it is not always the best path to take. Seriously consider every other possible alternative, and seek legal counsel before deciding on this solution.

Rethink your life.

Take time to re-evaluate your goals. Talk to your family and friends and try to think of other options you can take. Decide what additional sacrifices you are able and willing to make in order to see yourself through this period, with your family unit intact. This time will be a very unpleasant one that tests your relationship, but it's a time that must be gone through. Below are examples of options you could consider:

- Look for less-expensive housing. Move to an apartment or to a smaller apartment, perhaps further out into the country, away from the more expensive city life. Be sure

I take time to re-evaluate my goals and my life.

to consider the quality of life, schools and the opportunities for employment in your new location.

- If you decide to sell your home, be sure to weigh the emotional impact on all family members as well as the financial implications of moving. Is your home saleable in its present condition, or will you have to make any expensive repairs? Will you be able to sell it at a price high enough to cover your mortgages?
- Should you lower your salary expectations at the same time and seek a less-challenging position?
- Could your children temporarily leave college or transfer to a less expensive school?
- Do you have any relatives you could contact for a loan or for temporary housing?

By the time you get to this point, few options are open that offer you an attractive alternative. If you have no family obligations, the choices may be easier only because your decisions affect you and not your spouse and children. Regardless of your family status, when the collection agencies increase their efforts to seek money from you, little solace remains.

When the bill collector comes.

Even when your accounts have been turned over to a collection agency, you still have certain rights. You can write the bill collector saying that you want him/her to cease communicating with you. The collecting agent must then stop contacting you except to advise you of any legal action he/she intends to take. If a debt collector violates the law, you may notify the Federal Trade Commission ({202} 326 - 2222) or sue for actual and punitive damages.

Your rights under the Fair Debt Collection Practices Act.

The Fair Debt Collection Practices Act applies to any personal, family or household debt and covers debt collectors who regularly collect debts for others, but not the creditors themselves or their attorneys. Collection agencies are prohibited from harassing, oppressing or abusing you, as well as threatening to take your property without the right to do so. They also are not allowed to make untrue statements, for example statements falsely implying that they are attorneys or work for a credit bureau or Social Security.

My decisions are the best for my loved ones and our future together.

The law further prohibits collection agencies from contacting you at inconvenient times (defined as before 8:00 am or after 9:00 pm) or places. The collector may not contact you at work if your employer disapproves. If you wish to stop this practice, you need to notify the debt collector of this fact in writing. They also must not tell anyone else that you are behind on your debts, and they cannot use obscene language.

You may have to bite the bullet.

If you feel (after consultation with professional advisors) that you must take drastic measures, you might consider bankruptcy. But it should be a last resort, even though it may be the best move for you. Seek legal advice before making this move.

Don't be afraid of the word "bankruptcy." It can be a valuable tool. Federal bankruptcy laws were passed to protect you and to allow for relief from most unsecured debts. Bankruptcy laws allow you to make a fresh start and protect most of your personal property (under certain circumstances this includes some of the equity in your home).

Bankruptcy in any form is not desirable, but if you have staggering debt it may be your best option. Don't look at it as a financial (or social) disaster. If you deem it necessary to file for bankruptcy, you cannot apply for bankruptcy for another six years. So make sure your decision is well thought out and absolutely necessary. Before you make any lasting and final decisions, seek legal counsel about the options open to you:

1) **Chapter Thirteen (of the federal bankruptcy law).** It is sometimes called the Wage Earner's Plan and allows you to repay debts under bankruptcy court supervision while being protected from creditors' harassment and lawsuits. An advantage of Chapter Thirteen over straight bankruptcy is that you can usually keep all of your assets. In addition, you can do your own filing (there will be a $120 fee), but you may want to hire an attorney because of all the complications that could arise. When filing for Chapter Thirteen, you must submit a plan to repay your debt within 3 years (although you can take up to 5 years if the court permits). If your plan is approved, monthly payments are made to a trustee who distributes money to your creditors.

2) **Straight bankruptcy.** If all else fails, straight bankruptcy (Chapter 7 of the federal bankruptcy laws) may be your only option. The mechanics of filing require that you draw up and file a petition listing your assets and liabilities (your statement of net worth). There is a $120 filing fee, and if the court approves your petition, all of your assets (except for

---

I do something every day to achieve financial freedom.

certain items) will be sold and the proceeds distributed among creditors listed on your petition. Straight bankruptcy does not discharge all your debt. You must still pay alimony and child support, taxes, student loans, and anything else not listed on your bankruptcy petition. Be aware the bankruptcy information will remain on your credit bureau file for 10 years, and it could make getting credit and possibly employment or rental housing difficult in the future.

Utilizing your credit bureau.

Sometimes problems with debt collectors can keep you from restoring your credit rating after you go back to work. In this case you may want to contact a local credit bureau to review your credit record. Credit bureaus collect credit information about consumers for the use of businesses to whom consumers apply for credit. Credit bureaus can provide information only to:

- creditors who are granting or have granted you credit
- employers considering you for employment
- insurers considering issuing you an insurance policy
- government agencies reviewing your financial status in connection with issuing you a license

If you contact the credit bureau, it must let you know the nature and substance of all information contained in your credit report, inform you of the sources of its information, provide you with the names of employers, creditors and others who have recently received reports about you and re-investigate within a reasonable time any information you dispute. Take advantage of your rights with the credit bureau and make sure you are being treated fairly.

If in their investigation the credit bureau finds the information is inaccurate or cannot be verified, the information must be corrected or deleted. On the other hand, if the information is accurate, the credit bureau must allow you to write a brief statement of dispute and include it in all future reports. If any deletion or notation is made you may request that the new information be sent to any employer receiving information during the past two years and any other person receiving a report during the past six months.

If you are sued.

If you are unable to make your payments, the creditors can sue you to recover the amount of the bill. If you have wages or income and

---

I am a wealthy person in many ways.

have not made acceptable arrangements, your income may be garnished (money may be automatically deducted from your pay to pay off a debt). Garnishment can only be done by court order. You have a right to be heard before a garnishment can be ordered. You may avoid the garnishment if you can show the judge that you are doing your best. That's why it's so important to make any payment you can to show your good faith in meeting your obligations.

There's always hope.

It's not mandatory that you reach this stage in your finances. Something will come up when you least expect it that will help you through these tough times. Even going through bankruptcy proceedings marks the end of one era and the beginning of a new life. Do all that you can (and all that you must) to keep yourself and your family intact. Read Coping With Unemployment over again to help you deal with your finances and get your life back in order.

I am free of financial worry.

Chapter Thirty Eight

The True Benefits of Unemployment

Few things in life will challenge your emotions, strength and relationships as will a prolonged period of unemployment. It's a time that will test your resolve and belief in yourself. But from these ashes will rise a new person, one who has overcome a harrowing ordeal, and succeeded.

Most people think the benefits of unemployment are paid in terms of dollars over a limited number of weeks. This is not the case. The real benefit of being unemployed is what you *become* as you deal successfully with all the challenges throughout your search.

Once you accept a job offer, your initial feeling may be that finally there is an end to your pressure and worry. But this is actually a beginning. You're starting the rest of your life as a new person. You'll never be the same because of what you've gone through. A job search doesn't take something out of you, it gets something out of you. It doesn't do something to you, but for you.

The first indication of this is a feeling of self-respect. As you look back over all that you have accomplished, your self-esteem will improve immediately. You realize that you've triumphed over tremendous adversity and that you *are* greater than anything that can happen to you.

The new magnificent seven.

You'll discover that you've grown in seven significant areas. Unemployment has taught you to control your attitude, finances and actions and you've developed the self-discipline necessary to utilize and manage your time.

In addition, you now understand the power of commitment. Your unfailing determination has seen you through a great deal of personal suffering and misfortune. And because of that, problems will no longer seem ominous, because you've been challenged by one of life's

---

I do what I must to succeed.

greatest tests, and won. You overcame frustration, depression, financial and personal crisis, and succeeded. That is no ordinary feat.

The knowledge that you can overcome significant obstacles will have a positive impact on your confidence. Your self-image will take an enormous positive step and you'll walk taller with this increased self-esteem.

As you think back on all the rejection you withstood, you'll feel self-satisfied. You know that you had the courage to handle rejection, frustration and dejection even when you felt that you couldn't. In so doing, your creativity was tested and used adroitly. No obstacle in the future can withstand your ability to see the perfect form that lurks within it.

Your ability to focus all your efforts on the attainment of your goal will benefit you throughout your lifetime. Concentration upon a specific objective is rewarded with success, as you have discovered.

And from now on you'll find yourself evaluating and correcting all your major actions, so that future performance is improved. Competition with yourself takes the focus off what others are doing. You can now grow and succeed according to what's important to you.

The essence of Coping With Unemployment is related in a poem describing my feelings during a bout with unemployment:

IT'S ALL UP TO YOU
Brian Jud

When you first learn the verdict that you've lost your job,
Your heart starts to flutter, your brain starts to throb.
Your knees start to tremble, your mouth starts to frown;
Time seems to stand still and your world's upside down.

You look to the past when things were secure,
Without steady income your future's unsure.
The plans you had set for all your tomorrows,
Are dashed upon rocks as you wallow in sorrow.

Deep down you know you still have the chance,
To rise from the ashes, your life to enhance.
Unless you control the way that you think,
Your thoughts will get worse and continue to sink.

I triumph over unemployment because I'm committed to success.

"What will I do?" will run through your mind.
"I've a wife and two kids, and debts of all kinds."
"I've nothing in savings" you'll further lament.
To buy food and clothing, and still pay the rent.

The first thing you'll do is count all your cash.
What's left in insurance, what else have you stashed.
Once you've determined the size of your credits,
You'll try to balance it with all your debits.

It matters not how many times that you figure,
Somehow the difference only gets bigger.
It weighs on your mind, your family you tell,
To cut back on spending; you try not to yell.

From all your notations you'll come to a date,
That you must have a job, but it's hard to relate
To others the worry and pressure you feel,
With self-doubt and negative thoughts at your heels.

You may choose to allow an hour or two,
To think of the worst, to feel down and blue.
But if you allow these thoughts to persist,
You'll cripple your efforts, your mind you will twist.

You haven't the time to wait and to see,
Or worry and think "What will happen to me?"
You must reach down for a good attitude,
You can and you must, it's all up to you.

Control all your assets, especially your mind,
Ration them out and don't get behind
In making deposits both fiscal and mental,
'Cause keeping your balance is not incidental.

Talk to your spouse or significant other,
Seek out your friends, but don't let them smother
Your positive outlook and self-less persistence
To overcome odds and hapless resistance.

Every step I take is helping me form a new, stronger character.

Compete with yourself for what you can strengthen,
Work to get better, but don't even mention
The things that are yours but that you cannot change
Like sex, race and height, or years home on the range.

Your confidence lets you trust in your actions,
While courage helps you deal with the factions
That offer a negative view of your life,
Though trying to help, they can cut like a knife.

Constantly seek to apply innovation,
And daily utilize self-affirmations.
Commit all your efforts to finding success,
And sooner, not later, a job you'll possess.

Your clear mental image now helps you see,
The job that you want, and all you can be.
You'll send 500 letters, the price you will pay
To seek a position with your resume.

What words can you write that will make them see,
That you're the best person for their company.
You'll write a first draft and then yet another
As frustration re-sets, you'll think "Why bother?"

Again you'll reach down and lean on your strengths,
For you must keep on working and go to all lengths
To do what you must to see this search through
Just never forget it's all up to you.

A month will go by, perhaps even three.
You may even start thinking, "Why don't they want me?"
You've written a resume and cover letter,
Now sit down again, and make them much better.

You know it takes time for prospective employers,
To make up their minds, but it's still a destroyer
Of your self-esteem which continues erosion,
But courage wins out and this time you're chosen.

I balance my time among personal, family and career needs.

The call finally comes and your heart starts to pound
As you answer his questions about your background.
You hear that positive tone in his voice
That signals to you that he's made his choice.

"Can you come in next Friday at two?"
You agree on a time for your interview.
There's much to be done between now and then,
To prepare yourself and learn all you can.

As you walk toward his door your tension will mount.
You'll think "Here's my chance, on me I must count."
Before going in you say one last prayer,
Then smooth out your clothes and feather your hair.

As you firmly shake hands and walk to your seat,
Again you will feel your heart skip a beat.
But each passing moment reduces self-doubt,
You feel better by letting your natural-self out.

Your mouth starts to moisten, your shoulders unstiffen.
More questions he'll ask and carefully listen
To you as you answer and move and relate,
Your accomplishments, skills and talents to date.

The questions subside as he's trying to gauge
If you'll be a good choice, then you're on the stage.
The next phase begins, it's your turn to share,
The questions you have and how you've prepared.

Since you've planned all the questions to ask,
You sound like a pro and up to the task
Of filling the duties the job will entail,
He's almost convinced, you're the one who won't fail.

You're asked to come back, your spirits don't sag.
Although you're more hopeful, it's not in the bag.
You're afraid to start thinking that this job you've landed,
'Cause you've been there before and come back empty handed.

I am a better person for what I have conquered.

But after what seems like an infinite time,
There comes the conclusion, he makes up his mind.
You now sense what's coming, the tension starts mounting,
You hope the pay's more than on what you were counting.

You're breath you are holding, your fingers you cross
You want to get rid of your albatross.
Then the offer is made, you accept in a hurry,
There's finally an end to your pressure and worry.

You try to contain the elation you feel,
Until you're outside, then a moment you steal
Some time for a prayer to silently thank
Those who stood by your side and didn't break rank.

It's good to do that, but never lose track,
It was you who kept at it when things looked so black.
You planned and you worked but you never quit.
As the dollars kept dwindling, the bullet you bit.

You worried and fretted but kept reaching down,
For substance and courage and somehow you found
The will to keep knocking when others shut doors,
So when backs are all patted, make sure one of them's yours.

Don't give up.

Do everything that you can to reach your goal of finding a
suitable long-term career position. You can do it, and you will. It's all up
to you.

_____

If it's to be, it's up to me.

Appendix A

Motivational and inspirational messages can help you restore and maintain a successful attitude as you cope with your unemployment. Below is a list of quotations which have helped me get through some difficult times in my life, and I wanted to share them with you.

These statements are meant to be <u>used</u>, not just read. Study them as you would a textbook rather than as you would read a chapter of a fiction book. Think about the meaning behind the words as you read. Don't just scan the words trying to read as many as you can in one sitting. If you think about how you can apply each concept in your life, they become useful and beneficial.

Read several of them and think about what they mean or could mean to you. Write down your thoughts in your Career Journal and use them to stimulate other ideas that will help you feel better and renew your spirit. Copy your favorite quotations on 3" x 5" cards and keep them in your glove compartment, purse or briefcase. Then refer back to them when you need a little extra positive feedback.

My personal library consists of over eight hundred books and video tapes as well as forty (six-cassette) audio tape programs. I lean on these regularly as a source of information, motivation and relaxation. I have condensed the millions of words in these volumes into a few that I hope will provide you with the spark that you need to revitalize yourself and move you closer to your ultimate objective.

"You may have to fight a battle more than once to win it." Margaret Thatcher

"High expectations are the key to everything." Sam Walton

"Fall seven times, stand up eight." Japanese proverb

"The worst bankrupt is the person who has lost his enthusiasm." H. W. Arnold

Anthony Robbins (in his <u>Personal Power</u> audio tape program):

"There's always a way.

The past does not equal the future.

Live with passion."

"It is often hard to distinguish between the hard knocks in life and those of opportunity." Frederick Phillips

———

"Always give a hundred percent and you'll never have to second-guess yourself." Tommy John

"You can't build a reputation on what you are going to do." Henry Ford

"In life, as in a football game, the principle to follow is: hit the line hard." Theodore Roosevelt

"Courage is contagious. When a brave man takes a stand, the spines of others are stiffened." Billy Graham

"Better to ask twice than to lose your way once." Danish proverb

Maxwell Maltz (in his book Psycho-Cybernetic Principles for Creative Living):

> "It is within our power to set realistic goals and move to achieve them.
>
> Every day, tell yourself you were born into the world to succeed, not fail.
>
> When the breaks are going against you, try all the harder and stand strongly behind the one thing you can really count on: your faith in yourself.
>
> We turn a crisis into an opportunity when we call upon the memory of past successes to help us master it and move forward.
>
> Turning a creative thought into a creative performance should be a daily objective.
>
> Relaxation means total immersion in today. You must escape the catastrophes of the past and the uncertainties of the future.
>
> By letting off steam, you reduce the strain on your internal machinery and create a climate for growth.
>
> Symptoms of failure:
>
>> Frustration
>>
>> Aggressiveness (misdirected)
>>
>> Insecurity
>>
>> Loneliness
>>
>> Uncertainty
>>
>> Resentment
>>
>> Emptiness"

"If you wait, all that happens is that you get older." Larry McMurtry

"Ninety-nine percent of the failures come from people who have the habit of making excuses." George Washington Carver

"One of the most dangerous forms of human error is forgetting what one is trying to achieve," Paul Nitze

"I don't believe in pessimism. If something doesn't come up the way you want, forge ahead. If you think it's going to rain, it will." Clint Eastwood

"Better bend than break." Scottish proverb

"How we spend our days is, of course, how we spend our lives." Annie Dillard

Denis Waitley (in his tape program The Psychology of Winning):

> "Burning desire is the best antidote for fear and despair.
>
> It's not what you think you are that holds you back, it's what you think you are not.
>
> Winners build for the future but learn from the past."

"There are few things more consoling to people than the mere finding that others have felt as they feel." Frederick Faber

"Look at a day when you are supremely satisfied at the end. It's not a day when you lounge around doing nothing. It's when you've had everything to do, and you've done it." Margaret Thatcher

"It is one of the beautiful compensations of this life that no one can sincerely try to help another without helping himself." Charles Dudley Warner

"To think too long about doing a thing often becomes its undoing." Eva Young

"Unless each day can be looked back upon by an individual as one in which he has had some fun, some joy, some real satisfaction, that day is a loss." Dwight D. Eisenhower

"The greatest discovery of my generation is that a human being can alter his life by altering his attitude." William James

"Ideas are   like rabbits. You get a couple and learn how to handle them, and pretty soon you have a dozen." John Steinbeck

"Change starts when someone sees the next step." William Drayton

"A man cannot be comfortable without his own approval." Mark Twain

"Climb up on a hill at sunrise. Everybody needs perspective once in a while, and you'll find it there." Rob Sagendorph

---

Zig Ziglar:

> "Success is not a destination, it's a journey.
>
> Quit counting time and start making time count.
>
> You don't drown by falling into water, you only drown if you stay there."

"Don't aim for success if you want it; just do what you love and believe in, and it will come naturally." David Frost

"What I'm looking for is a blessing that's *not* in disguise." Kitty O'Neill Collins

"I have learned to use the word *impossible* with greatest caution." Wernher von Braun

Optimism is a cheerful frame of mind that enables a teakettle to sing though in hot water up to it's nose." Harold Helfer

"The day will happen whether or not you get up." John Ciardi

Goals are dreams with deadlines." Diana Scharf Hunt

"People often say that this or that person has not yet found himself. But the self is not something that one finds. It is something that one creates." Thomas Szasz

"Most problems precisely defined are already partially solved." Harry Lorayne

Robert Shuller (from several of his books, tapes and personal presentations):

> "Approach every door with a new attitude. Don't let previous negative experiences dictate how you will treat the next person or event.
>
> Tough times never last, but tough people do.
>
> Nothing is impossible until you stop setting goals.
>
> Aim at nothing and you'll succeed.
>
> The first "anything" is always the hardest.
>
> Believe there is a solution to every problem. You will never find the solution if you are undecided.
>
> Never look at what you have lost. Always look at what you have left.
>
>> Some men die by shrapnel.
>> Some go down in flames.
>> Most men perish inch by inch,
>> Playing little games.

When you can't solve the problem, manage it.

Start small and succeed. Then move on to bigger things.

It's better to do something imperfectly than to do nothing perfectly.

The demanding person runs into resistance, the defeated person runs into indifference and the dedicated person runs into help.

I affirm that I will never be defeated because I will never quit."

"A stumble may prevent a fall." English proverb

"Some men see things as they are and say "Why?" I dream things that never were and say "Why Not?" Robert F. Kennedy

"Few wishes come true by themselves." June Smith

"The same fence that shuts others out shuts you in." Bill Copeland

"Opportunity's favorite disguise is trouble." Frank Tyger

"One of the nice things about problems is that a good many of them do not exist except in our imaginations." Steve Allen

"Goals determine what you are going to be." Julius Erving

"A rock pile ceases to be a rock pile the moment a person contemplates it, bearing with him the image of a cathedral." Antoine de Saint-Exupery

Art Linkletter (in his book Yes, You Can):

"No matter how tough the job seems at the time, you only fail when you say "I quit." As long as you keep trying, you haven't failed; you just haven't succeeded yet.

It's a basic failing of human nature that we tend to emphasize our weaknesses rather than our strengths.

It's all right for things to go wrong.

Every problem can be an opportunity if you just try to find the lesson the troublesome situation can teach you.

A hard, persistent effort is necessary if you hope to achieve anything in life."

"The person who says it cannot be done should not interrupt the person doing it." Chinese proverb

"You can't think only in terms of "lack." That creates a condition of lack. In your thinking, you create the condition that actualizes." Norman Vincent Peale

"The harder I practice, the luckier I get." Gary Player

"Do the obvious when you should obviously do it, and don't do anything when you obviously shouldn't." Harvey MacKay

Maxwell Maltz (in his book <u>Psycho-Cybernetics</u>):

> "Our actions, feelings and behavior are the result of our images and beliefs.

> Your nervous system cannot tell the difference between an imagined experience and a real experience, It reacts appropriately to what you think or imagine to be true.

> Ignore past failures and act as if it were impossible to fail."

"Deep faith eliminates fear." Lech Walesa

"Facing it - always facing it - that's the way to get through. Face it." Joseph Conrad

"Far away is far away only if you don't go there." O Povo

"Easy *doesn't* do it." Al Bernstein

"When you need salt, sugar won't do." Yiddish saying

"When you reach for the stars, you may not quite get one, but you won't come up with a handful of mud either." Leo Burnett

"Worry often gives a small thing a big shadow." Swedish proverb

Norman Vincent Peale (in his book <u>You Can If You Think You Can</u>):

> "Believe that problems do have answers. Believe that they can be overcome, that they can be handled. Believe that you can solve them.

> Practice getting the feeling of tranquility by passing peaceful words and thoughts through your mind.

> Self-trust is the first secret of success.

> Change your thoughts and you change your world."

"The will to win is not nearly as important as the will to prepare to win." Bobby Knight

"There is no such thing as darkness; only a failure to see." Malcolm Muggeridge

"I like the dreams of the future better than the history of the past." Thomas Jefferson

"If you have a garden and a library, you have everything you need." Cicero

---

"No symphony orchestra ever played music like a two-year-old girl laughing with a puppy." Bern Williams

David Schwartz (in his book The Magic of Thinking Big):

> "Action cures fear. Isolate the fear and then take appropriate action.
>
> Look at things as they can be, not as they are.
>
> People who tell you it cannot be done almost always are unsuccessful people.
>
> Action must precede action. Nothing starts itself.
>
> The important thing is not where you are but where you want to go."

"Many things are lost for want of not asking." English proverb

"You cannot teach a man anything; you can only help him find it within himself." Galileo Galilei

"Once you believe something is true, whether or not it is, you will act as if it is." Mark Ortman

Benjamin Franklin:

> "Necessity never made a good bargain.
>
> He that can have patience can have what he will."

"I cannot give you a formula for success, but I can give you the formula for failure, which is: try to please everybody." Herbert Bayard Swope

"I complained because I had no shoes until I met a man with no feet." Arabic proverb

Professed by anonymous authors:

> "A man can fail many times but he isn't a failure until he begins to blame somebody else.
>
> A chip on the shoulder is about the heaviest load that anyone can carry.
>
> Adversity introduces a person to himself.
>
> It isn't your position that makes you happy or unhappy. It's your disposition.
>
> Fear is the darkroom where negatives are developed.
>
> It's not what happens to us that matters. What matters is what we let it do to us.
>
> It takes 72 muscles to frown, but only 16 to smile; so if

you're tired, smile.

Before you speak, you are a master of what you say; afterwards a slave.

You can tell a person's character by what he turns up when released from a job: his nose or his sleeves.

No dream comes true until you wake up and go to work.

The nearest to perfection that most people ever come is when writing their resume.

There are four steps to accomplishment: Plan purposefully. Prepare prayerfully. Proceed positively. Pursue persistently.

Every accomplishment, great or small, starts with the right decision, "I'll try."

The thing to try when all else fails is again.

Begin where you are but don't stay where you are.

Failure is not the worst thing in the world. The very worst is not to try.

The only thing you have to fear is not doing something about the fear you have.

Some people entertain ideas and other people put them to work.

If you itch for success, keep on scratching."

"When a situation becomes hopeless, there's nothing to worry about." Edward Abby

"Never say never and always avoid always." John Hazlitt

"Necessity is the mother of taking chances." Mark Twain

"Nothing echoes like an empty mailbox." Charles M. Schulz

"Whatever the mind of man can conceive and believe, it can achieve." Napolean Hill

"Imagination is more important than knowledge." Einstein

Maxwell Maltz and Charles Schreiber (in their book <u>Live and Be Free Thru Psycho-Cybernetics</u>):

> "It takes twenty-one days to experience a noticeable change in a mental picture.

Everyone possesses more talent than they use. Therefore, the measure of success we achieve is not dependent on how much we possess, but on how much we utilize.

You cause a turning point in your life when you recognize your duties and responsibilities to yourself and your family, and then accept and carry out them to the full extent of your ability.

Enthusiasm overcomes all obstacles. Nothing great is possible without enthusiasm.

As a man thinks, so he is. And as he continues to think, so he shall remain.

The art of relaxation: 1) keep life simple, 2) avoid listening for the knock in your engine, 3) learn to like your work, 4) have a good hobby, 5) like people, 6) make a habit of saying the cheerful, pleasant thing, and 7) meet your problem with decision

> If you think you are beaten, you are.
> If you think you dare not, you don't.
> If you like to win, but you think you can't
> It's almost certain you won't.
>
> If you think you'll lose, you're lost,
> For out of the world we find
> Success begins with your will;
> It's all in your state of mind.
>
> If you think you're outclassed, you are;
> You've got to think high to rise.
> You've got to be sure of yourself before
> You can ever win a prize.
>
> Life's battles don't always go
> To the stronger or faster man,
> But sooner or later the person who wins,
> Is the one who thinks he can."

"To be upset over what you don't have is to waste what you do have."
Ken Keyes

"Sorrow looks back, worry looks around, faith looks up." Quoted in
Guideposts Magazine

———————

No one can really pull you up very high - you lose your grip on the rope. But on your own two feet you can climb mountains." Louis Brandeis

"The time is always right to do what is right." Martin Luther King

"Be careful of your thoughts. They may become words at any moment." Iara Gassen

"What counts is not necessarily the size of the dog in the fight - it's the size of the fight in the dog." Dwight D. Eisenhower

"It's hard to detect good luck. It looks so much like something you've earned." Frank Clark

Maxwell Maltz (in his book Creative Living for Today):

>"You mean something if you mean something to yourself.

>You are what you think you are and you can do what you think you can do."

>No goal is too insignificant if it contributes to your sense of achievement.

>To cure loneliness, work hard at a job that needs to be done.

>Sleep *on* a problem, not with it."

Napolean Hill (in his book Think and Grow Rich):

>"By controlling your mind, you control your destiny.

>Persistence is power of will. It's a state of mind and is cultivated by: knowing what you want, desire, self-reliance, definiteness of plans, accurate knowledge, cooperation, will power and habit."

"There is a time to let things happen and a time to make things happen." Hugh Prather

"Simple solutions seldom are." Forbes Magazine

"Self-discipline is when your conscience tells you to do something and you don't talk back." W.K. Hope

"Character consists of what you do on the third and fourth tries." James Michener

"Start by doing what's necessary, then what's possible and suddenly you are doing the impossible." St. Francis of Assisi

"Standing in the middle of the road is very dangerous; you get knocked down by the traffic from both directions." Margaret Thatcher

"No man was ever wise by chance." Seneca

"An error doesn't become a mistake until you refuse to correct it."
O. A. Battista

"If you cannot win, make the one ahead of you break the record." Jan
McKeithen

"May you have warmth in your igloo, oil in your lamp and peace in your
heart." Eskimo proverb

———————

INDEX

Now you can order the latest job-search information by mail:

1. <u>Job Search 101</u> contains hundreds of proven and creative techniques that you can use to quickly find a new job. It shows you easy steps to writing persuasive cover letters and resumes, and will help you perform better on interviews.

2. <u>The Art of Interviewing</u> is a **NEW** 37-minute video program that demonstrates powerful techniques for asking and answering tough interview questions. You'll learn how to prepare for the interview and make a good first impression. This informative new video will show you how to effectively use and read body language to get more job offers.

3. Order additional copies of <u>Coping With Unemployment</u> for your friends and relatives in need of emotional support during their bout with prolonged unemployment.

If you have comments about <u>Coping With Unemployment</u> or suggestions for future editions, please send them to Brian Jud c/o Marketing Directions, Inc.

Please send me:

____ copies of Job Search 101 @ $14.95 _____

____ copies of En Busca De Trabajo 101 @ $14.95 _____

____ copies of The Art of Interviewing @ $39.95 _____

____ copies of Coping With Unemployment @ $14.95 _____

Free Pocket Guide with each order

Order Total _____

CT Residents add 6% sales tax _____

Shipping & Handling @ 10% _____

Total enclosed _____

Name _____

Address _____

City _____ State_____ Zip Code _____

Telephone ( ) _____

Marketing
Directions, Inc.

P. O. Box 715, Avon, CT 06001-9965
1 (800) JOB-HELP

_____

GARY BURNS
K'200